PRAISE FOR *AUTÉNTICO*

"An invaluable roadmap for career success. The insights will facilitate the development of a rich pipeline of talented Hispanic leaders who will make a significant positive difference for a world in much need of authentic and inspired leadership."

—*David Antonio Rodriguez, Ph.D., executive VP and global chief HR officer, Marriott International*

"At Korn Ferry we believe that great leadership begins with authenticity. *Auténtico* takes this concept further by spotlighting the criticality of addressing one's cultural identity for Latino executives and future Latino leaders. As a CEO, this book opened my eyes to how much more we can do to accelerate the overdue advancement of Latino leaders."

—*Mark D. Arian, CEO, Korn Ferry*

"From navigating corporate cultures, to wrestling with whether assimilation is an enabler to success, this book does an excellent job of presenting candid insights into what it's like to be Latino in contemporary corporate America."

—*Rohini Anand, SVP corporate responsibility and global chief diversity officer, Sodexo*

"It is my strong desire to see Apple's Latino employee communities around the world continue to grow and to thrive. This book offers insights that will help any organization with this objective."

—*Denise Young Smith, vice president, Worldwide Talent, HR, Inclusion, Diversity, Apple, Inc.*

"Two of the preeminent diversity and inclusion thought leaders have teamed-up to create the blueprint for Latino professional advancement. A must-read for anyone interested in the impact on corporate America of our nation's fastest growing demographic."

—*Pedro A. Guerrero, CEO Guerrero Howe, and publisher of* Hispanic Executive

"A thought-provoking and compelling read. With deep research and an experience-based approach, it lays out a road map for understanding and addressing nuances of corporate culture, navigating challenges, and driving transformative leadership."

—*Alan May, chief HR officer, Hewlett Packard Enterprise*

"As a big fan of Dr. Price Cobb's work on African-American corporate success, this is a wonderful tie-in to his groundbreaking work—and now we have the definitive must-read Latino career success guide."

—*Brian Tippens, chief diversity officer, Hewlett Packard Enterprise*

"A great resource for anyone wishing to understand challenges, opportunities, and best practices for Latino advancement in corporate America by two renowned experts on Latino leadership and diversity and inclusion."

—*Cid Wilson, president and CEO,*
Hispanic Association on Corporate Responsibility

"The combination of primary research, a review of the current literature, and the authors' own deep insights, has created the basis for a powerful Latino Executive Manifesto. An invaluable reference tool."

—*Gloria Castillo, president & CEO, Chicago United*

"The successful Latino leaders highlighted in this book will inspire young Latinos to learn strategies to achieve in their careers while embracing their culture and identity. It is a wake-up call to corporate America to increase their inclusion and to tap into the growing and dynamic Latino talent."

—Juana Bordas, president, Mestiza Leadership International,
and author of The Power of Latino Leadership
and Salsa, Soul, and Spirit: Leadership for a Multicultural Age

"A first-rate book that will undoubtedly change the way Latino professionals view and actively approach their careers. Its strategies and insights will bring them to the next level in corporate America."

—Michael Hyter, managing partner, Korn Ferry, and author of
The Power of Choice: Embracing Efficacy to Drive
Your Career

"The Latino Manifesto at the end of the book is comparable to the 10 Commandments for Latino executives. A true jewel."

—Jorge Ferraez, publisher, Latino Leaders Magazine

"As two of the most influential thought leaders in the diversity and inclusion space, Dr. Robert Rodriguez and Andrés Tapia have written a book that is a critical contribution for enhancing Latino self-understanding and for leaders to become more culturally competent in managing the growing Latino workforce."

—Mary-Frances Winters, president and CEO,
The Winters Group, Inc., and author of
We Can't Talk About That At Work: How to Talk
About Race, Religion, Politics, and
Other Polarizing Topics

"An indispensable resource for much-needed Hispanic executives. This book goes a long way toward addressing the Latino leadership gap in corporate America."

—*Miguel A. Quiñones, Ph.D., chair, Department of Management and Organizations, Edwin L. Cox School of Business, Southern Methodist University and academic director, Latino Leadership Initiative*

"Compelling personal biographies with powerful sociological insights into our Latino communities and their relationship with corporate America, this deep dive into Latino society, culture, and generational differences is a valuable education for anyone."

—*Sally Olson, chief diversity officer, Sidley Austin LLP*

"An unequivocal road map to mastering the art of navigating corporate culture and leveraging the insight for positive, transformational change—not just within a particular company, but at companies worldwide."

—*Dr. Yasmin Davidds, CEO, Latina Global Executive Leadership Institute, and author of* Take Back Your Power, Your Own Terms, *and* Empowering Latinas

"A smart, compelling firsthand analysis of what is required for Latinx executives to break through in the corporate ranks."

—*Bernard C. Coleman III, global head of diversity and inclusion, Uber*

"Curates the stories of an exceptional group of role models that will inspire and guide the next generation of Latino business leaders who will make our business community and our country richer through their contributions."

—*Nina Vaca, chairman and CEO, Pinnacle Group*

"A treasure trove of information that will not only guide thousands of Latinos to greater career satisfaction and success, but should be mandatory reading for any executive committed to truly unlocking the potential of their diverse workforce."

—Nadia Younes, diversity and inclusion advisor,
International Monetary Fund

"Full of wisdom with much needed practical advice that leads to self-discovery and shows a path to career success."

—Salvador Mendoza, vice president, Diversity and Inclusion,
NBCUniversal

"A rallying cry of a new generation of Latino leaders and their contributions to American society. An important read for people of all backgrounds!"

—Jane Hyun, leadership strategist, author of Breaking the Bamboo Ceiling: Career Strategies for Asians, *and co-author of* Flex: The New Playbook for Managing Across Differences

"A call to *acción* (action) to all of us, and the ecosystem of corporations, government, universities and nonprofits to focus on the power embedded in the growing segment of Latino talent."

—Maria Wynne, CEO, Leadership Greater Chicago

"With numbers too big to ignore, the ability to grow, develop, and place Latinos in key leadership positions is mission-critical for all companies and all industries. This book insightfully lays out how."

—Gloria Johnson Goins, chief diversity and inclusion officer,
Bon Secours Health System, Inc.

"The most important collection of knowledge yet on one of the fastest-growing populations of talent and consumers today by two of our foremost authorities on the Latinx experience."

—*Jennifer Brown, president & CEO, Jennifer Brown Consulting, and author of* Inclusion: Diversity, The New Workplace and The Will to Change

"An excellent read. By giving voice to the Latino experience through insightful stories, Andrés and Robert have penned a must-read for aspiring Latino professionals and diversity and inclusion practitioners."

—*Jim Evans II, chief diversity officer, Capital Group*

"If companies want to compete in the new global marketplace it is the time of urgency for addressing the advancement of Latinos and other underrepresented talent in organizations around the world. Unique insights into these challenges and concrete solutions are offered throughout the book. Especially powerful is the 10-point Latino Executive Manifesto."

—*Kristen Anderson, chief diversity officer, Barilla*

AUTÉNTICO

The Definitive Guide to Latino Career Success

A Latino Executive Manifesto

Dr. Robert Rodriguez & Andrés Tomás Tapia

LATINX
INSTITUTE
PRESS

Published by Latinx Institute Press

Library of Congress Catalog No.

ISBN: 978-1-946229-58-8

First printing: October 2017

Publisher's Cataloging-In-Publication Data
(Prepared by The Donohue Group, Inc.)

Names: Rodriguez, Robert, 1969- | Tapia, Andrés, 1960-
Title: Auténtico : the definitive guide to Latino career success : a Latino executive
    manifesto / Dr. Robert Rodriguez & Andrés Tomás Tapia.
Other Titles: Definitive guide to Latino career success
Description: [Chicago, Illinois] : Latinx Institute Press, [2017] | Includes
    bibliographical references and index.
Identifiers: ISBN 978-1-946229-58-8 | ISBN 978-1-946229-57-1 (ebook)
Subjects: LCSH: Hispanic American executives. | Hispanic American executives--
    Interviews. | Hispanic Americans--Employment. | Discrimination in employ-
    ment- United States. | Success in business.
Classification: LCC HD38.25.U6 R64 2017 (print) | LCC HD38.25.U6 (ebook) |
    DDC 658.40908968073--dc2

"Se hace camino al andar."

You make the path as you walk it.

—Antonio Machado

DEDICATIONS

Andrés:

A mi papá, who was that Latino executive who
role modeled thought leadership, relentlessness,
risk taking, and giving back.

A mi Tío Douglas, who through passionate Sporting
Cristal soccer weekends at el Estadio Nacional,
shared his love for me.

To Lori, who from the beginning saw
and loved the Peruano in me.

A m'hija Marisela y a Erick's (with the unique apostrophe s)
quienes viven el espíritu Latinx con toda passion.

Robert:

To Mom & Dad: Thanks for all the sacrifices you made
to help give me more opportunity and a better life.
This book extends your legacy of always giving back
to the community. All my love.

To Bailey and Benjamin: I can have no better ambition in life
than to be the best father I can be for you both. Hope you see
this book as a gift as it relates to your Latino identity.
Love you.

To Sofia: I feel so fortunate to be the subject of your grace
and favor. Thank you for helping me connect with
my inner Latino self. *Te amo.*

CONTENTS

Nationalistic Divides
Socioeconomic Divides
Racial Divides
Spanish Language and Accent Divides
Grew Up in Latin America versus Grew Up in the U.S.
Overcoming the Divides
The Power of an Integrated Cultural Identity

Latino Cultural Preferences and How They Compare
  to Corporate Culture
Locus of Control: God Helps Those Who Help
  Themselves versus *Si Dios Quiere* (God Willing)
Ascribing Status: Hierarchy versus Egalitarianism
Identity: I versus We
Process: Follow the Rules versus Go with the Flow
Time Management: Clock- versus Event-oriented
Managing Emotions: Stiff Upper Lip versus *Pura Vida*
Hired for Differences but Told to Assimilate

FOREWORD

Price M. Cobbs, M.D.
Author of *Cracking the Corporate Code*

Robert Rodriguez and Andrés Tapia have written a thoughtful and timely book. Most importantly, their research and experience provides persuasive information and insights that will help many men and women map out how to avoid pitfalls, strategize, and prosper in their careers. With Latinos presently at 17 percent of the United Sates population and growing rapidly, this group is an important part of the nation's workforce and will be even more crucial in the coming decades. In acknowledging these facts, this book serves as a primer—or as the authors describe it, *The Definitive Guide to Latino Career Success*. Beyond wanting to foster career success, the passion of the authors is evident in their desire to see more Latino executives take their place at the helm of organizations.

There are many barriers in place that make the Latino journey to career success difficult and unpredictable. Some of the barriers are personal, and can be overcome by determination and self-improvement and by applying many of the lessons offered in this book. Some are interpersonal, and can be mitigated— if not removed—by interactions, communications, and tough conversations about implicit bias and erroneous assumptions. Other roadblocks are organizational and institutional, and have to be acknowledged and identified, with much work to be done to remove them.

The authors' focus on these barriers is a reminder that in present day organizations one size no longer fits all. Today's most forward thinking leaders accept that and work to make their organization more diverse and inclusive. This valuable book is a tremendous addition in helping such leaders.

If our country is not successful in utilizing untapped Latino talent, then our economy will pay the price. Everyone suffers when a significant part of the American family does not realize its full potential. There are historical parallels we can learn from. The Industrial Revolution of the late nineteenth and twentieth centuries was successful because the latest immigrants were successfully assimilated into the workforce. In addition, Detroit led the way in expanding a black middle class as many workers migrated from the south to work in automobile factories. A tremendous challenge of the twenty-first century is finding new ways to replicate these earlier successes.

The interplay between cultural identity and success in an organization is an underlying dynamic throughout many portions of this book. It is this interplay and how it is resolved that is at the heart of how immigrants and the native born of previous generations were able to claim their part of the American Dream. It is worth noting that the concept of American Exceptionalism as defined by that great student of the U.S., Alexis de Tocqueville, was initially a specific reference to the U.S. as a country of immigrants, with immigrant assimilation a major part of that exceptionalism. So, in this important book, the authors are highlighting a theme that has reemerged in contemporary America.

The idea of this nation as a melting pot has been altered in the decades since America expanded by immigration in the late 1800's and the early part of the twentieth century. The melting pot originally meant people coming from Europe. In those days, many people would consciously choose to let go of all but nostalgic parts of their link to a mother country. Today, many recent immigrants (and those who have been here for generations) from Mexico, as well as Central and South America want to consciously maintain portions of the customs and culture of their former countries.

I think few would argue that to thrive in the U.S., one must adapt to this country's historic language, mores, and values. One must understand the culture and the rules and regulations, both written and unwritten. In the great migrations of recent decades the majority of people have arrived from south of our borders, the Pacific Rim and Asia, Africa and the Caribbean. Many of them assimilate or "melt" in ways different from previous centuries. This book focuses on those who choose to call themselves Latinos and how they must make their assimilation consistent with their ambitions and future success.

Where once children of immigrants were at times forbidden to speak the language of their parents' or grandparents' land of origin, now many are encouraged to be or remain bilingual. And, where once the term "hyphenated American" was considered a derogatory term, it is now used as a badge of pride. Theodore Roosevelt once stated in a speech, "there is no room in this country for hyphenated Americans;" one might wonder what he would say now. This book adds to the growing body of literature that speaks of an America that derives much of its strength from the diversity of its people, many of whom proudly refer to themselves and their group in hyphenated terms.

When Judith Turnock and I wrote *Cracking the Corporate Code* we were aware that although the book was about the success of the thirty-two African-Americans we cited, interest in the book would go far beyond that group. This will no doubt be true of this book. Its chapter "Power Ambivalence: The Achilles Heel" shines a light on this topic. People who grow up in a culture shaped by ancestors who look like them benefit from this and have an inherent leg up. They fit in. Others, who are outsiders and different by many standards, must understand and study power if they are to be successful. Merit is an entry card, but understanding organizational cultures, learning the unwritten rules and many other facets of organizational life are also necessary.

In my experience, every organization—large, small and in between—has a success model. A part of this model is known and written down; how you achieve success and how you interact with others is spelled out. But, underlying this are the unwritten rules. How you look, how you dress, how you speak and don't speak, and a thousand more nuances are indeed the marker as to how far you will eventually go in an organization.

This book makes more explicit how a better understanding of your individuality, your cultural identity and how all of this interacts with your success in a career. It is a must read, not only for aspiring Latinos, but for everyone seeking broader knowledge of this important component of contemporary America. ❧

INTRODUCTION

The Coming Latino Talent Boom
and the Urgency for
More Latino Executives

"Pies, ¿para qué los quiero si tengo alas para volar?"

Feet, what do I need you for when I have wings to fly?

—Frida Kahlo, Mexican painter

Why this book now? Because there are 55 million Latinos, over 40 million of whom are U.S. citizens. They are transforming American society—in politics, in the economy, and in the workplace—in underestimated ways.

But there are definitely too few Latino executives and senior leaders, and this must change. To do so, we need to be vigilant in defense and savvy on offense.

Defense is about neutralizing the many conscious and unconscious biases toward Latinos that create obstacles and then relentlessly diminishing them in decision makers' thought patterns. Also we must surface how these biases have been systematized in the ways talent sourcing, recruiting, retention, development, and advancement effectively sideline Latino and other traditionally underrepresented talent from rising to the top echelons of leadership.

While that work gets done, we must also move on offense. A key component that contributes to Latino advancement is highlighting successful Latino role models and the keys to their success that can be passed on to the next generation of rising Latino leaders.

Inspired by Price Cobbs's seminal work on the secrets of successful Black leaders, *Cracking the Corporate Code: The Revealing Success Stories of 32 African-American Executives,*[1] we set out to research and write a Latino version of the corporate success narrative.

To do so, we interviewed twenty successful boomer executives, and dozens of Gen X and Millennial Latinos and Latinas. As we listened to their stories of *éxito* (success) we looked for themes—convergences and divergences in what they faced in their career paths, how they addressed the challenges, and how they seized the opportunities—and with their narratives we captured the lessons learned that can be used by future Latino leaders.

In addition, we focused on Latino executives who retained their sense of Latino identity throughout their careers and, in fact, used it as an asset in their ascendancy and effectiveness in their

---

1   Cobbs, Price M., and Turnock, Judith L. *Cracking the Corporate Code: The Revealing Success Stories of 32 African-American Executives.* New York: AMACOM, 2003.

work. To us this cultural identity grounding was the basis of their being *auténtico* (authentic) a hallmark that contemporary leadership research reveals as a foundation for being a successful twenty-first century leader.[2]

The Context of Rising Latino Presence

Before diving into the leadership stories and the lessons they offer, discussing the context of the rising Latino presence in the U.S. is important.

Latinos are changing the popular culture, the marketplace, and the political landscape. Consider this: in the first decade of the twenty-first century, the number of Latinos increased at three times the growth rate of the rest of the population. Latinos are now the largest ethnic minority group, at 17 percent of the country's population and comprise 21 percent of the Millennial generation. Latinos accounted for half of the overall U.S. population growth. At this rate Latinos are expected to make up one-fourth of the U.S. population by 2025 and one-third by 2050. By 2060, the U.S. Hispanic population is estimated to reach 128.8 million.

Analyze the meaning of this large and growing Latino presence as it relates to professional advancement. Today Latinos represent 15 percent of the U.S. workforce and have a participation rate of roughly 68 percent. This is a higher workforce participation rate than among European-Americans, African-Americans, or Asians. Further, Latinos are expected to comprise 20 percent of the workforce by 2042 and these are not just blue-collar jobs. Latino high school graduates are enrolling in college at a higher

---

2 Cashman, Kevin. *Leadership from the Inside Out: Becoming a Leader for Life.* San Francisco, CA: Berrett-Koehler Publishers, 2008.

rate than all other ethnic groups including European-Americans[3] (69 percent versus 67 percent) and are poised to be the most highly educated generation of Hispanic Americans in U.S. history. This percentage is not just a student body ratio; it is the future workforce.

Latinos will not only make their presence known in the workplace, but as *Time* magazine declared in a September 15, 2016, feature story, they are also on pace to "...drive America's economic growth."[4] Some statistical highlights from the article:

- In 2017, Latinos, at 17 percent of the U.S. population, are estimated to have $1.4 trillion in purchasing power, surpassing the GDP of Mexico and growing at a rate of $100 billion a year as they move to become one-third of the U.S. population by 2060.

- Between 2010 and 2030, Latinos are projected to account for more than half of all new U.S. homeowners.

- From 2007 to 2012, Latinos launched new small businesses at a rate more than sixty times that of non-Latinos, and Latina-owned businesses grew at 137 percent over the last nine years.

- In 2007, Hispanic-owned businesses generated more than $358 billion in revenues and were projected to reach $486 billion in 2014.

---

3   Fry, Richard, and Paul Taylor. "Hispanic High School Graduates Pass Whites in Rate of College Enrollment." Pew Research Center's Hispanic Trends Project. May 09, 2013. Accessed July 29, 2017. http://www.pewhispanic.org/2013/05/09/hispanic-high-school-graduates-pass-whites-in-rate-of-college-enrollment/

4   "How Latinos Drive America's Economic Growth." Time.com. Accessed July 29, 2017. http://time.com/4494780/how-latinos-drive-americas-economic-growth/.

• In 2014, the growth rate of Latino businesses was approximately 43 percent (3.22 million businesses added). The growth rate for all U.S. businesses from 2007 to 2014 is only about 20.2 percent.[4]

• In 2012, Latino-owned businesses employed 2.5 million workers.

• The Hispanic market is not just a niche market; it is the market.

On the political front, Latinos played a meaningful role in the last three presidential elections. They helped elect Barack Obama twice and were then a central issue on both sides of the debate in Donald Trump's election. In 2016, 13 percent of the electorate was Hispanic/Latino, up from 11 percent in 2012, 9 percent in 2008, and 7 percent in the 2010 midterms. Between 2008 and 2016, the number of eligible Latino voters grew from 19.5 million to 27.3 million, a 40 percent increase.[5] Eligible Latino voters will number an impressive 30 million in the next election cycles. This is not a side constituency; it is a potential margin of victory.

The massive Latinization of the U.S. has reached every fabric of American culture from food to music to entertainment. On Latino influence of mainstream culture, we have Christina Aguilera driving *The Voice* on NBC, and Jorge Ramos on Univision anchoring the most watched newscast among *all* networks. Pitbull tops the charts time after

5   Krogstad, Jens Manuel, Mark Hugo Lopez, Gustavo López, Jeffrey S. Passel, and Eileen Patten. "Millennials Make Up Almost Half of Latino Eligible Voters in 2016." Pew Research Center's Hispanic Trends Project. January 19, 2016. Accessed July 29, 2017. http://www.pewhispanic.org/2016/01/19/millennials-make-up-almost-half-of-latino-eligible-voters-in-2016/.

Latino Share of the U.S. Population

2017 17%

2030 30%

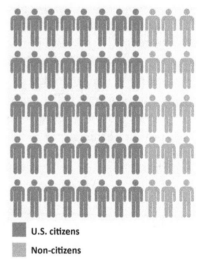

55 million Latinos, 40 million of whom are U.S. citizens

U.S. citizens

Non-citizens

Latinos are projected to account for more than half of all new U.S. homeowners.

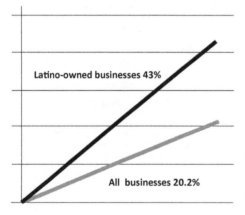

Latino-owned businesses 43%

All businesses 20.2%

Latino-owned businesses are growing at more than twice the rate of all businesses

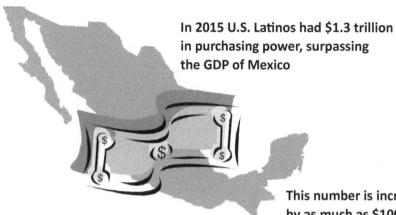

In 2015 U.S. Latinos had $1.3 trillion in purchasing power, surpassing the GDP of Mexico

This number is increasing by as much as $100 billion a year. It's expected to reach $1.7 trillion by 2020

Jorge Ramos of Univision anchors the most-watched newscast among all networks— and has won eight Emmys

In 2016, 13 percent of the electorate was Hispanic/Latino, up from 11 percent in 2012, and 9 percent in 2008

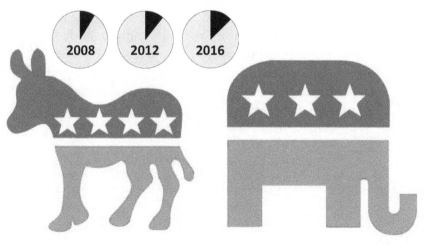

2008 2012 2016

time with cross-ethnic, crosscultural collaborations. Salsa has long surpassed the all-American ketchup as the number one condiment in the U.S. Peruvian cuisine is garnering top restaurant status in some American cities. Andean quinoa is as ubiquitous as Quaker oatmeal.

The Gap

Yet as Latinos increase their presence in the marketplace, popular culture, and political arena, they do not find prospects as bright in the workplace. According to the Hispanic Association on Corporate Responsibility (HACR), in their 2016 Corporate Inclusion Index, Latinos held just over 7 percent of board seats among the participating companies and a little more than 4 percent of executive officer positions.

On boards this is only a marginal improvement from HACR's 2013 Corporate Inclusion Index when Latinos held only 6 percent of corporate board seats among HACR's participating companies, and pretty much unchanged in the number of Latinos in executive officer positions.[6]

Behind these low representation numbers, a 2013 Harris Interactive poll found that over 75 percent of Latinos feel people with their background are discriminated against by not being hired or promoted for a job and being called names or insulted. According to a 2016 study published by the Center for Talent Innovation, *Latinos at Work: Unleashing the Power of Culture*, most Latinos in the U.S. do not feel that they can bring their whole sense of Latino-ness to the office. The study found that the vast majority of Latinos (76 percent) repress parts of their personas at work.

---

6   "Ya! The Time Has Come for Latinos to Claim Our Place in American Society."
    Latin Post. September 15, 2014. Accessed July 29, 2017. http://www.latinpost.com/
    articles/21389/20140915/ya-time-come-latinos-claim-place-american-society.htm.

In spite of these headwinds, as college educated Latinos become a greater percentage of the available labor force, companies who are unsuccessful at sourcing, attracting, and engaging this talent pool will see their talent pipeline shrivel up. Corporations sit at the edge of a yawning talent divide when it comes to Latinos in the U.S. While the number of Latino executives is still very small in corporate corridors of power, Latino talent is burgeoning—not only in hourly workers but also in the professional ranks. Without a doubt the workforce of the future will have an increasingly Latino identity.

So Let's Look at Latino Leaders

Most companies are still asleep at the wheel, failing to recognize that there is an exploding Latino workforce. Even worse, most do not understand what will entice Latinos to come work for them. Companies that wake up to this gap first will be best poised to win the talent war for future generations.

We will start by looking at those leaders who made it in spite of the obstacles. Our book is grounded in primary and secondary research, illustrated by stories of those interviewed, and interpreted through our personal experiences. Ultimately we seek to offer the keys to success that have served successful Latinos, and to codify what we believe will provide a guide for the next generation of Latino executives.

The research we undertook included the following:

- In-depth interviews with twenty Latino and Latina executives

- A targeted survey completed by a total of twenty Latino executives and senior leaders

- Five focus groups with up-and-coming Latinos and Latinas under age forty in the geographically dispersed locations of New York City, Dallas, Chicago, and Los Angeles

- A targeted survey filled out by over three hundred Latinos and Latinas under age forty

- Secondary research synthesis of over a dozen studies on Latinos in the workplace, Latino advancement, and markers of success

- A journalistic look at major sociocultural, economic, political, and corporate trends that mark the impact the growing Latino presence is having on U.S. society and business

This research approach and the subsequent insights shared in this book were filtered through our own personal and professional journeys. We both have dedicated our careers to the inclusion and advancement of traditionally underrepresented groups. Robert's focus has been on enhancing the effectiveness of employee resource groups in general and in addressing the specifics of Latino talent acquisition, as well as Latino leadership development and advancement. Andrés has focused on enterprise-wide diversity and inclusion strategies, on the leadership development of traditionally unrepresented talent, as well as on improving the capabilities of all executives and senior leaders to lead more inclusively.

We have a collective thirty years of corporate experience in the topic, serving more than two hundred clients. These clients have been in nearly every for-profit sector (retail, finance, manufacturing, managing consultancies), government (regulatory, law enforcement, military, intelligence), healthcare, and not-for-profits (education, social services, advocacy groups). These companies have been domestic as well as global.

We have organized the book in the following way:

Part 1, "Outer Forces: The Challenges of Being Latino in Corporate America" explores the unseen cultural challenges that many Latinos face in their quest to give their best at work and, in doing so, find the pathway to advancement in leadership roles. What are these challenges, why do they exist, and what is the often unintended, yet very real, detrimental impact on the contributions Latinos can make in the workplace?

All this in turn forces identity questions for Latino talent. Should they bury their own unique Latino identity and instead assimilate into the corporate culture, or should they instead double down without apology on what it means for them to be Latino and try not to deny their identify? These are among the most urgent and vexing questions many Latino professionals face today.

With the context set for what it's like to be Latino in corporate America, in Part 2, "Inner Forces: Successful Strategies of Latino Executives," we turn to what we learned from the executives we interviewed asking how they personally addressed their dilemmas. In listening to them as a cohort, we extracted themes of convergence and divergence. With convergence, we looked at which issues emerged consistently for these successful executives. For divergences, we looked at their journeys and the choices made in their career paths that were not linked to social and cultural patterns, but influenced more by each person's personality and uniqueness.

Among the themes we found were the role of education, and how Latino culture can be both an inner asset as well as something that produces dilemmas and challenges in ascending the corporate ladder. We also mapped out what these leaders shared as the keys to becoming a transformative leader.

The lessons learned and bits of advice offered by the boomer executives set the stage for the chapter "The Next Generation of Latino Leaders: Latinx Learns, Challenges, and Rises," where we compare and contrast their experiences and effective strategies with the two Latino generations that followed them: the Gen Xers and Millennials. We lay out some fundamental socio-historical and cultural generational differences and how these affect advancement—or lack of—within their organizations. We identify their needs and techniques for resolving those needs. In addition, we point out how they would benefit from the experience and wisdom of those Latinos who did make it to the top.

Finally, in our Conclusion we take a step back from what individuals have done to break through barriers and seize opportunities to look at what government, corporations, not-for-profits, and educational entities can do to address still existing institutional resistance to Latinos and their heritage.

The Feeling of Being Latino

Having outlined the intellectual basis and approach to the book, we have one final word on the soul of this book.

We recognize that there is vast diversity within and across the Latino experience. Latinos, wrote Carlos Fuentes, are *una raza cósmica* (a cosmic race)—a fusion and amalgam of ethnicities, races, social classes, and religions. But through it all there is something intangible, some *esencia* (essence), that captures what it means to be Latin whether we are first, second, third, or fourth generation, Boomer, Gen X, or Millennial, Spanish dominant or English dominant, or somewhere in between.

This variety is what both of us, Robert and Andrés, also bring to this book. Robert, the son of Mexican immigrants, grew up in Minneapolis without much of a sense of his Latino heritage.

Andrés spent his childhood in Lima, Perú. His Peruvian dad met his American mom during his medical residency at the Cleveland Clinic. They fell in love and married, and when Andrés was a year old, the family moved to Lima, where he grew up and the time finally came for him to attend college in the U.S.

There are the basics of language, food, dress, surnames, and music that Latinos share. However, leaving home is often when the feeling of being Latino is challenged and each must confront this experience in their unique way, navigating a majority European-American culture.

So what is that feeling of being Latino? Let's explore this by taking a short journey into the mysteries of one form of Latin artistic expression: flamenco.

Andrés's twenty-something daughter, Marisela, is a professional flamenco dancer with much formal and informal training including many performances. Recently he joined her in Seville, Spain, the mecca of flamenco, where she was obtaining some master training in this ancient dance form. Like Latino culture itself, flamenco is an amalgam of influences beginning in India and coursing through the Middle East and the Baltics before landing in Moorish Spain.

To his surprise and delight (as well as trepidation), Marisela had enrolled him in a flamenco class during his visit. Knowing that this twelve-beat art form was exceptionally complex in technique, Andrés was skeptical as well as apprehensive about how much he could learn—not to mention how much he could do so without a high level of embarrassment—in the three scheduled sessions.

Marisela explained that this was the perfect class because the accomplished dancer who was the instructor was focused not on the technique of flamenco but on the *feeling* of flamenco. In fact, the instruction takes place with tennis shoes so students will not be distracted by the drama and performance activation that the flamenco shoes' staccato elicits.

The lessons begin with the music. The instructor, Luis Peña, invites participants to listen, not just with their ears but with their whole bodies. Then they can allow that physical resonance caused by the guitar string, the *jota* (flamenco yodeling) and *palmas* (rhythmic hand clapping) to elicit a feeling. Only at that time should they release their bodies to move in response to *la música*. Their feet will find the beat, their hands and arms will channel the surge that emanates from within, and their heads will lurch in the direction of an invisible presence.

When they have found the feeling—felt it, channeled it—then, and only then, are they in the right place to learn the complex techniques of the seemingly infinite twelve-beat variations of flamenco.

And so it was with Andrés. His uncertain steps and the sense of being in over his head gave way to allowing his feeling for the music to surge through his legs, feet, arms, and hands. Suddenly the surge made his body move in a flamenco way. His technique may have been far from perfect, but there he was in full, true flamenco expression.

Andrés's journey in learning the feeling of flamenco is not unlike the journey to cultural identity that many Latinos face. While there is a concrete aspect to the Latino reality (how to dance salsa, how to prepare *arroz con pollo*, or how to speak Spanish correctly), these are secondary to the feeling of being Latino.

While Andrés grew up with a Latino feeling as a young person in Lima, things were different for Robert. As one of the very few Latinos in Scandinavian Minneapolis, he did not have a strong feeling of Latino-ness. With *mamá's* spices spreading their aroma in the kitchen at home, he experienced some feeling of being a Latino, but he had not internalized it. Robert did not learn Spanish (researchers have proven there is an inextricable link between language and cultural meaning). Nor did he participate in Latin dancing. And what passed for "Mexican" food in Minneapolis did not come even close to the real thing.

Thus Robert grew up without that Latino feeling. Yet in the middle of his career, he began to long for it, especially after he had begun his research of Latino talent. It was this work that awoke in him a need and a desire to discover that Latino feeling. Just as in Andrés's flamenco class experience, Robert realized that while learning the details of a language or a cuisine were important, being Latino was about a feeling. He began to connect with the artistic vibrations emanating from Latino authors whose works he had not read, and from the music he had heard only with his ears but not his body. He paid more attention to the stories of Latino identity that he heard repeatedly in the course of his work. He also connected more with Latin culture by studying Latin American history and visiting Latin countries including the Dominican Republic, Panama, and Argentina. As he did this, he began to allow the feeling of Latino-ness to course through his body to the point when he knew what being Latino meant. *Lo siento, lo hago.* (I feel it, I do it.)

That is the spirit of this book. When we talked with these executives and the up-and-coming Latino leaders and saw the patterns in their stories, we not only listened to their words but also sought to capture their feeling of what being Latino means and how they desire to more fully express that Latino-ness.

Welcome to the journey of Latino *éxito*—while remaining *auténtico*. ❧

"Welcome. We love your differences—now be just like us."

PART 1

OUTER FORCES: THE CHALLENGE OF BEING LATINO IN CORPORATE AMERICA

Latino executives and aspiring leaders must confront forces both outside of themselves (discrimination, unconscious biases, pressures to conform), and within (sorting out their career aspirations, defining their Latino cultural identity) as they press on to ascend as leaders.

In addition, like other underrepresented groups in corporate America, Latinos face seemingly irreconcilable corporate pressures on one hand to assimilate in how they look, talk, and behave, and on the other in how they handle personal pressures to be different as Latino leaders.

How do they overcome these pressures without burying their own diverse identity for the sake of fitting in? For many Latinos who come from cultural backgrounds and environments quite different from that of most individuals in corporate America, this dilemma is particularly acute.

Part 1 traces these invisible—yet very real—forces and the different types of trajectories the leaders chose and why, and how corporate America responded. Let's look at how these encounters led to both conflict and resolution.

CHAPTER *1*

The Myths of Meritocracy and Color-Blind Corporate Cultures

"Cuando estás convencido que una causa
es justa, continua luchando."

When you are convinced a cause is just, keep fighting.

—Rigoberta Menchú, Guatemalan human rights activist
1992 Nobel Peace Prize

Meritocracy—that uplifting concept defined as a workplace ethic that rewards those who show talent and competence as demonstrated by performance—is one of corporate America's most cherished ideologies. According to this value, getting ahead in the workplace is based solely on individual merit.

Latinos, and other traditionally underrepresented groups buy into the idea of meritocracy, often pursuing corporate careers precisely due to its promise. The trouble is that when considering Latinos and other minority groups, companies fall seriously short of living up to this ideal.

Why does this happen? To explore the causes of any system failure, we first must understand how the system is supposed to work.

Meritocracy Design

Merit tends to be viewed as a combination of innate abilities, hard work, and intelligence.

The meritocracy ideology is very much aligned with the "American Dream": the U.S. as the land of limitless opportunity where individuals can go as far as their abilities and desires will take them. When placed in a work context, supporters speak glowingly of a singularly meritocratic environment where everyone has equal opportunity and where the workplace is a level playing field. The tenets of meritocracy put work environments on a path that is supposed to be colorblind and gender-neutral.

In a meritocracy, a fair and equitable work environment creates a competitive system. Those who outperform their peers get promoted. In a meritocracy, hard work pays off and each person, judged solely on results, rises to the fullness of their potential. Proponents of a meritocracy say the issues of race, ethnicity, and gender do not matter because merit is all about performance.

Ask most Latino leaders and executives and they too believe in the meritocracy ideology. In fact, that is what Latinos want. They do not want to be promoted because of their Hispanic ethnicity, but rather they want to get ahead based solely on their capabilities.

Meritocracy Illusion

However, a review of the top of the organization charts and the profile of most corporate boards tells us something is not quite right. If the level playing field is indeed as equitable as meritocracy proclaims, then the racial, ethnic, and gender makeup of our corporate leaders should be distributed equally, mirroring that of the available labor force. A true meritocracy should espouse proportional representation of all kinds of talent because the law of averages would be at work. When a meritocracy is real, there should be no shortage of women and people of color in top leadership positions.

Ask a corporate executive—or most members of our society for that matter—if they believe that women and people of color are inherently inferior to European-American men, and the answer is a resounding "no." Indeed, believing otherwise would be racist and sexist.

However, if we as a society don't believe women and racial and ethnic minorities are inferior, and if we believe that a meritocracy is fair and based solely on performance, how do we then explain the shortage of women and people of color in top corporate roles? What could be holding our organizations back from delivering on the promise and the value of the intended outcomes of a meritocracy?

This gap between how society believes people are promoted in our organizations and how organizations actually promote people unveils what we, and various other writers, refer to as the myth of the meritocracy.[1] What we must realize is that while merit does indeed affect some who advance and receive promotions, other forces vastly diminish the perception of merit.

For Latinos in the workplace, the reality is that they don't tend to come from the same backgrounds as the majority culture. In fact, Latinos face different types of headwinds to their advancement, which creates a drag on their ability to progress. This and

---

1   Hyter, Michael, and Judith L. Turnock. *The Power of Inclusion: Unlock the Potential and Productivity of Your Workforce.* Ontario: Wiley, 2006.

other non-merit factors suppress, neutralize, or even negate the effects of merit, creating barriers to individual Hispanic mobility in corporate America. We must recognize those forces that keep Latinos in roles and positions that they currently occupy regardless of the extent of individual merit.

The 4 Percent Shame

The myth of the meritocracy is that it holds that those who "make it" do so because of their excellent ability; in a true meritocracy, what you do, and not who you are, matters.

As the HACR 2016 Inclusion Index (described in the Introduction) documented, Latino representation in top roles in corporate America proves that meritocracy is not fulfilling its true promise. Only a little over 4 percent of executive officer positions in Fortune 500 firms are held by Hispanics. Worse news is that Hispanic females hold fewer than 1 percent of those positions. Further, HACR research shows little movement at all in the representation of Hispanics over the past several years.

The myth of meritocracy continues for Hispanics when you review representation on corporate boards of directors. While HACR's index of participating companies came up with a 7 percent representation, the Alliance for Board Diversity reports that Hispanics/Latinos held only 3.5 percent of Fortune 500 board seats in 2016. In either case, whether 3.5 or 7 percent, this is a woeful gap from the 17 percent representation of Latinos in the U.S. population. This is not to suggest that the percentage of board positions needs to be 17 percent at this time, since we do need to account for an eligible pool with certain educational and leadership credentials. However, while we must still address the legacy of educational disparities, this yawning 10 to 13.5 percent gap cannot be explained away simply with the "there's not an available labor pool" argument.

If a meritocracy is supposed to result in a normal distribution of leadership opportunity based on merit, then companies must address what we refer to as The 4 Percent Shame. Something besides merit is preventing Latino and Hispanic advancement to these executive officer positions in Fortune 500 firms. The gap points to the reality that favoritism, discrimination, and bias do exist in most corporate cultures. What supporters of a meritocracy don't realize is that the current system reinforces ideals that shore up existing power structures and privileges.

We must also think through the pressures faced by those 4 percent of Hispanic and Latino executives who have demonstrated merit and moved to the very top of the corporate ladder. Their relative scarcity at the top of a meritocracy system places them under a microscope by other Latinos in the workplace who are desperate for role models who look like them. Many of these Latino executives may prefer to simply not be identified by their ethnic affiliation so they can avoid being associated with what they perceive as negative stereotypes that members of the majority may have of Latinos. At the same time, the organization is eager to highlight their presence in leadership ranks as, what turns out to be false evidence that the meritocracy system does indeed work for Latinos.

Latino executives who do not appear to connect strongly with their ethnicity or who are not seen actively advocating for Hispanic issues may be inadvertently sending a message to younger Latinos that the road to success within a meritocracy requires assimilation and the denial of their Hispanic heritage.

Data suggests that this phenomenon is already happening. In the 2016 study conducted by the Center for Talent Innovation (highlighted in the Introduction), we saw that more than three out of four Latinos expend energy repressing parts of their persona in the workplace, downplaying their ethnicity. Having to expend energy related to their identity is energy not available for use in improving their workplace performance, and thus lowers their chances of success. Some could conclude that Latino executives who chose not to connect visibly with their Hispanic identity in the workplace are unintentionally complicit in the myth of meritocracy.

Conscious and Unconscious Bias

These realities of Latinos experiencing discrimination and bias in the workplace are what undermine the promise of meritocracy. Several of the Latino leaders interviewed for this book described experiencing conscious bias in the workplace. As an example, one of our Hispanic executive interviewees described an outing with an executive from a previous employer:

> We went to this Hispanic event together, and at the event we were selling our product. As he was walking around he said, "What are these people wearing? Do they even have cars to drive?" So I said to him, "You know I think it's best you leave because you're probably going to do more damage to our company's brand than good at this point, and what you said is extremely offensive." So he left the event. Fast-forward a week after and he announced a reorganization and the result of the whole reorganization was the elimination of just one job—and that job was mine.

Darren Rebelez, current president of IHOP, recalls working many years ago at a different company whose leader was in his mid-seventies. While at an informal work gathering, someone innocently asked Darren about his ethnicity, to which Darren responded that he was Mexican. He described this leader's response on hearing his answer:

> He said, "No, you're not Mexican." I said, "Well, sure I am." Again he said, "No, you are not a Mexican." I didn't realize it until that moment, but he was a bigot. The notion that a Mexican could have risen to such a high level within the company, it just blew his mind.

Luis Ubiñas, former senior partner at McKinsey & Company, past president of the Ford Foundation, and current corporate board member and advisor, adds this experience:

> I say this with no bitterness, but what you need to remember is that we don't come from a place where race doesn't matter. I remember being at a meeting, as one of McKinsey's leading experts on newspapers, where the head of a small regional newspaper turned to the senior partner who's introducing me to them and said to my face, "Is this the best you can do?" All he knew about me was that I was Hispanic.

While examples of conscious bias such as these may not be rampant, their negative impact on Latino upward mobility in the workplace can be formidable. Just a handful of stories become part of the corporate lore which then gets repeated a hundred-fold.

Equally impactful is the unconscious bias Latinos face at work. That bias permeates the workplace at all levels because we all have prejudices. Numerous studies confirm that people harbor unconscious bias even when they explicitly believe that prejudice and discrimination are wrong.

Unconscious bias is subtler but often no less corrosive to Latinos attempting to reach the fullness of their own potential. Even well-intentioned people who wouldn't say they are biased sometimes display unconscious bias against Latinos, assuming certain inaccurate stereotypes, and potentially hurting Latinos' career advancement. Victor Arias, senior client partner at Korn Ferry, recalled a meeting he had with a previous employer earlier in his career. The meeting, scheduled in a conference room, was with the CEO of the company at that time:

> I walked into the meeting at the appropriate time and on the table there is a meal place setting. Then the CEO came in and he said, "Well, I think it's really important that we teach you how to have lunch." I was very insulted. I just said, "You are making the assumption that I don't know this already." "No, no, no," he said. I asked, "Do you do this for everybody?" His response? "No."

And there was the time he walked into the locker room of the upscale health club he belonged to and another member attempted to hand him some wet towels and asked him to bring some dry ones. Victor put him in his place.

Acts of unconscious bias lead people to wrongly assume that Latinos are not leaders. One Latina executive interviewed for this book describes some of the meetings she attends where such bias is still on display:

> I've had vendors come and present to me and to my team, and these vendors assume that I'm not the one making the final decision. When they present, they looked at

everyone else but me. When I ask questions they would look at others and answer the question. That's usually when I just get up, walk away, and not finish the meeting.

These biases create additional headwinds that some Latinos are not able to overcome because it saps their motivation. Misunderstandings may arise when cultural differences in how Latinos respond to feedback, in how they prefer to complete their tasks, and in how they express emotions may make their non-Latino managers uncomfortable because those managers come from different socio-psychological backgrounds. (We will look at these specifics in Chapter 4.)

The Shadow of Anti-Immigration Walls

Making it even more difficult to overcome the myth of meritocracy is the current sociocultural environment in the U.S., leading to the rise of anti-immigrant sentiments and policies. Most Latinos will not soon forget the statements Donald Trump made during his announcement speech for his candidacy for U.S. president in June 2015:

> When Mexico sends its people, they're not sending their best. They're sending people that have lots of problems, and they're bringing those problems with us. They're bringing drugs. They're bringing crime. They're rapists. And some, I assume, are good people.

This then set the tone for YouTube video clips capturing incidents across the country of people telling Latinos to "Go back to where you came from," or "Why don't you learn to speak English?" Newspapers routinely publish stories of increased violence about Latinos or Latino schools being vandalized with graffiti that reads, "Build the wall higher."

These sentiments also convey perceived negative economic costs associated with job competition and an undue burden on education and social services. While some anti-immigration advocates won't admit it, there is a concern that Latino immigrants will cause a change to traditional American identities and values.

Anti-immigrant legislative bills are being driven by isolated incidents of crimes committed by undocumented immigrants as justification to eliminate sanctuary cities and to enforce harsh immigration policies. The increase in immigration raids is creating fear and stress within the broader Latino community. A recent study by Dr. Edward D. Vargas, published in a 2017 issue of the *Journal of Health Politics, Policy, and Law*,[2] found that Latinos who believe that where they live is unfavorable toward immigrants are 70 percent more likely to report poor health, regardless of their own legal or immigration status. Additionally, the study found that Latinos who know about a family member or friend being deported are one and a half times more likely to report needing to seek help for emotional or mental health problems such as feeling anxious, sad, or nervous.

Currently arrests are happening while people are at home, when they drop off their children at school, or when they receive a speeding ticket. Planeloads of deported Latinos are landing daily in Mexico City; these are people who came to the U.S. when they were very young; they don't know Spanish, and culturally see themselves as Americans.

This anti-immigrant sentiment is definitely being noticed by Hispanic executives. Grace Lieblein, former president of General Motors Mexico and current director on the Southwest Airlines and Honeywell boards told us:

---

2   Vargas, E., Juarez, M., & Sanchez, G. (2017). Fear by Association: Perceptions of Anti-Immigrant Policy and Health Outcomes. *Journal of Health Politics, Policy and Law*. 42(3). Pp. 459-483.

I think it's scary. It [anti-immigrant sentiment] worries me, it really does. It worries me from a lot of different perspectives. It makes me feel very unsettled...and I think it's very sad.

The fear of many Hispanic executives is that such negative sentiment may make it more difficult for Latinos to advocate for Hispanic inclusion and equality in an increasingly polarized country. Such sentiment may make even more Latinos want to downplay or hide their Hispanic heritage because a growing number of people in the U.S. are equating being Hispanic as somehow meaning that they are "less than" in some capacity.

Latino Response

Even though anti-immigrant rhetoric appears to undermine Hispanic achievement and progress while conscious and unconscious biases still create obstacles to overcome, and even with the reality that our corporate cultures are not color-blind and that meritocracy has its limits, Hispanics are not giving up hope.

Luis Ubiñas reminds Latinos not to let bias or discrimination beat them:

Any Hispanic who tells you they haven't been exposed to moments of inequity is not telling the truth. The question isn't "Are you going to face moments of discrimination?" but rather "What are you going to do when you do?" Are you going to let them be barriers, or are you going to let them be a motivation? Of course, I've faced discrimination; of course, every Hispanic has faced discrimination. Is that a problem? Of course! Is it something that should be a barrier to Hispanic success? Of course not! Latinos need to ask themselves if they will use discrimination as an excuse to lamely lay down and fail, or are they going to use it as motivation? Remember, at the end of the day this country has been built by people who were first excluded and then led.

In spite of all this, today's Hispanic executives still believe in the power of meritocracy and of the American Dream. Their grandparents, parents, and even some of these executives gave up too much in their immigrant journey in a quest of success to simply stand by and have those dreams unrealized or taken away.

The setbacks have made them even more determined than ever to hold corporate America accountable to the idea that Latinos can reach positions of leadership. ❧

CHAPTER 2

Identity Crisis: Assimilate, Opt Out, or Double Down?

"Uno no puede pelear consigo mismo, porque esta batalla tendría un solo perdedor."

One can't fight with oneself, since this battle has only one loser.

—Mario Vargas Llosa, Peruvian author
2010 Nobel Prize in Literature

Being Latino is as much about the choices as it is about the heritage. This means that Latino identity relies heavily on how individuals choose to deal with their cultural surroundings. They can accept and internalize them, deny them, or change them.

Choosing is more complex because Latinos face a myriad of pressures in their journey to define themselves in a society that often disparages their identity and seeks to impose definitions on them rather than allow self-identification. This identity struggle often gets carried into the corporate world experience of many Latino professionals.

This struggle was true for many Latino executives in our research study, who at some point had to come to grips with their own sense of Latino identity and ways to express it in the workplace—or even try to hide it during certain phases of their careers. The executives who did not lose their Latino identity along the way worked through these difficult organizational waters. Throughout this book we will share the lessons they learned.

This key "to be or not to be" decision by the Latino executives was at the heart of the professional journey of many of the leaders we interviewed. The confluence of cultural and family pride currents flowing from one side, and of stinging discrimination currents flowing from the other, presented continuous dilemmas on how to best manage their own expression of cultural identity in the workplace.

Exploring how they dealt with these crosscurrents is further complicated because there is little uniformity in the formative years of these leaders. For some, their early years were fully immersed in Latino culture, while for others they were the minority, sometimes the only one, in a mostly European-American culture. Further, a handful of others grew up in racially mixed environments with Blacks, Asians, and other minorities.

Thus, there are multiple variations in how the executives dealt with their cultural identity when confronted with stark choices about whether to assimilate, opt out, or double down as they pursued their ambitions to be leaders in their organizations.

In their seminal 2001 essay, "Racial Identity Development and Latinos in the United States,"[1] Bernardo Ferdman and Plácida Gallegos describe Latino identity as the lens through which Latinos "see" themselves. The messages that Latinos receive about their group can be positive, negative, or neutral, depending on the identity lens they choose to use.

Based on our research and personal observation, we have categorized the different lenses used and paths Latinos leaders have taken in the following way:

Unapologetic Latinos
Have fully embraced their Latino identity and chosen not hide it, even in the most non-Latino of environments.

Equivocal Latinos
Have some boundaries about their Latino identity because of European-American values they were heavily exposed to in their formative years and during their educational and career pursuits.

Retro Latinos
May have grown up as an equivocal Latino but, who, for a variety of reasons in adulthood, have gone back to their Latino roots to discover or rediscover those elements of a distant or submerged heritage and culture.

Invisible Latinos
Have fully denied and disowned any connection to Latino culture deliberately, whether they grew up in a Latino environment or not.

---

1   Ferdman, B., and P.I. Gallegos. 2001. "Racial Identity Development and Latinos in the United States." In *New Perspectives on Racial Identity and Development*, C. Wijeyesinghe and B. Jackson, 32-66. New York University Press.

In our sample of leaders, we found all of the first three types, but it's no surprise that we found no Invisible Latinos. By the very nature of this book's subject, those agreeing to be interviewed came to the conversation with a sense of ownership and pride in their Latino heritage.

As we will see, their stories varied in terms of their upbringing, their journeys of Latino identity, and their resulting positions as leaders. Yet one thing they almost all had in common was that each at some point in their educational and work journeys were confronted with a need to *choose* how much their Latino heritage would be part of their leadership identity.

In contrast to Black executives, who by the very nature of the color of their skin don't have a choice, many non-Afro-Latino leaders' do have a choice of how much their Latino heritage will be part of their leadership identity.

This is because Latinos are not one racial group but rather an ethnic group that is a combination of races including Caucasian, indigenous, Asian, and Black. For some this makes it possible to *pass* for a member of the majority culture, if they choose to do so. Therefore, most of the Latino executive stories we collected brim with self-aware narratives of multiple choices made along the way.

The Unapologetic Latino

The stories of two of our leaders, Lisa Garcia Quiroz, senior vice president of cultural investments at Time Warner, and Victor Arias, senior client partner on the executive search side of Korn Ferry, illustrate the leader who chooses to double down on their ethnic identity when faced with conscious or unconscious peer pressure to assimilate.

To understand their stance, one must first know the story of their formative years. Here is Lisa's narrative of growing up in a fully Latino household in the midst of a white working-class neighborhood, and the way this shaped her own sense of Latina identity. Both the arc as well as the details of her story contain the anchors for her daily decisions as a leader to be unapologetically Latina in how she presents herself:

> I grew up on Staten Island, New York. I'm the oldest of three. My mother is Puerto Rican; my father is the son of Mexican immigrants.
>
> I grew up in a very Latino household. It was like the dichotomy to the external world I lived in. I spoke Spanish before I spoke English. My mother had only been here from Puerto Rico for a couple of years, and she barely spoke English by the time I was born, so I grew up with a strong sense of both the Mexican and Puerto Rican cultures. Growing up, a lot of people would ask me if I felt more Puerto Rican or more Mexican. I felt both equally.
>
> We'd spend weeks at a time in Puerto Rico in a rural part of the island. And my Mexican grandmother ensured that we all grew up with a strong sense of our Mexican roots, which meant that if Tony Aguilar was coming into Madison Square Garden, off we'd go. She was a great cook, so we grew up with the food, the music, and the culture. Then we had these epic trips where she'd take us to Mexico for a few months at a time to make sure we knew where we'd come from.
>
> These connections to our roots were pivotal for my identity because growing up in such a white neighborhood with both overt and unconscious racism, they were what allowed me to survive and even thrive in that environment. It gave me such a strong sense of self and pride about who I was and where I came from that nothing

could shake that. This was so important, especially when I think of how easy it would've been for my parents to have said, "No, no, no, no, no—we're going to raise you only as an American."

When you look at my school pictures, I was like the one brown spot in my kindergarten class, my first grade class, my second, and third. Because I was also a really good student, including being the valedictorian of my elementary school class, I got into a great high school, an all-girls Catholic school on Staten Island, where I was a top student. I then went on to Harvard and Harvard Business School. Even today, as the only Latina in the C-suite at Time Warner, the situation is consistent with how it's always been all my life: one brown spot.

Victor Arias also grew up in a Latino household, but in contrast to Lisa, was mostly part of a majority Latino culture in El Paso, Texas. He had some adjusting to do when he entered business school and the mostly Anglo and privileged world of Stanford University. He did so while still maintaining his deep Latino roots, sometimes with surprising outcomes.

I grew up in El Paso, Texas, known as the "Ellis Island of the South" because that place has so many families that have gone through there as a transition ground before they took off to different parts of the U.S. Although El Paso is in the U.S., the community is very Mexican. My first language at home was Spanish. Every Sunday we went to Mass, listened to Mexican music, and either hung out with the *abuelos* (grandparents) or visited with friends and shopped in Ciudad Juarez.

So it was very much a bifurcated existence because on the one hand, it was all Spanish, but when you started going to school, you had to know English. My growing up was in a very safe environment with a very big family. My mom came from a family of fourteen so I had lots of *primos* (cousins) and incredible grandparents. My dad was only one of two, so he gravitated to my mother's side of the family because it was just so special to have so many *hijos* and *hijas* (sons and daughters) and relatives.

My grandmother from my dad's side was a role model of how you can survive. She was a single mom who had come from Chihuahua, Mexico. My dad and my *tía* (aunt) were both born in El Paso, where they lived in a two-room apartment with an outhouse in the back. When we spent the night with my grandmother, we were all cramped up, and I remember having to go to the bathroom at night in the dark to the outhouse with the *cucuy* [boogeyman]. As I reminisce about those times of hardship and her work as a domestic, I just remember what those experiences meant for her and her dignity. I know that background impacted my dad, who was a latchkey kid since his mother had to work all day. It set the tone for my dad's motivations to achieve things for us that he didn't have growing up. It gave him drive, energy, and persistence, yet he was always sincere and humble.

My friends were predominantly Latinos, mostly Hispanic in a community like El Paso, but my first experience with mixed cultures was when I went to a Catholic grade school that was supposed to be a good school where there was a good mix of Anglos and Mexicanos. I'd hang out with Anglo friends and that's how I learned a lot of things about them.

Growing up in El Paso, a lot of "Spanglish" was spoken. It was different from the very proper Spanish that my compadres from Ciudad Juarez on the Mexico side would speak. In some ways they would look down on us because we didn't speak Spanish. So I started to feel that kind of difference. Also most of the guys from Ciudad Juarez came from privileged families, and I felt a little discomfort with that.

Then it came time for Victor to leave familiar El Paso and go to Stanford to get his MBA. This was his first time truly feeling different.

My first day at Stanford I headed to a wine and cheese reception feeling intimidated and thinking, "What the hell am I doing here?" So I wore my best dark blue velour sweatsuit and my best baseball cap. I found this guy who said, "I want you to meet these other friends of mine." So I said, "OK," and he took me over to the middle of the courtyard with all these guys who were the height of preppiness. The last guy, about six-foot-four, sandy-haired, had brown corduroy pants, Topsiders (which I just called boat shoes), two Izod shirts with collars turned up, and a sweater draped over his shoulders. I said to him, "Kurt, how are you? Nice to meet you. Do you have any idea the collars are up on your shirt?" I went behind him and turned his collars down. He got really red. The others thought I was messin' with him. They said, "Wow, this guy is really bold and kind of crazy to do that." From that day, I got accepted by the rest, and they became my best friends, though Kurt didn't talk to me for two years.

Through their exceptionally successful educational trajectories and their stellar careers neither Lisa nor Victor lost their sense of being Latino, and in fact, it is a salient characteristic of their identities in the workplace. Here's Lisa again:

> I had a very strong commitment to ensuring that there were more Latinos and Latinas when I left than when I came in. I will tell you that's been a theme in my life, certainly in my corporate life: not just bringing in more Latinos, but bringing in more people of color as well as more women to any position I have available. My staff is 100 percent diverse. I always want to leave a place better than when I got there.

There are other Unapologetic Latino executives in our sample group whose formative experience stories were quite different—growing up outside the U.S. and migrating as young adults, or having been an expat in different countries due to their parents' work, or coming from more middle-class backgrounds—but they too are grounded in their ethnic cultural identity. They expressed no ambivalence about it. For example, born and raised in Costa Rica, Paul Raines, CEO of GameStop, shares:

> First of all, Spanish is a beautiful language. In many ways, much, much richer than English. You know, I'm blessed because my mother was one of these people who insisted I speak Spanish as a kid. I see kids today and they sort of go, "Aah, not sure I wanna be speaking Spanish." And I say, "Man, you are missing the greatest opportunity. Nobody says you have to exclude English so you can speak Spanish. What you should be thinking is, "I want to be multilingual."

Yet to be successful in corporate America, these people with diverse backgrounds also had to find ways to adapt to what are the very different and contrasting patterns of being, acting, and speaking that are part of any corporate culture. In fact, the overuse of the unapologetic approach can lead to being misunderstood, not fully accepted, or less effective as leaders.

"I feel that when we're in the corporate world we have to tone down our more expressive selves, for it doesn't allow us to be as authentic in what we're trying to project to the people we're working with," a young Latina professional told us at the focus group we conducted at the University of Southern California in Los Angeles.

A key attribute of Unapologetic Latinos is that they can appreciate the beauty of being Latino and at the same time be able to recognize certain features, those attributed to Latinos that others may perceive as negative, and adjust accordingly without being any less Latino.

Juan Galarraga, a senior vice president at Target who grew up in Venezuela and came to the U.S. as an adult, concurs:

> We are loud, we like to challenge, we tell it like it is, and in multiple households, at dinner or wherever, that's how we talk. We're not really fighting, but Anglos often think we are.

So did he adapt?

> Yes, I have. As I've grown in different professional roles, I've realized that our forwardness is one of those areas where it can really hurt us. I do take a lot of pride in what I have to offer, but my *how* in how I present myself has changed over time. Maybe instead of making a strong statement such as, "I think this is stupid," I may

ask an open-ended question to lead folks in the room to say, "This may not be right."

Another cultural preference that is especially true for Latinos who grew up outside the U.S. is a different sense of what being on time means. Juan says:

> We tend to be late to a many events. It's normal; it's who we are and how we are. If we say come at 7, we would never come at 7; we'd come at 7:30 or 8. But at work you have to be cautious of that habit, so I have adjusted and you'll never see me being late to a meeting in the U.S.

In a New York City focus group we conducted with Latino and Latina Millennial leaders, a young media professional spoke of watching his parents begin to deny their Cuban heritage when they moved to Florida from New York. This was at the time he was beginning to embrace his Latino heritage unapologetically, in direct contrast to his parents:

> My parents are snowbirds now. They loathe Miami. My dad refuses to speak Spanish when he's there. He hates the fact that he gets better service when he hits 2 for Spanish than when he hits 1 for English. He is hardcore. "Why are you assuming when I walk into CVS that you should be speaking to me in Spanish?" my dad wonders.

The Unapologetic Latinos can maintain their cultural selves while still being sensitive and compassionate toward others. However, these Unapologetic Latinos are always crystal clear about who they are, as summarized by Sandra Rivera, a vice president at Intel:

> I do feel like one of my big responsibilities is to make sure that in all of my leadership talks and all the men-toring and sponsorship that I do of Intel employees, is

that I bring up my Colombian identity as part of who I am. I talk about it in a very public way, so that Latinos who have similar backgrounds can feel proud as well.

The Equivocal Latino

The Equivocal Latino profile often emerges from an upbringing where European-American culture was quite predominant in the person's life without deeply infused Latino cultural values being instilled by the family. This often sets the initial parameters of a person's identity. According to Ferdman and Gallegos, for those we refer to as Equivocal Latinos, parents and extended family members tend to instruct the children about the boundaries of their Latino identity. What they learn at home about themselves as Latinos (for example, "We are better than others," or "We are less than others," or "We are no different than others" etc.) lays the foundation of their Latino identity.

The *familia* (parents, aunts, grandparents) may have been deeply rooted themselves in the Latino culture, but unlike in Lisa's or Victor's case, the cultural messaging and acculturation was missing or done with a lighter touch. This often takes place because of the parents' desire for their children to be assimilated—and therefore accepted—by mainstream American society. In some of these households, the parents actually chose not to speak Spanish to their children, and encouraged them to socialize as much as possible outside the Latin culture because they saw it as an opportunity to increase their children's chances of breaking out of the *barrios* they themselves felt trapped in.

This distancing from Latino culture was further exacerbated when their families chose to move to predominantly non-Latino neighborhoods where the process of acculturation could happen in more undiluted ways.

IHOP President Darren Rebelez grew up in San Diego as a third-generation Latino. His mom was Irish. He comments:

> For me there was more of a heritage in the food than the language. That's one thing I'd harass my dad about all the time; he did not speak Spanish to us. I had to struggle learning it on my own. My grandparents would speak it in the house and then they'd switch over to English for us unless they were chewing us out, which they'd do in Spanish.

The Equivocal Latino dynamic can also be circumstantial when it is played out in the workplace but not in personal lives. Equivocal Latinos sometimes define themselves situationally and are astute about fulfilling the perceptions and expectations of others. Thus their identity is based more on their personal interactions than their Latino background. Darren explains:

> Personally, I think of myself as being Mexican, but professionally, I don't wear that on my sleeve. And it's not because of anything that I'm ashamed of or don't want to talk about; I just never wanted to stress that identity as if I was looking for something. I didn't want any special treatment.

> Frankly, I view myself as an American first, and I think the great thing about being an American versus being of any other country is that you can have two identities as an American: American and Mexican. I can do both and can be proud of both because that's what we do in America. We embrace our heritage because we're a melting pot, people coming from everywhere.

> My background is an important part of my life personally, but when I'm at work, I just am who I am. From

time to time my being Mexican comes up, of course. I'm there to support, but I don't lead with my ethnicity.

I've mentored people over the years, and they ask, "How did you get where you are?" I always tell people, "Just focus on getting results. Don't focus on your heritage as part of your job." I worry that my being Mexican may be used as a reason for a handout. I agree that your heritage is who you are, and I wouldn't shy away from it. But it's difficult to argue with results.

In a conversation Andrés had with his colleague Jorge Farías, a senior client partner at Korn Ferry, he sounded a bit wistful about the choices he made considering the pressures in his career:

I remember what it was like during the times right after affirmative action, immediately following the ground-breaking civil rights movement, and well into the 1990s. It felt to me as though many companies and industries still did not view people of color as equally intelligent as those of the dominant culture.

My internal voice told me to just do the best job in whatever situation I found myself. I naively believed it would be hard for people to deny me what I deserved if I performed at high levels. I trusted my inner voice but still worried about external and unknown factors that could hinder my development, my progress, and my success.

To this day, I wonder if my lighter skin, my intense focus on education (earning a doctorate), and my working hard to avoid any hint of an accent—in effect, my efforts at assimilation—weren't ultimately the key that opened doors for me. But I do wonder at what cost to me personally.

The Retro Latino

It is possible for some individuals to maintain an orientation throughout their lives with little or no movement or change. But life as an Equivocal Latino is not predetermined as something people have to stay with if they do not want to. Latinos constantly make choices about how they see their difference and how they accommodate societal messages about themselves.

This happens regardless of whether there had or had not been much Latino cultural influence during the formative years. Ultimately cultural identity is a lot about choice.

The Retro Latino goes to great lengths to reconnect, rediscover, or discover those roots for the first time. They end up taking Spanish, learning how to dance salsa, bachata, or reggaeton. They start reading Latin American literature, begin hanging out with more Latinos, or joining Latino organizations for the first time. Others even start to date Latinas or Latinos, something they had never done before.

A few stories:

Jorge Figueredo, executive vice president of HR at McKesson Corporation, was born in Cuba. When his young parents immigrated to Union City, New Jersey (a place with many Hispanic families) and then to Harrington Park, New Jersey (overwhelmingly Anglo), he did not speak for a while as a child because he was confused as to which language to use.

There were several scuffles with some of the local kids on the streets because they made fun of him. This mistreatment continued all through middle school, with a few locals making it clear they didn't appreciate having a Latino in their community.

Due to these experiences with being different, before college I had always stressed my Americanism and tried to suppress my Cuban identity. But I had an awakening regarding my Latino-ness at Fairfield University, a Jesuit institution in Connecticut. Suddenly there were more Latinos as I met students from Puerto Rico, Cuba, and other parts of Latin America. I took a course in Latin American studies at the urging of a Cuban professor who was also a Castro sympathizer.

In fact, I began to realize that I *was* different in trivial as well as more profound ways. For example, growing up we were always late for things when my mom took me because she had a different perspective on being "on time" versus being "late." Also my parents would have a big party each year and my large extended family eventually became a part of the social fabric in my childhood community. Further, politics was always a topic debated passionately in the house.

My parents were worried that America was changing for the worse due to drugs and the sexual revolution. In addition, my college education led me to have some intense political debates with my dad, an exile from Castro's Cuba. But I also had debates with my Marxist professor. I saw myself as less ideological and more pragmatic.

Emblematically, how he manages his name is a full fusion of this complex dual identity. He never changed the spelling to "George," yet he introduces himself to others with the English pronunciation.

Yvonne Garcia, global head of client solutions for State Street Corporation, started her Retro Latina journey as a teenager and fully realized the process in her twenties. But in contrast to Jorge, she took the Latina identity further.

As I was growing up, I wondered if it was okay to be Hispanic. Perhaps there was an underlying force within me that taught me not to highlight it as much (maybe it was just survival skills) so I could just fit into an all-white school. I think I had learned this behavior of, "OK, cool, your last name is Garcia and you're Dominican, but maybe you don't need to promote it as much."

Being Latina probably didn't become a cool thing to me until mid-high school years where I started to meet other Hispanics and other women who were like me.

Then I moved from the underlying notion of "I'm Latina but the world doesn't need to know; they'll figure it out," to now as an adult I'm the opposite: I lead with the fact that I'm Latina.

These complex dynamics of identity did not manifest themselves just for many of the executives but also for many of the young professionals in our focus groups.

Here are the comments of a Latina, a professional in the finance industry from our USC focus group:

I work in Newport Beach, a California community that is predominantly Anglo. So my attitude was more of a hide your Latino-ness, tone it down because when you go to these events there are C-level people and senior vice presidents and your top Ivy League, typical white-person-with-money crowd.

I totally figured out their culture and their norms and modified my way of speaking to people. But the cost was that I couldn't be myself, be authentic.

It took me being in the Latina Leadership Academy at USC to start to own who I was, own my Latina-ness, own my culture, and really relate to people as fully myself as I embraced my culture and became authentic. Because the more you hide your Latina-ness, the more you're not being yourself. You can't be as successful as you want to be when you're not being authentic because you're hiding who you really are.

For me it has always has been challenging to be the Latina that I am, but then as I accepted who I was and accepted my Latina-ness, I started to brand myself around it. Now people know who I am. When people ask me what my name is, I say "Janet *Perez*." You'll never hear me just say just "I'm Janet." No, "I'm Janet Perez." "Do you speak Spanish?" "Yes, I speak Spanish." I learned to embrace who I really am because when I was walking into these huge networking events, I would just be in a corner by myself. When I accepted who I was, that's when I became more confident, surer of my identity.

Remember that some Retro Latinos may not have been fully exposed to their Latino background, history, or culture during their childhood. But as individuals mature and change their surroundings, the lens with which they view their Latino-ness may widen.

Several of the leaders we interviewed who grew up in mostly European-American environments had their Latino identity awakened when they moved to a place where there were more Latinos or where Latinos made the effort to find each other and network.

When this happens, feelings of isolation are more easily pushed aside by the simple presence and interaction with other Latinos. In the myriad Latino affinity settings of employee resource groups and professional associations that Robert has operated in, he frequently hears from many Latinos of how refreshing it is for them to see so many Latinos who are extremely proud of their Hispanic heritage and who wear their Latino identity as a badge of pride.

In many, this pride awakens a desire to let those aspects of their Latino heritage peek out, slowly at first, and incrementally revealing themselves more fully until it becomes a combination of a cultural identity blossoming from within, accelerated by increasing the number of Latino culture inputs, leading to an identity metamorphosis.

The Invisible Latino

The Invisible Latinos are the ones who ignore or even disown their Latino heritage, often won't even acknowledge that they speak Spanish, don't want their parents to come visit them, or just pretend to be as white as their college friends or workmates even though they did grow up with a Latino experience.

They prefer to identify themselves and others as "just people," and claim to be color-blind because of their preference to view each person as distinct from their ethnic or racial background. Juan Galarraga, another Unapologetic Latino, also must fight the temptation not to judge:

> As you go higher and higher in organizations, I've seen some Latino leaders almost forget that they're Latino. I don't know if it's the pressure of fitting in.

Juan goes further and indicates that rather than giving in to that peer pressure to fit in, he actually embraces being different:

> When people make fun of my accent, I cannot be prouder of my accent. After all, I know who I am, and I stay

grounded by understanding what's important in life and by not forgetting where I came from.

Some Latinos who may have more Anglo features, such as blonde hair and blue eyes, may chose to connect more closely with their European-American features and all that is connoted by them over their Hispanic heritage. They see their whiteness as the essential and primary element of their identity, and view the world through a white-tinted lens. Invisible Latinos also tend to view the shortage of Latinos in senior roles as the result of individual failure and not as bias or discrimination against Latinos.

Consider the Latino or Latina who hears about some Latino professional organization and says, "You know what, I don't want to get involved." We asked Victor Arias how he would respond:

> I can be a little judgmental when people tell me that. However, I have to think about what stage in their life they're at. When I see young Latinos who are just making their way into corporate America, I say, "The most important thing you need to do is to be extremely successful at your job." That may take a toll time-wise on their involvement in the community, so I tend to give them a pass and support them building an incredible reputation in whatever role they're trying to pursue. But where I am less understanding is with those that have clearly done well. If they are not giving back, it tells me that, one, they don't care about the community, and two, there are some real insecurities about being perceived as Latino. I tell them, "You've been to college. Do you think you're the exception to the rule?" "Oh yeah," they say, "we're very fortunate." I say, "You've been given a lot, and it might be good to think about helping others, don't you think?"

The fact that none of the executives we interviewed disowned their Latino identity tells us that a dimension to strong leadership is authenticity. We don't believe it's any coincidence that these individuals are successful leaders and that they never gave up and disowned their heritage.

Don't get us wrong. Invisible Latinos can attain success, but this book is a *Latino* executive manifesto, not just an executive manifesto. The invisible ones may be executives, but they're not *Latino* executives; they've disowned that part. They're not *manifesting*. This book is the manifesto of leaders who are successful and who definitely embrace their Latino-ness.

This journey into Latino-ness is not only about inner individual identity work as we have seen in this chapter, but it also demands outer communal identity work—defining who we are as a Latino community in the U.S. And here we have a lot of work to do, as we will see in the next chapter, "Intra-Latino Divides: Truth or Consequences." ❧

CHAPTER *3*

Intra-Latino Divides:
Truth or Consequences

"La cultura consiste en conexiones,
no de separaciones: especializarse es aislar."

Culture consists of connections, not of separations: to specialize is to isolate.

—Carlos Fuentes, *Myself with Others: Selected Essays*

Previously we delved into the dynamics of cultural identity crisis and resolution through the lens of the individual. But cultural identity must also be seen through a group identity perspective. Who do Latinos say we are collectively? Suddenly a simple question gets complex.

Now we must look at a more negative view as we explore the shadow side of Latino reality in the U.S. We will eventually delve into the inspiring and uplifting Latino story, which includes a rising pan-Latino consciousness unfolding in corporate America and in the country as a whole. First, however, we need to acknowledge the barriers we ourselves create that further complicate the obstacles we find in corporate America.

Elements that divide us include our nationality, our socioeconomic and racial backgrounds (whether or not one grew up in the U.S.), plus the languages we speak as well as the accents we may retain.

Nationalistic Divides

There is vast diversity beneath that umbrella labeled "Latino" because Latinos can be economic or political refugees, or both. Others are descendants of families who lived in the part of Mexico that was annexed by the U.S. in the Spanish-American War. In addition to the immigrant waves of first-, second-, third-, and fourth-generation Latinos, other Latinos include the Spanish-, English-, and Spanglish-dominants, the Millennial, Gen Xer, and boomer Latinos, and the racial spectrum of White, Indigenous, Black, and Asian, as well as the twenty-seven different nationalities that comprise what being Latino means.

In the U.S., the most divisive differences among Latinos are the ones around national heritage. While a seemingly harmless issue, and even fun when it comes to World Cup favorites and bragging rights, these nationalistic fissures are the most debilitating in terms of Latinos gaining collective power commensurate to their rising numbers.

This phenomenon is caused in part when Latinos view themselves primarily in terms of their nationality and not necessarily identifying with Latinos of all other nationalities. Having great pride and viewing one's own nationality positively is not wrong or destructive. But as Ferdman and Gallegos point out[1], it does create a problem when these individuals identify

---

1   Ferdman, B., and P.I. Gallegos. 2001. *Racial Identity Development and Latinos in the United States*. C. Wijeyesinghe and B. Jackson, 32-66. New York University Press.

themselves exclusively with their country of origin and view Latinos from other nationalities as deficient or inferior. When this happens, the result is a more narrow and exclusive view of their Latino identity.

Until Latinos can collectively and cohesively address this dimension of Latino identity, they will be responsible for their lack of advancement. The nationality differences have become more fissures than features. George Herrera, CEO of Herrera-Cristina Group, describes it this way:

> When growing up in New York City, we had no issue across the different Latino groups. It was a true melting pot; you had Puerto Ricans, Cubans, Dominicans, Peruvians, Chicanos, and we just got along.
>
> But when I got to the U.S. Hispanic Chamber of Commerce in 1998 I saw the underpinnings of what was keeping the Hispanic community down in America—an ethnic turf. The feeling was that there was no way a Mexican in L.A. was going to let a Puerto Rican out of New York be a spokesperson for them. "Hold on a second," was my response. "We're talking about an economic development agenda, and so what are you guys fighting over? If anything, you are fighting over the crumbs anyway because you're being nickeled and dimed by white America."

Comcast Corporate SVP Myrna Soto agrees:

> I often think about our broader Hispanic community, and how we often hurt each other because of our subcultures. The Mexicans versus the Cubans versus the Venezuelans versus the Colombians. I think about the

power we have as a collective. And for some reason, there are these subcultures that create diminishing returns for our advancement.

Socioeconomic Divides

Socioeconomic differences often overlap with the national identities divide. Cubans who fled the island during Castro's revolution have a higher per capita income than Mexicans and Central Americans, causing some elitist attitudes. Puerto Ricans are U.S. citizens by birth and can sometimes have a condescending attitude toward Mexicans and others whose parents, or they themselves, are here undocumented. Another factor is the classic *Us vs. Them* dynamic that develops to allow groups of people to judge and negatively stereotype other groups. This causes Latinos to fall prey to the very forms of discrimination they themselves face in white corporate America.

The Latino community also carries a legacy of classism that is more powerful than racism in Latin culture. For example, Myrna talks about living in the Miami area:

> If you were fortunate enough to live in Coral Gables, you were viewed as a little higher up in the class. Those who lived there saw themselves as more refined with a little bit more panache and prestige. Hialeah on the other hand, where I grew up, was more blue collar, grassroots, working class. And those distinctions held as Latinos across Miami interacted with one another.

AT&T's Patricia Diaz Dennis experienced this as the child of an expat when they lived in Santiago, Chile:

> There were a couple of guys I dated while in high school who just stopped dating me because I wasn't wealthy, which they had assumed I was because we had

come from the U.S. But once they came to our home, saw where we lived, they realized I wasn't what they viewed as the typical American. I was brown-haired and darker skinned like they were. I remember when one of them broke up with me, he told me about his earlier girl-friend who had a big house; her father was an officer in some big American company. I felt so powerless because I was being judged by things I could not control.

Racial Divides

Latinos can also carry biases against people of different races. As a people we have not been exempt from expressions of racism toward those with darker skin or Asian physical features within, or outside, our own communities.

Facing up to this racial prejudice in ourselves can be difficult because many of us have been on the receiving end of discrimination. We may bristle at the idea that racism may be present within our culture. However, there is an unmistakable pattern in our Latino communities: the darker one's skin, the less favored they may be in the eyes of the public, employers, and even family members. The stories are plentiful of lighter skinned siblings faring better than their darker-skinned kin.

In Latin American countries where almost everyone is ethnically Latino, the visuals are stark. Those who are darkest skinned tend to be lower on the socioeconomic ladder. In Brazil, which is about 50 percent Black or mixed race, or in Colombia, where that figure is 25 percent, there is a near-zero Black Latino representation among executives, senior leaders, and managers. Even at corporate diversity conferences in these countries, the highly committed participants from major corporations have a hard time assembling racial diversity, even in token ways. Across Latin American countries, myriad varieties of deprecatory statements about those with darker skin tones can be heard.

In the U.S. this legacy shows up in underlying racial tensions between Latinos and African-Americans. It's a complicated dynamic, since as we have seen, many Latinos are also Black racially. But lighter-skinned Latinos often must look in the mirror to see that they too may be susceptible to unconscious racial biases toward Afro-Latinos, Afro-Americans, Afro-Caribbeans, and Africans. These interactions are further complicated by an economic system that often pits Latinos and Blacks in competition with each other for low-paying jobs.

Racial tensions don't surge just among these different people of color. They can also show up in negative attitudes toward European-Americans that can then spill over into judging fellow Latinos and Latinas for their associations with them. "I was criticized for marrying an Anglo by a Chicano law student in an article in the La Raza newsletter," shares Patricia Diaz Dennis. She elaborates:

> One guy wrote an article about amphibians that are "...neither at home at land or sea. They adopt white man's ways, they take a white man's side, they marry white men."

Spanish Language and Accent Divides

Latinos can also be judged by other Latinos for their accented Spanish or English, or for not speaking Spanish at all. Victor Arias of Korn Ferry shares this story:

> When I was working at the bank in Houston, my accounts were all in Mexico. So I used to go to Mexico but my Spanish wasn't very good and it veered more toward

Spanglish. I remember one of the first meetings I had with a client in Monterrey. The guy says, "*¿De donde eres?*" (Where are you from?) I said, "El Paso." He said, "Aaah," like, "OK, I get it now." That embarrassed and hurt me. They thought less of me because I was not from Mexico. I developed this insecurity about that.

So I went back and learned Spanish really well. A few months later, I was back down there with other clients and I get that question again, "*¿De donde eres?*" "*Norte, buey,*" (from the North), which I chased with some Mexican slang. In fact, I had started to use "*buey*" a lot. This time I got a different kind of "Aaah." I now had a different kind of acceptance there.

Accents and language are indeed heartfelt and important topics to many Latinos in defining their cultural identity. After a successful diversity conference a few years ago, Andrés was at a dinner in Boston's North End, at the outdoor patio of Ristorante Fiore, an Italian restaurant on Hanover Street. A group of Latinos—some sipping wine, others espresso, between bites of bruschetta and raw oysters—began discussing and debating the role of accented English as it related to Latino identity in the workplace.

As the alcohol and caffeine took their effect, the conversation about how we sound dipped into a discussion about identity and success for minorities. Why it is that having a French or British accent is seen as a plus, but having a Spanish accent a minus? And because of this, should Latinos who speak English with a Spanish accent work at reducing their accent?

The answers were not easy, the implications uncomfortable. Here we are, a table of Latinos from different countries and with different migration stories, each having made different choices.

What path should each of us take? One person described facing ridicule and teasing at best, discrimination at worst, due to his heavily accented English during visits to the U.S. when he was young. This experience motivated him to work on losing his Spanish accent when he came to this country for college.

As he calibrated his inflections, pitches, and tones, the change in responses to his words clearly shifted toward more positive reactions. From that point on, it became clear to him that many English-dominant European-Americans heavily weighed their assessment of the value of words by the density of the accent of Spanish-dominant speakers.

But others around the table at Ristorante Fiore had made different choices, equally valid. How they sound, including their accented English, is part of their Latino identity. It is a marker of who they are culturally in the same way that rolling one's r's or pronouncing Martínez, Ochoa, Jimenez, and Castillo in the original Spanish rather than in American English are language markers of a Latino identity that is so paramount that even when they could use the more Anglicized name, they don't. On the other hand, others do choose to always use the more Anglicized names.

Grew Up in Latin America versus Grew Up in the U.S.

One of the most apparent divides left unspoken is the sense that Latinos who grew up in Latin America may, in relation to Latinos who grew up in the U.S., enjoy preferential treatment from corporate America when companies seek to increase their Latino diversity.

While we have not been able to track down comparative statistics, this is spoken more in whispers than in pronouncements from the stage: observations are often made that the

Latino executives being extolled by companies as evidence of their commitment to diversity are not Hispanic Americans, but rather Latin Americans. While this was not true from our sample of executives for this book (13 of the 20 were born in the U.S.), the perception is real and creates underlying unrest.

What could be contributing to the possibility of preferential treatment? A few thoughts:

- Latin American-born professionals who immigrate to the U.S. often have a socioeconomic advantage in that they are more likely to have been raised in middle-class or even upper-class environments than many Hispanic Americans whose small town or rural immigrant parents may have started with less education and fewer resources.

- These Latin American elites often have easier access to networks within the U.S., which, through cocktail parties, dinners, and business conferences, provide opportunities for seamless acculturation to corporate American ways and access to a greater number of career opportunities.

- Latin American–born Latinos often feel they can't relate to Hispanic American Latinos who grew up in, or in close proximity to, mainstream American culture to the point many of them don't even speak Spanish. The Latin Americans struggle to understand how this can be possible.

- Because those raised in Latin America read and write Spanish as their primary language, they are better able to take advantage of opportunities that require Spanish fluency, thus giving them access to more opportunities.

- Conversely, Hispanic Americans perceive that the Latin Americans are not tuned into the realities of being Latino in the U.S.—that they have a rarefied view of American life that is far removed from East L.A., the Bronx, or San Antonio.

- Some of the executive roles available in corporations that make it a priority to seek out Latino talent are for Latin American operations where these corporations make the assumption that those from the area would have an advantage in having connections and knowing the region, compared to those born in the U.S.

Overcoming the Divides

Obstacles to a greater sense of common purpose and unity among Latinos still exist. However, the Latino experience in the U.S. is replete with powerful stories proving there is Latino unity. Some of that unity has always existed as illustrated in the stories of many of our executives who came from pan-Latino, multiethnic Latino enclaves and who joined organizations representing that unity. Some of this cohesiveness is new as Latinos begin to connect with the reality that their growing numbers will only translate into greater power and influence if there is greater sense of common purpose. This sense has also accelerated as the anti-immigrant and anti-Latino walls have gone up. External threats such as we are currently experiencing make those intra-Latino fissures trivial in comparison to what is truly an existential threat from rising xenophobia against people that don't look like white America. Victor Arias talks about when his sense of identity sharpened:

> When I moved to Chicago, that's where I think the true Latino-ness really started, because that's when I ran into second, third generations, whether they were

Puerto Ricans, Mexicans, Salvadorans, who had sort of mixed. You had *Mexiricans* and you had *Salva Mexicans* and all these other things. My mind thought, this is really cool, this is what is the fabric of America, what I think of as Latinos in America. So I became much more open to seeing Latinos as a much larger group than just my own Mexican-American experience.

And Patricia Diaz Dennis explains:

We shouldn't be asking, "How American are you or how Latino are you?" All of us are unique individuals; there should be no litmus test. People feel self-conscious if they don't speak Spanish well. My mother keeps telling me I sound like a gringa.

The driver at one of the companies on whose board I serve is from Puerto Rico and he said to me, "I can't tell you how proud I am you're on this board. I can't tell you what it means to me." I cried. When I leave that board, he's going to be one of the people I go to dinner with. Because they are brethren—or sisters— right? It's really critical to me to not forget where you're from.

Authenticity really matters. How do I want to feel with a group of Latinos? I want all of us to be authentic with each other and not pretend to be something we aren't. I was born in this country so of course I'm going to sound a little different. I came from New Mexico, but I also think that we are helping each other whether we speak Spanish or not.

The Power of an Integrated Cultural Identity

Latinos are a bicultural people. In his book, *The Hispanic Condition*,[2] Ilan Stavans describes the concept of Latino identity as being almost like a labyrinth because of its maze-like qualities. For some Latinos, trying to find their way through this labyrinth is frustrating and exasperating because it can be curved, distorted, wandering, and complex. This may help us understand why these Latinos chose to reject this chaotic Latino identity situation because of its tendency to infuriate, confuse, and disorient them.

Imagine the difficulty these Latinos face in trying to explain to non-Latinos why a new immigrant from Venezuela shouldn't be assumed to have the same exact needs as a fourth-generation Chicano or a Manhattan-born Latino with Newyorican parents. When we make that assumption, we can begin to grasp why they chose not to deal with the issue of Latino identity altogether.

Others choose to face the cultural dilemma head on. How much do they (or do they not) want to identify with their ethnic roots versus how much do they want to embrace mainstream American culture as the core of who they are?

The Latino executives featured in this book, for the most part, learned not to view this tension as an either/or dilemma but as a both/and celebration. Their key to not being lost in the cultural identity maze is *to embrace a bicultural identity*.

The Unapologetic Latinos tell stories of how they modulate their Latino selves skillfully to be crossculturally adaptive toward those who don't share their same cultural heritage. Equivocal Latinos, who often become Retro Latinos, embrace their lost or weakened heritage with more enthusiasm.

---

2 Stavans, Ilan. *The Hispanic Condition: The Power of a People*. New York: Rayo, 2001.

This is how many Latino executives become bicultural, fully embracing their Latino heritage whether it was always there or whether it blossomed later in life. At the same time, they successfully and smoothly operate within the norms of corporate America. It's a duality they all manage. Victor attributes his Latino upbringing to broadening his view of other cultures:

> My upbringing was very rooted in respecting people from all walks of life. That's who I am. I'm very proud of being American, and I'm very proud of being Latino. I can value other cultures even though I'm American and Latino. I love to talk about other cultures, languages. Key experiences in both cultures really shaped me, and I learned how to bob and weave. And that's when I felt I belong here in the corporate world. Nobody's going to tell me I don't belong.

Latinos in the U.S. are a multistage, multiethnic, multiage phenomenon. The Super Bowl and La Copa Mundial (World Cup). McDonald's and *arroz con gandules* (rice and pigeon peas). *American Idol* and *telenovelas*. The American Dream and *la patria de mis padres* (the country of my parents). No surprise then that according to Pew Hispanic Research, seven in ten young Hispanics report they regularly blend English and Spanish into a Spanglish hybrid.[3] These young Latinos epitomize the new Latino-American multidimensional identity.

In fact, half of Latinos in the U.S. are English-dominant Millennials who, paradoxically, also tend to identify with their parents' country of origin (Colombia, Costa Rica, Argentina, etc.).

---

3 "Mapping the 2012 Latino Electorate." Pew Research Center's Hispanic Trends Project. September 30, 2012. Accessed July 29, 2017. http://www.pewhispanic. org/2012/10/01/mapping-the-2012-latino-electorate/.

Latino talent, like the leaders interviewed for this book, embodies these multidimensional characteristics. Fully both bicultural and tricultural, they identify equally with their Latino and mainstream American selves. Their patter often flows back and forth between English and Spanish. Even in business conversations in English with other Latinos, Spanish expressions provide color commentary. Their stories of not fitting in live side-by-side with stories of professional success in spite of the odds they've overcome.

Many Latinos actually straddle the fusion of more than two identities. Millennial Latinos are more likely to come from mixed ethnic and racial backgrounds, and they self-identify with the blended identities of Blaxican, Mexipino, or China-Latina. Plus the creative tension caused by the generational diversity of boomers, Gen X, Millennials, and Gen Z when they interact with each other also shows up in Latino communities.

Further, that same study by Pew found that only 16 percent of Millennial Latinos see themselves as White, compared to twice as many older Latinos. This means that they are less likely to be assimilationist in mindset than were their first-generation parents who, as they faced discrimination due to their limited or accented English, chose not to teach their children Spanish.

We pick our cultural identity spots. *Este es quien soy.* (This is who I am.) Increasingly for more Latinos, particularly Latino Millennials, the assimilation survival tactics of their parents are not as necessary or desirable. Their modern path forward has been to embrace both the Latino and mainstream American culture. It's biculturalism.

Given all this variety, Latino identity cuts across a wide spectrum of choices of how much of that identity to embrace. This spectrum can range from the fiercely nationalistic to the fully assimilated into mainstream American culture.

Indeed, the range of choices of how to express their Latino selves in American society are as diverse as the people who make up the Latino/Hispanic fabric *en los Estados Unidos de America.*

Whether one is an Unaware Equivocal, a Consciously aware Equivocal, a Retro, or an Unapologetic Latino, cultural identity is a choice.

The successful Latinos we have chosen to highlight have taken into account the benefits of not only embracing their Latino identity but also letting others know they identify as themselves as Latinos. They have been able to successfully educate others about racial and ethnic diversity, as well as challenge prevailing stereotypes held by others about Latinos.

This biculturality, this tighter embrace of Latino identity we see in the executives and in the Gen X and Millennial generations, sets the stage for conflict with some of the key cultural markers and preferences of corporate America.

We'll turn our attention next to this conflict. What are these cultural tensions, how have successful Latino executives navigated them, and where does corporate America need to make adjustments if it's going shed its shame of having only 4 percent of the Hispanic workforce in executive officer positions in Fortune 500 firms? ❧

Hispanic or Latino?

These terms are often used interchangeably in the media but have meaningful, but not-so-simple-to-explain differences in their origins, in who uses them, and how they are used. People often are concerned about using the "right" term. No worries; neither is offensive.

While there are complex grammatical debates about their usage, it comes down to how people prefer to be identified. "Hispanic" was introduced in the 1970 U.S. Census by American government officials seeking a generic term to describe all who came from, or who had parents from, Spanish-speaking countries. Mexican Americans, the largest Spanish-speaking nationality in the U.S., are most at ease with the term Hispanic. The use of the Spanish-language term "Latino" in the U.S. is more recent. Immigrants from South America and their offspring embrace this term more naturally.

Choosing which term to use is only the tip of the iceberg. When we say "Latino" or "Hispanic," are we referring to the first-, second-, third-, or fourth-generation Latino? The boomer, Gen Xer, or Millennial Latino? The English-, Spanish-, or Spanglish-dominant Hispanic? The Peruvian immigrant or the Honduran-American born in Wichita? Or any of the other hyphenated Latinos coming from twenty-seven different national heritages?

That's why, when in doubt, just ask.

CHAPTER *4*

Culture Clash: Can Corporate Cultures and Latino Cultures Be Reconciled?

"La preservación de la propia cultura no requiere desprecio o falta de respeto hacia otras culturas."

Preservation of one's own culture does not require contempt or disrespect for other cultures.

—César Chávez, American labor activist

Herein is the conundrum: corporate America says it wants more Latino managers and leaders. Young Latino professionals in growing numbers aspire to this leadership. Yet, as we have seen so far, what should be mutually reinforcing trends to speed up advancement are instead two forces increasingly in conflict due to deep differences between corporate culture and Latino culture.

If businesses are to overcome the 4 Percent Shame, they must go beyond the necessary public declarations in support of diversity and take a zero-tolerance stance toward overt bias. This requires facing up to unconscious cultural biases that can negatively affect the evaluation of both the performance and the potential of Latino talent and generate work environments that are unattractive to many Latinos. Corporations should become more conscious of Latinos' demands that they demonstrate for greater crosscultural agility. Doing so will require the following:

- Gaining a deep understanding of the archetypical cultural preferences of Latinos
- Nurturing self-awareness of the current cultural preferences of the corporation
- Determining how to bridge the gap in a mutually-reciprocal way

Latino Cultural Preferences and How They Compare to Corporate Culture

Often when Latinos have graduated from college and gain their first corporate job, the signs that their past experiences haven't adequately prepared them for this job begin to surface. The trivial becomes precursor to much more profound differences. Charlie Garcia, former CEO of Sterling Financial Group and current CEO of Association of Latino Professionals for America (ALPFA), grew up in Panama. He tells this story:

> My first roommate at the Academy was trying to break the ice by telling me a joke about *Mork and Mindy*. I innocently asked, "Who's Mork and Mindy?" He replied, "What planet did you get off of?" Later I would put my salsa music on in the weekend and people would knock on the door yelling, "Turn that s*** off. We're in the United States." Then somebody changed my nametag from Garcia to O'Garcia, and they started calling me Ogarsha because they said I looked Irish.

The differences are cultural as well as socioeconomic. Patricia Diaz Dennis tells of the time peer lawyers were talking about taking a ski trip:

And then I said to the person next to me, "So where do you go to rent skis?" He just looked at me and said, "Oh, no need, I *own* mine." I had no idea that this was even possible.

While these more surface differences are fairly innocent and can lead to entertaining cocktail reception conversation, they are just the tip of iceberg of differences in cultural values and assumptions that lie deep below the surface of polite interactions. Clueless assumptions lead to the unconscious biases by individuals in the dominant culture, and those biases get codified in talent management systems (leadership competencies, development programs, performance assessment, high potential identification) in ways that systematically reinforce the glass ceiling for Latinos.

Dismantling these bias reinforcement mechanisms requires having a grasp of the cultural differences between mainstream corporate culture and Latino culture.

Before elaborating on this, let's provide a primer on how to talk about culture comparisons. We are going to compare *archetypes*, the general tendency of a particular group to behave in certain ways, without falling into *stereotype*s, the assumption that every member of that group behaves according to the archetype.

Sociologists and interculturalists specialize in the study of what happens when people from different cultures come into contact with one another. They have been able to trace the normative, bell curve behavior of groups, fully recognizing that there are many who, for a variety of reasons, do not adhere to these norms. However, understanding the group norms is helpful in ferreting out patterns that could be in conflict and could keep Latinos from advancing.

Let's look at six cultural dimensions (taken or adapted from the various works of interculturalists Geert Hofstede,[1] Fons Trompenaars, and Charles Hampden-Turner[2] and applied to the Hispanic American context) where these two cultures can be at odds with each other.

Corporate Attitudes: European American vs. Hispanic
Locus of Control
God helps those who help themselves vs. *Si Dios quiere (God willing)*
Ascribing Status
Egalitarianism vs. *Hierarchy*
Identity
I vs. *We*
Process
Follow the rules vs. *Go with the flow*
Managing Emotions
Stiff upper lip vs. *Pura vida*
Time Management
Clock vs. *Event-oriented*

As we point out the differences, it will raise the question: whose responsibility is it to close the cultural gap? The leaders we interviewed stressed the concept of reciprocal adaptation. However, for too long the full burden has been put on Latinos to assimilate into

---

1　"Geert Hofstede." The Hofstede Centre. Accessed August 03, 2017. https://geert-hofstede.com/cultural-dimensions.html.

2　Fons Trompenaars and Charles Hampden-Turner, *Riding the Waves of Culture: Understanding Diversity in Global Business* (2nd ed.), New York, NY: McGraw-Hill, 1998.

the dominant culture. As we saw in the previous chapter, doing so can be detrimental to Latinos' own sense of personal identity and empowerment. Plus corporations lose the benefits of the differences in perspectives and backgrounds that Latinos bring to the workplace.

There may be some cultural dimension, depending on the cultural gap, where resisting adaptation to the majority culture could be a losing battle. At the same time, there are other areas where standing our ground—and in fact, influencing adaptation on the part of the other party to match a Latino cultural preference—might be the healthiest way to optimize personal and organizational performance.

Let's explore these cultural gaps and how the Latino leaders navigated their way among the cultural tensions. There is no clear-cut right or wrong way to do this, but these Latino and Latina leaders tended to be self-aware of the choices in front of them.

Locus of Control: God Helps Those Who Help Themselves versus *Si Dios Quiere* (God Willing)

Different cultures have their own beliefs about whether they can control the environment around them. *Internal control* cultures believe they have that control while *external control* cultures believe they do not. European-American culture, and by extension corporate America, tends to believe the former while Hispanic American culture believe the latter.

The belief that a person's destiny and path in life is determined by God is the mindset of fatalism. Such a belief leads many Latinos to have a yielding view of life, and thus prepare themselves to consent to God's predetermined fate for them. A study conducted by the Pew Hispanic Center in 2002[3] shows how prevalent this feeling is in the Latino community: 53 percent of Latinos in the U.S. agreed that it doesn't do any good to plan for the future because one has no control over it. Patricia Diaz Dennis, explains a behavioral outcome of this *si Dios quiere* passivity: "Many of us, rather than volunteering to take on a new assignment or role, instead wait to be invited."

Cari Dominguez, former Bank of America executive and former chair of the U.S. Equal Opportunity Commission, explains how this difference can play out for a good number of Latinos wanting to climb the career ladder:

While Anglo-Americans may believe that one can dominate the environment and external circumstances, Latinos often believe that it is not up to us, that things may be out of our hands, out of our control. This can lead to behaviors embedded in our different cultural consciousness such as "toot your own horn" versus "humbly wait to be noticed." Many of us Latinos have a hard time tooting our own horns, but it is a behavior that is necessary to get ahead in corporate America. Instead we hold on tightly to lessons from *mamá* to not be proud, not call attention to our accomplishments, but instead allow others to point them out. So as we look at this cultural gap, we need to realize that we can't be culturally bound and wait for somebody to do something on our behalf. We need to do a better job of marketing ourselves and touting our accomplishments.

---

3   Generational Differences. (2004, March). Retrieved from http://assets.pewresearch. org/wp-content/uploads/sites/7/2011/10/13.pdf

In our research sample, we did notice that there was also a gender dimension to this cultural dynamic. While both Latinos and Latinas wrestled with this similar upbringing acculturation, it was clearly more deeply rooted and, therefore, more of an articulated struggle, for the women. For example, Lisa Garcia Quiroz, senior vice president, cultural investments for Time Warner, struggled with the religious aspect of our culture. She explains:

> I think that the disadvantage, and I hate to call it a disadvantage, in our culture is that we value humility so it's not in our DNA to brag about ourselves. It's a very Catholic thing, right? The meek shall inherit the earth.

Former vice president of General Motors Grace Lieblein layers on another behavior that stems from this lack of competitiveness:

> I am one of the least competitive people I know. It's probably to a detriment, frankly, but it's just not in me. Life to me is "What you see is what you get," and I'd just as soon help the person who's next to me than push him off the ladder. Sometimes that worked, and sometimes I probably didn't get as far as I could've if I'd been more competitive. But I'd rather be myself than be somebody else and get higher in the organization.

Corporate American culture on the other hand, is premised on leaders, managers, and employees taking more entrepreneurial initiative within the corporate structure, whether providing innovative ideas or taking charge of their own careers.

The rallying cry of "You own your own career," while making complete sense as a default belief for the majority culture, feels foreign to many Latinos and can actually be disengaging and even marginalizing. Many Latinos are reluctant to ask for things they want and need.

The idea of "owning your career" may be one of the rules of the road that is difficult to buck if Latinos seek to succeed in corporate America. Many of the executives we interviewed had to learn to speak up for themselves, and doing so is one of the first principles these leaders teach other up-and-coming Latinos. We further explain how they accomplished this speaking up for themselves in chapter 6 where sample leaders explain how to see ambition as honorable.

Ascribing Status: Hierarchy versus Egalitarianism

Latinos can tend to be hierarchical compared to the egalitarian European-American approach. This tendency can cut both ways in terms of emerging Latino talent either engaging more senior leaders too deferentially without sufficient assertiveness, or Latino leaders acting with too much forcefulness as they gain positional authority.

The historical, religious, and anthropological roots of these two very different views of status go back to Reformation times in the Middle Ages and Colonial times in both British and Spanish colonies in the Americas.

Martin Luther's Protestant Reformation was a direct challenge to the Roman Catholic Church's interpretation of divine hierarchy, which vested the priests with the powers of being the only ones through which the faithful could connect with God. Luther's theology of the "priesthood of all believers" was enabled by the disruptive technology of that time, the printing press, which put German language Bibles in the hands of the laity, thereby democratizing access to God.

As Catholicism made its way south and Protestantism north, the Spanish colonies were conquered by soldiers under a full top-down military structure. In contrast, the British colonies were settled by families fleeing religious persecution. While the racism of the British settlers resulted in near-annihilation of the indigenous people—as it also did at the hands of the racist Spanish *conquistadores*—their in-group values played out very differently when it came to more Protestant egalitarian processes and structures. In contrast, the Spanish colonizers engrained their military and Catholic-influenced hierarchical structures into most aspects of Latin American society.

Fast-forward to the twenty-first century and these long-ago legacies still have residual effects. Many Latinos grow up in strong matriarchies or patriarchies. Given the deeply held value of family and its structures that are inherently hierarchical, they tend to be more deferential to authority. This leads to the more prevalent passivity among Latino talent. This hierarchical view of status reinforces the belief among Latinos that not much is in their control, which in turn leads towards a sense of having less self-agency—the ability to give voice to one's aspirations, hopes, and needs.

The management practice of paternalism has a long-established history in Latin America. A key feature of paternalism is a set of benevolent management practices where the *patrón* (boss) provides for employees' welfare. Paternalism has been a strong force with workers because it is derived from traditional, gendered family roles, and established Catholic precepts that cast employers as caretakers of an employee family. The employment equation then is that employees simply have to work hard and the *patrón* will take care of them. Some Latinos still subscribe to the paternalism phenomenon and feel there is no need to call attention to their contributions or apply for promotions because their boss will automatically reward them for their hard work.

Identity: I versus We

As much as it may sound like a cliché, *familia* is exceptionally important to Latinos, but it is profoundly true and companies chronically neglect this reality.

This all-in enveloping of *familia* in the Latino ethos comes from a sense of communal identity—*who I am is defined by whom I belong to* versus the more European-American interpretation of individualistic identity—*who I am is defined by my self.*

This too is why Latinos tend to be more group oriented when it comes to workplace dynamics. Carmen Matos, a senior consultant at NBCUniversal, put it this way in a recent conversation with one of the authors:

> We Latinos tend to be very relationship-driven, and strong relationships unleash our best selves. When we have that sense of community at work, our talent and hearts find a home. This means that quality of time spent with coworkers in the workplace versus solely what is accomplished can take on added significance. As an example, a 9 A.M. meeting in corporate America may start with a quick hello and grabbing coffee as people rush to pen portfolios and get down to business. In Miami or Mexico City it will often start with warm hellos and an extended recap of weekend and family events. Then we get down to business. At the end of the day, much will have been accomplished in both worlds, but the Latino employee feels like he or she is working with colleagues who could be considered friends and extended family members. It makes for a sense of belonging at the workplace, which feeds engagement.

She adds that there was a time when this relaxed dynamic was more prevalent and valued in the U.S. before the waves of "downsizing" and "rightsizing" made the corporate picnic obsolete:

Before that time it was easier for employees to feel like they mattered and were more than a number. But now the workplace has unfortunately become more transactional and more focused solely on getting the work done. A growing number of workers feel they must leave their hearts at home or in the parking lot. This sacrifice of culture in the workplace has been difficult for many. And it has been acutely painful for communal-oriented Latino talent.

The high value of community is not just about work-related get-togethers. It shows up in how many Latinos would prefer that workplace performance would be more about group results than individual results. There is a high sense of importance in achieving group goals, a desire to have equal distribution of regard within a group, and a strong sense of loyalty to a group. This, of course, collides with the more prevalent corporate America best practice of setting achievement and accomplishment goals and rewards at an individual level.

Community also goes a long way in explaining the Latino tendency to highly value networking, not just for socializing purposes, but to actually get things done. Like African-Americans, who are also more communal, Latinos (compared to European Americans) overemphasize attending work- and industry-related events. It is through the relationships made and nurtured at these events that business and new career opportunities get transacted. This kind of networking is, of course, common among European Americans, but it goes into hyperdrive with many Latinos.

This communal "we" preference also affects how answers to classic interview questions can trigger unconscious biases that can be detrimental to Latino job candidates. Picture this common interview dynamic between an individualistic hiring manger and a communal Latino:

> Hiring manager: "Tell me of a time you led a team to success."

> Candidate: "What my *team* did was…. What my *colleagues* contributed was… What *we* collaborated on was…"

Back in the debrief session, the hiring manager and recruiter look at each other and say:

> "I don't think that person did anything. I think he rode the backs of everyone else."

> Unconscious bias referee: "Really? Are you sure? Maybe it's that very kind of collaborative competency and value that our organization needs more of."

If corporate America can be more adaptive in catering to Latino communal values, it could benefit directly from more of this ethos in its midst. The American workplace's worship of the individual can be fraught with an internal competitiveness and reduced spirit of collaboration that can hinder optimizing performance.

Today's complex, hyper-interconnected, and volatile world demands fewer individualist superheroes and more group collaborators across various platforms, countries, disciplines, skills, and backgrounds. Resolving this cultural clash does not necessarily mean an *either/or* choice, but perhaps a *both/and* approach. Bicultural Hispanic Americans often value both individual recognition coupled with rewards based on the accomplishments of their teams.

Yvonne Garcia, senior vice president at State Street Corporation, thinks one reason that Latina initiatives have been more prevalent of late is because companies want to build cultures that are more collaborative. She has used this insight to successfully lead Latina initiatives across the country through her involvement with ALPFA. She explains:

> From an organizational perspective, companies are starting to realize the value that women in general, and Latinas in particular, bring to the workplace: a stronger sense of collaboration to get things done, determination, perseverance—these are all traits that are highly correlated to our culture.
>
> A lot of studies have been done by Google and others that show when teams are led by women, or when there were women on the team, they tend to be more successful—for a variety of reasons. Women tend to embrace the whole team spirit more, the whole collective approach. Women aren't afraid to ask questions. So I think that companies are starting to see that the data points to high-performing teams are highly correlated with women, and in particular Latinas, being part of that.

Conversely, this sense of *familia* can become a barrier to Latino career advancement when the ties that bind hold them back from seizing opportunities that require them to move farther away from their families and communities of origin.

In the focus group we conducted in Los Angeles, several of the Latinas clearly stated they would turn down a job opportunity, even if it meant a greater title and money, if they had to move away from their families. One young Latina focus group participant said, "I'm very close to my family. That's my support system. That's why I say no to relocation opportunities." Another young Latina added, "I would not relocate, because of my family and because I love California."

Another participant in the Chicago focus group shared how wrenching it was for her parents when she chose to move from a suburb in Chicago to downtown—just ten miles away. After she took that step, she has moved no further, even when opportunities have presented themselves.

All the executives we interviewed who faced the choice to stay near family or move for greater opportunities did choose the latter. George Herrera, CEO of the Herrera-Cristina Group sees it this way:

> In the Latino community, we're very culturally attuned to each other, we love family, and we want to be in the family. But if you're born and raised in Miami and that opportunity is in Boise, Idaho, you'd better go.

Comcast Corporate SVP Myrna Soto adds:

> I grew up in and spent the majority of my early adulthood in South Florida as a typical Hispanic family member where we are very enmeshed, we all live close to each other, and we don't necessarily move too far from the nest. But when the opportunity presented itself, I broke that chain by moving away.

Darren Rebelez, IHOP president, explains:

> It's not a matter of whether it's right or wrong. That's always going to be a personal decision since sometimes, depending on what's going on with the family, it's more important to stay than to pack up and pursue another

career opportunity. But you've got to recognize that the rest of the world is going to move on regardless of the decision you make.

Process: Follow the Rules versus Go with the Flow

European-Americans tend to seek reassurance in the rules, while Latinos can tend to seek redress in the particulars of each circumstance. Trompenaars and Hampden-Turner were intrigued by their research that showed how multinationals with strong corporate cultures, such as IBM, still struggled with national differences preventing their being able to work as effectively as they wanted. To better understand what was going on, they created an extensive survey with a series of "What would you do?" scenarios.

Here's one: You're riding in a car with a friend who you know is speeding. Suddenly, the flashing lights of a police car appear in the rearview mirror. After pulling the car over, the officer asks you, "Was your friend speeding?" What would you answer? The answer depended on one's nationality. Ninety-seven percent of Swiss would say, "Yes, my friend was speeding," but only 32 percent of Venezuelans would give the same answer. What's going on?

The authors had come up with seven cultural dimensions to explain the different ways people from various cultures would approach the same scenarios. In the case of the speeding car, they developed a construct that identified what individual cultures determine is fair. Some cultures believe that rules apply to everyone equally. Trompenaars and Hampden-Turner referred to them as *Universalist*. Other cultures determine what is fair based on the context of the situations. They referred to these as *Particularist* cultures.

In returning to the case of the speeding ticket, you can now imagine the judgments flying. The Universalist turns to the Particularist and says, "How dare you lie to a police officer!" while the Venezuelan turns to the Swiss and retorts, "How dare you betray a friend!" Both want the same thing—fairness—but they have different ways of interpreting what fairness is. In their book the authors explain how these kinds of worldview clashes happen daily in the workplace as workers try to figure out whom to confer status to, how to get work done, and how to manage time, projects, and emotion.

Lou Nieto, former president at ConAgra's Consumer Foods, describes how he went against company rules and established protocol, following an approach that felt more appropriate to him based on his cultural lens:

> During my first year, I think it was 2005, there was a national organized labor boycott. Latinos were going to walk out of their jobs for one day in protest of how Latino immigrants were being treated and to help people understand how this country would run without Latino employees. We had fourteen manufacturing plants, three of them majority-Latino. There was a senior VP who ran manufacturing and operations and reported to me. I asked if we would be affected and he said, "Yes, we have three locations that are primarily Latino, but we're prepared for it. First, we're telling everyone that anyone who walks out on Monday will not get paid for that day and also will get suspended for two more days without pay. In addition to that we're prepared to bring in supervisors from other plants to help cover. We will continue to operate with a skeletal crew, but we're not going to let them shut down our plants."

And I said, "Hmm. I've got a different idea. I don't want to be punitive because these employees are part of our family and we value them." He said, "We can't just let them walk out; it sets a terrible example." I said, "We can't do it that way. What I'd like to do is tell all our plant employees, we're going to have an additional personal holiday this year, and people can choose to take it whenever they want to. Anybody who wants to take it two weeks from today when that walkout is going to occur, just let us know a week ahead of time and we'll give you this personal holiday so you can in solidarity support other Latinos across the country." He said, "What about all the non-Latinos? What happens to our plants?" I said, "Oh, they get another personal holiday also, so everybody wins. Additionally, you've got a plan to run them with a skeletal crew, but you don't have to punish anybody." He said, "OK, OK, if that's what you want." I said, "That's what I want." And we did it. Morale was so strong after that.

Co-workers addressing business issues with these contrasting worldviews are going to end up clashing regularly, leading to accusations dripping with moral judgments. Note that in this example, this contrast in values stems more from the primacy of relationships in Latino culture, even above the primacy of rules and processes.

In a corporate world governed by external industry, state, and federal regulations, and internal policies, this difference in cultural preferences is often difficult to reconcile—especially since many of the regulations that must be followed cannot be arbitrarily ignored without consequences for the organization. However, not all situations are governed by regulations. There are many policies or norms that can be challenged like Lou did for the sake of inclusion before the planned national organized labor boycott.

Time Management: Clock- versus Event-oriented

What is time? Is it what is scientifically defined by the clock, with 60 seconds to the minute, 60 minutes to the hour? Or is it ruled by the circumstances of the moment? Does the meeting end at 11 A.M. on the dot because the schedule says it should, or does it go overtime because the conversation in motion has not yet arrived to its final destination?

European Americans tend to be ruled more by the clock (referred to by interculturalists as being "clock-oriented") whereas Latinos are regulated more by the event ("event-oriented")—the former making the task at hand the top priority, the latter making the *gestalt* of the whole group most important, making them more likely to stay in the moment rather than cutting it short artificially due to what the clock says.

This is one cultural value difference where the distance between the two narrows with each successive generation of Latinos in the U.S. As evidenced by our interviewees, those born and raised outside the U.S. who then emigrated to study and/or work, tended to struggle most intensely with this divide than those Latinos who grew up in the U.S.

As mundane as the question of meeting start and end times can be, differences in the interpretation of time can be a source of great tension in the high-stakes corporate environment. Ultimately, the event-oriented Latino leaders figured out that it was a losing battle to get corporate America to be more time flexible. The stakes were too high. Having team members waiting for the one executive or leader to arrive to start a meeting had too much negative domino impact on productivity since the entire organization's meetings were premised on things starting and ending on time. Their lateness showed a lack of respect for others' time.

Several of these leaders found ways to retain the value of "the moment" by recognizing when an employee needed more compassion, attention, or coaching, and giving that person the needed time, a moment that would not come back again. These leaders moved from a default of always going with the flow and the moment, to qualifying those moments on a more selective basis. But it was their event orientation that continued to serve them well in discerning the power of the moment.

Lou Nieto describes such an instance when employees needed extra attention and nurturing due to a ConAgra decision to divest a business that first needed to be turned around financially. His leadership approach, shaped by his Hispanic ethnicity, dictated a more compassionate way to handle the situation:

> The decision was made to make a public announcement about the planned divestiture. As the president of the business to be divested, I realized that it would make the turnaround incredibly difficult. Our employees in the business unit would not be motivated because they would know that they would no longer be part of ConAgra.
>
> I decided there was only one way to approach this—a way that felt right to me regardless of whether it was culturally the right thing for the corporation. So I quickly flew to our fourteen manufacturing plants and to our corporate headquarters for that business in Chicago. I delivered the following message: "We are no longer going to be part of ConAgra. Even though we'll be a part of

ConAgra for maybe two or three years, effectively we're not part of the company anymore. We're by ourselves. So I'm asking you to work really hard even though we don't know what's going to happen. I'm not asking you to do it for ConAgra, I'm asking you to do it for your family, for the people that you love and care about, whomever they may be. Because that's why you come to work. You come to work because you're working for your family, your loved ones. If you look around, the people next to you, they're doing the same thing. Now the catch is, just working really hard by yourself isn't going to help you be successful. You have to work as a team with all these other three thousand people in order for us to be successful. Because if we're not successful, it's going to affect your family." I changed the whole focus of "Let's do this one for the company." Instead it was, "Let's *not* do this one out of corporate pride, and let's *not* do this one because you're going to get big bonuses. Let's work hard because this is the only way you can provide financial security for your family." That really resonated for me culturally, and it was a message that really connected with the employees.

Managing Emotions: Stiff Upper Lip versus *Pura Vida*

This one is fraught with the potential to stereotype and caricature. We have seen too many exaggerations—from Ricky Ricardo to Sofia Vergara—on mainstream American television that make many Latinos cringe. But it is true that the normative Latino behavior is to be more expressive than many of their European-American counterparts. Also many Latinos have stories of being coached to "tone it down" when presenting or engaging in the corporate America context.

Myrna Soto speaks from the heart in describing this:

> There was a point in time where some of the leaders above me said, "Hey, just settle down, just because every time we have a meeting you're always kind of like...whatever." They couldn't even say the words. It made me feel bad at first. But then I defended it. "Hey, this is the way we talk; we're passionate, we talk with our hands, we're not yelling, but we're excited about something so our voice may get a little elevated."

Different interpretations of how to manage the reality of human emotions are at play here. We all have them, but Latino culture tends to value showing the emotion, while European-American culture is more about restraining the display of emotion. Like other cultural dimensions discussed, neither is right nor wrong, but they are different. In the workplace these differently inter-preted behaviors can clash and lead to team dysfunction.

While most of the Latino executives we interviewed had stories of adapting to tone down their style just a bit, many found that Latino passion just kept bubbling to the surface no matter what the topic: advancing in their careers, making a difference in the world, helping raise the next generation of Latino leaders, etc. It was this intensity that gave several of these leaders a differentiated edge in their career trajectories. Costa Ricans have a wonderful expression that captures this ethos: *pura vida* (living life fully).

For several of the interviewees, to hold back emotions or to pos-sess that stiff upper lip seemed a technique to use in situations that would ensure effectiveness with those being addressed. But this technique could not hide the deep rivers of emotion from which they drew their inspiration—and by which they inspired others.

Monica Lozano, former CEO of ImpreMedia and current program chair of Latinos and Society at the Aspen Institute, recalls having to inform employees who were going to be laid off from her family's business as one of the hardest things she has ever done, because she viewed employees as part of a family. She did so by emotionally connecting to them:

> I still choke up thinking about it. We'd made the hard decision to close the production facility and I carried the message to the company's press crews. Although we'd done everything we could to avoid layoffs and helped to place many of them in other companies, I had to tell long-term employees who'd been there more years than me in some instances, about the layoffs. I was having a hard time getting through my remarks and toward the end, one man stood up and says, "You know, *Señora Monica*, on behalf of my family I want you to know that because of you and your family, I was able to not only put food on the table, but I got my daughters through college, we own our own house and have property in Mexico. Thanks to you and your family we have a life here, and I don't want you to forget that." That really affected me. I couldn't believe that I'm telling somebody that this was their last day at work, and he's thanking me for what we meant to him and his family.

Hired for Differences but Told to Assimilate

Some of the very actions Latinos are criticized for are those that are valued and nurtured in Latino culture. Unconsciously, the corporate values that are exalted and held as universal standards for how a great leader and executive should look come from the European-American context. The challenge for corporations who want to attract more Latinos is to do some soul searching about their own cultural values and realize that what often are seen as must-haves are much more subjective than the gatekeepers think they are.

Corporate America must make a distinction between true job requirements and cultural preferences that are not vital for job success. This requires self-awareness of what is preferred and why, curiosity and education about Latino culture and its differences, as well as similarities, to corporate culture. Proactive steps must then be taken to simultaneously affirm the many dimensions of mainstream culture that have given corporate America its strength and resilience, while at the same time becoming open to new ways of growing and strengthening their companies.

These changes are not needed just so Latinos will feel more welcome and not feel they must keep sacrificing their identity at the altar of conformity. Change is also required so companies can truly benefit from the differences Latinos bring to the workplace. As demographic trends predict, the future workforce will be represented with an increasingly Latino identity so the current unilateral approach of requiring Latinos to do all the adjusting must change.

Bottom line? Corporations need to stop saying they want to hire Latinos for their differences and subsequently coach them into assimilation by asking them to set aside those differences. ❧

"Al mal viento, buena cara."

To bad winds, a good face.

PART 2

INNER FORCES: SUCCESSFUL STRATEGIES OF LATINO EXECUTIVES

In spite of the many strong, negative, and invisible forces detailed in Part 1, the successful Latino executives we interviewed found ways not only to overcome the obstacles but also to thrive because of them.

Their intuitive as well as calculated strategies revolved around drawing from inner forces: optimizing educational opportunities, seeing their unique Latino backgrounds as assets, and then bearing down on mastering key leadership traits and competencies. We cover these topics in the chapters that follow in Part 2.

Yet the mastery of key leadership skills does not come without challenges such as certain Latino culture legacies being liabilities and the underlying ambivalence about power that many Latinos wrestle with—topics we explore here as well.

We wrap up Part 2 by looking at how the leadership lessons learned by the Latino executives converge and diverge from the early- and mid-career experiences of Latinos.

CHAPTER 5

Reaching Outward: Education at All Costs

"Hasta que tengamos igualdad en la educación,
no tendremos una sociedad igualitaria."

Until we get equality in education, we won't have an equal society.

—Sonia Sotomayor, U.S. Supreme Court Justice

One overarching commonality the successful Latino executives we interviewed have had is a college education, many at a graduate level. For most, this achievement was not a given. Several were the first in their families to ever go to college. The odds were against entering college, but most importantly, graduating with that degree in hand.

Here's what the odds would have been for them today, these odds were worse when the executives we interviewed began their journeys. If you begin with 100 Latino freshmen in an urban public high school, 12 of them will drop out before graduating. Of the 88 who do finish high school, only 35 will go on to a two- or four-year college; the other 49 will have entered the job market

Of 100 Latinos who enter high school...

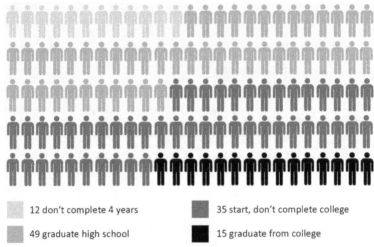

| | 12 don't complete 4 years | | 35 start, don't complete college |
| | 49 graduate high school | | 15 graduate from college |

instead of furthering their education. Those 49 might work as mechanics, hotel housekeepers, waiters, salespeople, landscapers, storekeepers, or teachers' aides. Some may succeed financially, but most will live paycheck-to-paycheck. The 35 who do go on to college will find many obstacles to success. A large number of them will drop out during or after the first year. Ultimately, only 15 of the original 100 high school freshman will become four-year degree graduates, meaning that 85 percent will not have reached that goal.[1]

These stats speak to a paradox many Latino immigrants feel: not being quite sure how to value the very thing they sacrificed so much for. Like all immigrant groups, Latinos who came to the U.S. did so seeking an opportunity to make better lives for themselves and their children. Many of these immigrants arrive

---

1   Krogstad, Jens Manuel. "5 Facts about Latinos and Education." Pew Research Center. July 28, 2016. Accessed July 13, 2017. http://www.pewresearch.org/fact-tank/2016/07/28/5-facts-about-latinos-and-education/.

without even a high school education, and thus face limited employment opportunities. As strong believers in the American Dream, they seek the recipe for the "secret sauce" to achieve it. Hard work, rewarded more in the U.S. than it had been in their home countries, is a plus in their lives that they grasp tenaciously. However, regarding a higher education as important proves more elusive given the relentless demands of a hand-to-mouth existence.

Most new arrivals and first-generation Latinos are often satisfied and parentally proud with their offspring if they graduate from high school, something they themselves may have been unable to do. They believe that with a high school diploma in hand, their sons and daughters will be able to find good jobs. Given the economic struggles faced by many of these families, the need for their children to go to work as soon as possible is seen as crucial so they can contribute to the family's survival. Going to college can be dismissed as a waste of time and money, possibly considered a luxury.

The avenues for advancing into the middle class have become more limited. The decline of manufacturing in the U.S. means fewer middle class jobs are available to those with limited education. Often, the only path left for advancing into the middle class is a college diploma. To achieve success and a high-level career position in corporate America, it's the only way.

Cari Dominguez, the former executive with Bank of America, commented on the need to combine the values of hard work and a good education:

> My parents never begrudged their circumstances because they just felt that it was well worth a sacrifice on their part for us to live in freedom and to get a good education. So what they said to us was, "You have to work hard,

you have to get a good education, and you have to pay it forward whenever you have the opportunity. Make sure that you help those who are coming behind you because this is a nation of immigrants. Everyone starts from the bottom and moves ahead with hard work and a good education.

Hard work will not be enough to advance Latinos in meaningful numbers into executive and senior management ranks. The *Latino Executive Manifesto* proclaims we must tackle this challenge with urgency and effective strategies that address the root causes of low Latino participation rates in college enrollment and graduation.

Latino Educational Achievement Trends

In its 25th anniversary report in 2011,[2] the Hispanic Association of Colleges and Universities (HACU) noted, "Hispanic high school graduation rates and readiness for college are much lower for Latinos than their peers. In addition to (and in part because of) socioeconomic realities such as low income and low parental educational attainment, Hispanics are far more likely to attend under-resourced PK–12 schools." The report continues: "More limited school finances lead to inadequate and lower quality educational services. These socioeconomic and school resource and quality factors explain much of the research findings on dropouts and high school graduation."

There are positive trends as well. Even though Hispanics trail other ethnic groups in earning bachelor's degrees, there is steady improvement as their high school dropout rate has fallen dramatically, and college enrollment increased. The Pew Research Center reports that while in 2000, 32 percent

---

2   "1986-2011: 25 Years of Championing Hispanic Higher Education." HACU.net. 2011. http://www.hacu.net/images/hacu/about/HACU_History_1986-2011F.pdf +.

Hispanics lag other groups in attaining a 4-year degree

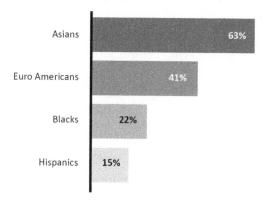

of Latinos did not complete high school, by 2014 that rate had fallen 20 points to just 12 percent. That same year, 35 percent of those aged 18 to 24 were enrolled in either a two- or four-year college, up from 22 percent in 1993, a 13 percent increase. The number of European-American college students in that age group rose just 5 percentage points, to 42 percent; Black enrollment increased to 33 percent, rising 8 points in the same timeframe.

Even with this increase in enrollment, just 15 percent of Hispanics have a bachelor's degree or higher, compared to 41 percent for European Americans, 22 percent for Blacks, and 63 percent for Asians. This is partly because they are less likely to attend a four-year college, choosing instead to enroll in two-year programs at community colleges (the highest share of any ethnicity), and are more likely to live at home while working and attending school part-time. (One bright side to this is that Latino households have significantly lower amounts of student debt.)

Because they are affordable, local, and positioned to serve a first-generation college student's needs, two-year community colleges—many of which have been designated as Hispanic-serving institutions (HSIs)—provide an opportunity for many Latino students who couldn't otherwise afford a four-year program.

HSIs were the result of legislation that emerged in 1992 when the Hispanic Association of Colleges and Universities (HACU) urged Congress to begin targeting campuses with high Hispanic enrollment for federal appropriations. Two- and four-year institutions must have a Hispanic enrollment total of more than 25 percent and be designated as an HSI to receive an increase of funds. Currently HSIs in the U.S. represent less than 10 percent of all higher education institutions nationwide, but together they enroll more than two-thirds of all Hispanic college students. Most HSIs are found in areas with increasing Hispanic populations including Miami, Detroit, Philadelphia, Chicago, Los Angeles, and San Antonio.

However, the welcome increased enrollment on the part of Latinos in community colleges, HSIs, and other four-year schools is eroded by their higher dropout rate compared to European Americans. This must then be the next area of focus: to increase the Latino college graduate pipeline.

Why do Latinos falter? Put simply, they're often unprepared for college since they can't rely on the shared experience of their parents having some college education to thus guide them. It's not that the families aren't willing to help them, rather they just don't know how to do so.

The stakes are high to be able to enter college, and are high to remain there. Latinos often feel a sense of alienation and sometimes face animosity or unconscious biases. Many of the issues discussed in the earlier chapters about corporate America also relate to education. Lisa Garcia Quiroz, senior vice president, cultural investments for Time Warner, reflects:

> I know plenty of people who went to Harvard, colleagues of mine, Latino students who entered the same time I did but who were back home by year's end because the environment was so alien and so white. The university wasn't great about supporting those students.

While the challenges are considerable after Latinos enter college, many headwinds prevent their even enrolling in the first place. Let's look at those issues.

The legacy of high interest rates

Many Latino immigrants came from countries with very high rates of interest, sometimes more than 50 percent which discourages going into debt. As a result, Latinos are uncomfortable with the idea of taking out loans for college. This leads to students paying cash for a semester and then taking time off when they can't afford the next tuition payment. They hopefully work to save enough to return to school. This pattern becomes a slippery slope: When they start taking semesters off, they extend the time it takes to get a degree, resulting in more of a challenge.

Peer pressure

Latino kids' friends who are not college-bound often accuse someone who wants higher education of being "uppity" or "trying to be white" rather than understanding that they're simply trying to increase their chances for career success. Grace Lieblein, former vice president for General Motors, states:

> The gift that my mom gave me was a belief that I could do anything. I grew up thinking I can be anything I

want to be. When we were seniors in high school, I told my friends I wanted to be an engineer. They were horrified; "You're going to be what? Is that on a train?" "No," I replied. My friends clearly did not understand me, but I had no fear of going into a nontraditional field at all.

Large families

When younger children in large families who are living hand-to-mouth need basic necessities such as shoes or clothes, parents often discourage college attendance for the older children as an unaffordable luxury. As soon as children graduate from high school, they are expected to begin working full-time to bring in additional income. In these households, college tuition is not seen as an investment with future returns, but rather as an immediate cost that should be avoided.

High rates of teenage pregnancy

Although the rates of teenage pregnancy for Hispanics have fallen dramatically since 1990, one in three Latinas under age twenty becomes pregnant, which is one and a half times higher than the national average. Obviously having the responsibility of raising a child lowers the likelihood of women attaining college degrees.

Family ties

Sometimes the strong emphasis on family prevents bright Latino students from going to the best schools because their families want them to remain close. This factor limits the number of colleges and universities some students even consider. And young Latinas face more pressure to remain close to family than do many European-Americans.

Former ConAgra Consumer Foods President Lou Nieto recalls how this scenario played out in his family. Although he stayed close to home precisely because of the family pull, he was fortunate that the college close to home was a first-rate one. He recalls:

> I applied to a bunch of Ivy League schools and some in the Chicago area. My dream was to go East. I was accepted at Harvard College, and thrilled about my fulfilled dreams. In late April, before I had to accept the East Coast school offer, my mother pulled me aside and asked if I would stay home in Chicago and not go away. I said yes, of course. I don't regret not going East because I certainly got a strong education at the University of Chicago.

Current political and budgetary climate

As if the headwinds facing Latino students were not enough, the current political landscape—driven by certain legislatures and governors who are not diversity-friendly—does not bode well for increasing educational opportunities for Latinos and other people of color.

Many states are cutting back dramatically on their support for public colleges and universities, at a time when the cost of higher education is growing at an almost exponential rate.

Illinois is a striking example: In 2017, Governor Bruce Rauner and the state legislature were at a budgetary standoff so the state had no budget for three years. This resulted in draconian cuts at all state-supported institutions, including Northeastern Illinois University in Chicago, which serves a large number of first-generation and minority students, including many Latinos. In May 2017, NEIU was forced to eliminate about

180 full-time jobs. The cuts included 130 civil service and 50 administrative and professional employees: a quarter of the staffing in both categories. These cuts are particularly harmful to Latino students. "They're your resources, your advisers, your mentors," Ashlei Ross, a NEIU senior and president of the student government association told the *Chicago Tribune*.[3] "They're the staff that are the ones who are really holding your hand. To lose that is a dramatic thing, especially for first-generation students because they don't have that resource at home. They can't ask their parents."

Attitudes About Education

In spite of these headwinds, the growing push for education among Latinos feeds a telling contrast between Latino and European-American families. Often in middle-class Anglo communities higher education is seen as a given, almost part of the air their children breathe. The assumption is that their offspring will further their education, and when they don't choose to do so, those children are breaking the norm. In contrast, if young Latinos from low-income families do go to college, *that* is breaking the norm.

It is anecdotally shared among many Latinos that when you ask both Latino and Anglo parents if they're involved in their children's education, they'll each say yes. For the Anglo parents, that answer will likely mean they join the PTA and go to parent-teacher conferences. When the Hispanic parents say they're involved, it means their son or daughter has clean clothes and pencils. Although the Hispanic parents push their children to

3   Rhodes, Dawn. "Northeastern Illinois University to Cut About 180 Jobs: The Devastation Increases." Chicagotribune.com. May 31, 2017. Accessed July 13, 2017. http://www.chicagotribune.com/news/local/breaking/ct-northeastern-illinois-university-budget-problems-20170530-story.html.

get good grades and better themselves, it's a different dynamic. They don't know the pathways: applying to schools, taking college tours, or discovering how to pay for an education.

Pew Hispanic Research reveals that the importance Latino families place on attaining a college education has markedly increased over the past few years. 88 percent of Latino families agree that a college degree is necessary to get ahead, versus only 74 percent of European Americans having the same attitude.[4] This shift in attitude is a driving factor in the growing numbers of Latinos enrolled in college. Luis Ubiñas, board president of the Pan American Development Foundation, points out:

> Education is an anchor value of Latinos. We as a community take any scrap of opportunity for education. You see it in factory workers who try to send their kids to a better school in a better neighborhood. The mothers take extra jobs to pay for tutoring. Children are being raised with the idea that their education and subsequent opportunities are their responsibility. From both personal observation and my knowledge of higher education, I feel that the Latino community is desperate to get the educational advancement that is required.

These improvements in higher education have been fueled partly by Latino parents who figured out this key ingredient in the secret sauce of the American Dream, even if great sacrifice is required. Lou Nieto recalls those sacrifices made by his parents:

> I attended a small parochial school in our almost exclusively Latino community and the Franciscan sisters

---

4   Stepler, Renee. "Hispanic, Black Parents See College Degree as Key for Children's Success." Pew Research Center. February 24, 2016. Accessed August 05, 2017. http://www.pewresearch.org/fact-tank/2016/02/24/hispanic-black-parents-see-college-degree-as-key-for-childrens-success/.

told my parents that St. Ignatius Prep (a Jesuit school) was the best school in the city. They added, "Your son should go there because he's a really good student." My parents sent me there, thus changing my life. My dad was a Teamster, so we were very blue collar. We weren't poor (I wouldn't try to pretend to be that) but we didn't think of ourselves as middle class either. My dad took a second job and my mom, a part-time job to be able to send my brother and me to Ignatius Prep. There was no financial aid back then. So just paying the high school tuition was a big sacrifice for my parents. They were big believers in education, and it paid off because it got us into good colleges.

In addition to parents who understand the role of education in creating more opportunities, other socioeconomic factors have contributed to the slow but steady increase of Latinos attending college. The onset of the 2008 recession led to a rise in unemployment for Latino youth, and ironically this increased their long-term economic prospects since many chose to attend college in light of there not being any jobs.

Darren Rebelez, president of IHOP, told us:

My dad had not gone to college; no one in his family did, yet he demanded that I get an education. He didn't know how we were going to pay for it and he didn't know what I needed to do to get in, but he just expected it, and I needed to figure that out.

Grace Lieblein, who grew up middle class and had parents who attended college, did not necessarily face the same challenges that other Latinos who are from lower income families face:

My father was a huge proponent of education. His brothers and sisters were highly educated and had left Cuba, after Castro had taken over, with basically the clothes on their back. They were able to make good lives in other countries. Therefore he always said, "Material things can be taken away, but your education can never be taken away." If I was going to college was never in question. The assumption was always yes.

The Many Roads to the College Experience

The successful executives we interviewed had a wide range of educational experiences, depending on their family and community backgrounds.

Some grew up in Latin America in affluent families and came to the U.S. later in life, while others came from barrios in El Paso or Los Angeles. A few were the only Hispanics in their neighborhoods, while others came of age in communities of mixed ethnicities. There were those who attended prestigious colleges such as Stanford or Harvard, and others who began their education at local community colleges. Some faced discrimination and isolation because of their Latino backgrounds, but for others it didn't seem to matter. Cubans in Florida, Mexicans in Texas or California, Venezuelans in Illinois—all had interesting stories to tell about their experiences from grade school through college. All credited their educations as helping them to learn skills for their career path, and also in socializing with other ethnic groups, which enabled them to participate more fully in a broader society. Following are some of their stories.

Different school experiences

Gilbert Casellas, former chairman of the U.S. Equal Employment Opportunity Commission and current chairman of Omnitru Technologies shares:

> I went to an all-black parochial school for the first six years. It was the same school my parents went to. The school had been founded in 1894 by Sisters of the Holy Name. When they established the school, the surrounding neighbors—who were all white—burnt it to the ground and posted a handwritten note on a tree nearby saying, "You educate these colored kids, they're not going to want to work."

Victor Arias, the senior client partner at Korn Ferry, talked about attending Cathedral High School in El Paso:

> I remember there being more Mexican-Americans than there were non-Mexican Americans. There was also a good number of Mexicanos from Ciudad Juarez, making the school population an interesting sort of mix. Even though I wasn't aware of it, those who actually lived in Ciudad Juarez were very different. I started realizing the differences between those who were just purely strong Mexican citizens versus the Mexican-Americans, versus the gringos. Still everybody really excelled.

Intel Vice President Sandra Rivera, discussing her parents' emphasis on education, told us:

> The importance of education—and more than that, the culture and the love of learning—was instilled in us. From a very early age we were taught that an education, a good education, was the path that would really open up all these opportunities in life.

Former McDonald's Executive Vice President José Armario recounts how his time in a military school helped him succeed:

> Through grade school and middle school, I first attended the public school system and then a private military school, Miami Aerospace Academy. That experience, while it was very tough, created a lot of good habits for me in terms of study, homework, testing—attaining success early in life by being very disciplined.

José graduated from Miami Dade Community College with an associate's degree in business administration. He then began attending a local college in pursuit of his bachelor's degree, but left the program because he just didn't find it inspiring. He rose rapidly through the corporate hierarchy at Burger King and was busy launching a successful career. College really didn't matter at that point. Ultimately, when he was in his forties, José decided that he wanted to finish his education and acquired a master's degree. Speaking of his experience at the University of Miami, he told us:

> They had an advertisement for pursuing a master's degree that didn't require a four-year degree. When I met with the admissions officers, they said, "Since you don't have the four-year degree, but have extensive experience, we just need you to take the graduate admissions test. If you do well on the test, we always admit one student who doesn't have a bachelor's degree." I was that student! Fifteen months later I had a master of science in management."

Lou Miramontes, a retired KPMG partner, lived at home while attending California State University, East Bay. He recounts his experience:

I think about my parents' income and how they really didn't have the college funds for us, although college wasn't that expensive back then. Given their income level and our situation, sending me to college was still going to be an effort, so I lived at home. I remember telling my dad that everybody else had a bunch of roommates and were living in dorms. He said, "You did pretty well at home in high school, *amigo*." I had no problem understanding that because I was close to mom, dad, and my brothers. Since I didn't want to incur any costs for them, I lived at home and kept working hard at college.

Lucky breaks and mentors

Many of these successful executives had a lucky break that changed the course of their educational careers. Darren Rebelez remembers attending a college fair with his father after having attended his less-than-challenging high school in Southern California:

> I was just grabbing the normal California college giveaways from the U.C. system, San Diego State, and others. West Point happened to have a booth there. My dad asked, "Why don't you go talk to those guys?" I countered, "How am I going to get in there, Dad? You're not a congressman or a general." He said, "Shut up and get an application." I did, I applied, and I was accepted.

Some executives had caring mentors who helped them greatly in getting accepted by top-notch schools. For Gilbert Casellas that guidance came from a priest and a doctor who helped him get into Yale. He recalls:

In my senior year in high school as I'm applying for colleges, one of the priests came to me saying he had been at a dinner party where the doctor who was the host was a graduate of Yale and Harvard, and was really interested in recruiting minority students. This priest said, "Y'know, I told him about you, and I thought you should talk to him and consider applying to Yale and Harvard. I'm going to put you in touch with him and he's going to contact you."

I added Yale to my application list. I received a thick envelope from them on April 4, 1970—you don't forget certain dates. I was stunned and will remember forever my dad's words when he read the letter, "Hell of an opportunity!" That's all he said, and that did it for me. I accepted.

Education as the Great Equalizer

It's clear that a college education expands horizons for first-generation students by exposing them to new understandings of the broader world. They learn middle-class conventions and new values of speaking, dressing, critical thinking, problem-solving, and more. These lessons don't come from going to class, but instead are embedded in the way the students absorb the college life. No matter how smart you are, if you don't go to college, you will very likely miss out on so much that underlies the middle-class corporate culture.

Most importantly, during college, students begin to build and take advantage of personal networks, which leads to contacts who can later open doors in the business world. Latino organizations such as Society of Hispanic Professional Engineers (SHPE) and ALPFA have college chapters that offer opportunities for Hispanic students to join together and expand their networks. University alumni associations also provide another way to make important connections.

These expanded horizons create a ripple effect that goes beyond the individual students, spreading through their immediate and extended families, and into the community at large. Graduates who earn degrees and begin working in corporations enlarge their social circle and may travel the U.S. and even other countries. They share those experiences with family and friends giving others a glimpse of more possibilities for themselves. Rather than being viewed as "uppity," these people become role models for others in their community who begin to seek similar opportunities. This ripple effect encourages others to follow a similar path.

Here's Victor Arias, speaking of his experience at Stanford University:

> I learned how to bob and weave because of the challenges I faced, and that's when I felt, "S***, you know, I belong here. Nobody's going to tell me I don't belong." I gained incredible confidence about what I could accomplish. I learned that having attended Stanford opened a lot of doors, so I just feel a tremendous amount of gratitude toward Stanford. I didn't have a lot of money so I decided to give them a lot of my time when I got out of school, and I did so. Stanford's a very special place, and I reiterate that it opened many doors for me.

Luis Ubiñas, who grew up in a poor neighborhood in the South Bronx with a father who had substance abuse issues, describes how he was able to rise above his home circumstances:

> I had the good fortune of having, through financial aid, a scholarship to go to private schools in Manhattan. After that I ended up at Harvard College where I graduated magna cum laude and got accepted to Harvard Business School.

Luis recalls being accepted by the other students in the tony private schools, occasionally spending nights at their homes—although it was out of the question for them to come to his:

> Going into those friends' homes was like going on a vacation, perhaps a safari. You may feel welcome, but you don't necessarily feel comfortable. When you are from the projects—buildings burning on the horizon and criminals literally blocking your path from your front door to the subway—arriving at a heated, private school on the Upper East Side where there was a fantastic education awaiting me was nothing short of a blessing.

Unintended Consequence: Education as an Un-equalizer

There is also a potential pitfall to Latinos attaining a college degree: education as an un-equalizer. This situation occurs when the first-generation college graduate comes away with a sense of superiority to their less-educated family members and friends. It may lead to alienation, distrust, embarrassment, and other destructive emotions. This works both ways, as the young man or woman with the college degree may see their family or friends as uninformed, naïve, unmotivated, or dull, while the other side sees the graduate as pretentious, dismissive, and even in denial of their Latino heritage—trying to be European American.

Recognizing this unconscious bias against your own culture requires courage and self-awareness, and then humility to overcome it. When graduates don't address their attitudes, this unequalizing factor causes some to become Invisible Latinos.

Ultimately, education has created both the foundation and the propulsion to success for the Latino executives we interviewed.

Completing college required supportive parents or self-agency if parents weren't supportive, mentors and sponsors, scholarships, straight luck, and blessings. Individuals had to have the tenacity to face the myriad headwinds as Lisa Garcia Quiroz explains:

> I was used to being the only one [Latina] and saw persevering as a challenge. I had a sense of being given an incredible opportunity that I couldn't fail. To me, it wasn't even an option to go back. Go back to what?

Advancing their education is becoming easier for Latinos. Graduation rates are improving both for high school and college. HSIs are helping two-thirds of Latino college students. Other Latino organizations providing help are college alumni associations. For example, the Latino Alumni Association at the University of Southern California (USC) has given over $15 million in scholarships to Latino students since 1973, while at Cornell University the Latino Alumni Association focuses on the recruitment and retention of Latino students.

A recurring theme of the executives we've profiled is their commitment to pay it forward. Nowhere is this more important than working to improve the prospects of college-bound Latinos.

As demographic trends continue to indicate, the workforce of the future will have an increasingly Latino identity. Challenges that impact Latino student success is an issue not only for Latinos but also for the entire U.S. As Latino education attainment rises, so does economic opportunity for the entire country. ❧

A Bold Way to Build the Diverse Talent Pipeline

In its May-June 2017 issue, *Harvard Business Review*[5] details a successful program in Boston to integrate all the efforts of various nonprofit organizations focused toward the goal of Latinos and other minorities successfully completing college and securing a good job. It profiles State Street Capital CEO Scott Nobles. When Scott was appointed to a Massachusetts public/private workforce development program, he saw a lack of coordination among agencies.

Given the challenges of urban education, he realized that effective intervention must go beyond what happens in classrooms. He said, "Getting students through school, into college, and then into good jobs requires managing a series of hand-offs and transitions. For example, some nonprofits do a great job of coaching high school students to improve their study skills or to perform better on college admissions exams. But rarely do those same organizations help the students with the college search and application process, which is the logical next step. Other organizations do that, but many kids can't navigate between the two. Then, when students get into college, they need mentoring and coaching to help them stay enrolled and succeed, which requires a different kind of support. After that they need help getting ready for a job and finding one. It's similar to a hospital experience: The patient may be treated by several specialists, and they have to communicate well with one another to achieve overall success."

In 2015 the State Street Foundation set up a program called Boston WINs (Workforce Investment Network). They staged a Shark Tank–like competition for local nonprofits, committing to an investment of $20 million over the next four years and to hiring 1,000 of the program's graduates. The goal was a seamless program that combined all the necessary expertise to support youths from high school through college and into the workplace. They chose a handful of nonprofits who had proven records, gave them funding to scale up, and taught them to coordinate their efforts so they were no longer working in isolation.

After seeing a successful outcome over two years, Nobles concludes, "We're nearly halfway through our four-year commitment to Boston WINs, and we've already hired two hundred grads. We're already thinking about how to scale the program beyond Boston, to other parts of the country and the world."

5   Hooley, Joseph. "State Street's CEO on Creating Employment for At-Risk Youths." *Harvard Business Review*. April 26, 2017. Accessed August 05, 2017. https://hbr.org/2017/05/state-streets-ceo-on-creating-employment-for-at-risk-youths.

CHAPTER 6

How to Be: Three Key Traits of Transformational Leaders

"El que sigue la consigue."
Who perseveres, achieves.

—Anonymous

Battle hardened by facing the outer forces of corporate culture biases and cultural identity crisis, Latino executives have also developed and honed particular leadership competencies, traits, and philosophies enabling their success as transformative Latino leaders.

One of the key objectives in our research was to discover these secrets to their success. So far in this journey we have extensively explored the foundational requirement of being *auténtico,* which the *Latino Executive Manifesto* declares must entail both defining and embracing our Latino cultural identity.

On top of the foundation of cultural authenticity, what did the executives we interviewed learn and put into play to become transformational leaders? Six key elements surfaced—three traits and three competencies:

Traits

- Embracing ambition as an honorable intent
- Risk taking as a catalyst for growth and getting noticed
- Deeply valuing relationships

Competencies

- Political savvy about corporate culture
- Establishing and shaping one's own leadership style
- Giving back to the community

We elaborate on the three traits in this chapter and on the three competencies in the next.

Embracing Ambition as Honorable

The executives' response to the inherent fatalism of Latino culture discussed in Chapter 4 is recognizing that corporate America is not waiting for Latinos to wake up and take their seat at the executive table. Latinos must pursue these positions with vigor and ambition. It is thus of little surprise that each of our Latino executives demonstrated elevated ambition and a deep desire to be successful in all aspects of life. They wanted to feel success and to be seen as successful, oftentimes to be seen as role models for other Latinos, or to be a tribute to their families for the many sacrifices made on their behalf.

It's easy to confuse ambition with aspiration, but they are not the same. Mere aspiration tends to focus on a particular goal; ambition is more of a trait or disposition, and as such, is persistent and pervasive. The word ambition comes from the Latin word *ambitio* (a striving for honor, recognition, and preferment). To be ambitious is to achieve—not just for the sake of achievement itself but also for distinguishing ourselves from others.

Ambition is also different than hope. Hope is the desire for something to happen, and anticipation of its happening. In contrast ambition is the desire for achievement and distinction *combined* with the willingness to strive for—as well as take—the necessary steps for success. Ambition is more self-propelled than hope.

Let's look at some of the characteristics of ambition.

Achieving success requires a deep-seated commitment

The Latino executives we interviewed proved to have talent and ability, but most importantly, they also had *ganas,* that hard-to-translate Latino cultural term that alludes to pursuing endeavors with total heart, body, mind, and soul. Their ambition drove them to dedicate their lives to long hours and hard work, the perfection of a craft, and a willingness to sacrifice for the sake of reaching the level they wished to attain.

It's clear that most come from family environments full of ambition and determination, the foundation for their own personal ambition. Many described parents whose attitudes led them to overcome obstacles and to triumph against significant odds. Immediate and extended family demonstrated the dream and the drive that proved having ambition was more important than having natural ability or access to resources.

For example, Gilbert Casellas's father was a high school dropout, yet he always encouraged his son to do well in school—even when Gilbert was required to attend segregated schools in Tampa. Yvonne Garcia's father did not go to school past the seventh grade, yet he recognized that education was the key to freedom and economic mobility. Lou Miramontes remembers his dad having to go to work at four in the morning as a migrant worker, always working extra hours so he could support the family. Getting a good education and going to a Catholic school was so important to Victor Arias's family; his dad worked two jobs so they could afford school tuition.

When Lou Nieto's school was forced to desegregate after the *Brown v. Board of Education* ruling, his mom, a civil rights activist, fought the school administration to make sure Lou was enrolled in the best classes at his school. She had big ambitions for him, hoping that he would someday become a U.S. Senator. Lou's own goal was to become the CEO of a Fortune 500 company.

Charlie Garcia's ambition to be in public service was influenced by his father, who served the government of Panama in various roles throughout his career. With that model of public service, Charlie studied at the Air Force Academy and began a military career. His mom was a public school teacher for twenty-two years, sparking Charlie's passion for education—which eventually led him to serve a White House Fellowship for Bill Bennett (Secretary of Education) and five years on the State Board of Education in Florida.

Monica Lozano's grandfather crossed the border into the U.S. from Mexico. He very much believed in the power of the press and was ambitious enough to eventually start two newspapers, one in San Antonio and one in Los Angeles. Luis Ubiñas's grandmother came from Puerto Rico with eight children, eventually settling on the Lower East Side of New York City. His mother, the eldest of those children, had to leave school early to work helping support the family. Luis earned scholarships to attend private schools, often having to avoid gangs and violence on his way to class. He would later attend both Harvard College and Harvard Business School.

Several of our executives come from families courageous and ambitious enough to flee Cuba and the Castro regime. Grace

Lieblein's father left Cuba in 1951, shortly before Castro seized control. He came to the U.S. to attend college but ended up enlisting in the Army and serving in the Korean War.

José Armario's father was an outspoken critic of the Communist regime and had to flee Cuba for fear of his life. José and his family soon followed.

Cari Dominguez's journey to the U.S. happened in reverse of José's because her father was under house surveillance when she left Cuba at age twelve with her mom and two sisters. Her dad eventually joined the family in Maryland six years later. Myrna Soto's father was a political prisoner for a time before leaving Cuba in exile. Even though Myrna's mother did not graduate from high school, her parents always expected her to do well in school.

Ambition provided the stimulus for State Street's Yvonne Garcia to seek out leadership roles to be in a stronger position to drive change:

> I've always felt comfortable in a leadership role. I've never really liked being second place, I never really enjoyed being vice-chair, and I don't enjoy being a vice-president. I've always enjoyed leading something because I have this combination of the ability to be strategic. But I also have a strong bias toward execution. I feel that when you are in charge of leading something, you're able to take action much quicker, influence people much faster, and drive change faster because you're able to make decisions.

What all these stories demonstrate is that transformational Latino leaders found motivation in the struggles and sacrifices their families faced. They felt an obligation to be ambitious and to give extra effort. The opportunities afforded to them were fought for and won by past family members. However, these opportunities were given to them with an implicit contract—that they make the most of them. Anything less than a high level of success and ambition would dishonor the efforts demonstrated by their families.

Forget the naysayers

While immediate family may have been mostly supportive of their early ambitions, what further distinguishes these executives was their ability to overcome naysayers who deemed their ambitions as a negative trait. *¿Qué te crees?* is a Hispanic sentiment that loosely means *Who do you think you are?* It was a term they often heard from classmates, neighbors, and eventually other Latino professionals who considered them to be cocky for having such ambition. Lou Miramontes recalls some of his Hispanic friends making fun of him for trying so hard in his classes and hanging out with the smart Anglo students. They mocked him by asking, "Are you trying to be white?" Lou's response was, "No, I'm trying to be successful."

The secret to becoming a transformational leader is not merely having ambition, but keeping a distance from those who feel that big ambition is something to be ashamed of. What Latinos must learn is that outside of this small group of detractors— rarely the role models anyway—denying your ambition does not make you look humble, but rather insecure. Denying your ambition does not make you look unpretentious; it makes you appear unfocused. It does not make you look modest; it makes you look like you aren't in control of your life.

What distinguished our Latino executives was not a denial of the strain of fatalism that courses through Latino culture, but rather a higher sense of self-efficacy. *They held a strong belief that their ambitious actions could produce the outcomes they desired.* This belief provided them the added motivation to embark on their pursuits and persevere in the face of adversity. Heavy ambition is not to be confused for greed or hubris but rather a desire to escape mediocrity.

Another distinguishing factor for the Latino executives was to make sure they succeeded *because* of the naysayers. They saw their detractors as doubtful, critical, and envious. They used the negative noise to fuel their ambition and prove the naysayers wrong via an "I'll show them" mentality. For example, on his acceptance into Yale University, Gilbert Casellas recalls his high school guidance counselor telling him that Yale was a hotbed for radicalism and that "Yale is going to screw you royally." Gilbert's response: "Talk about a motivator. I'm going to show you. I never saw him again, but in terms of the drive, those are the kind of remarks that cut deep."

Many of our Latino executives were at one time considered underdogs, but through their ambition were able to demonstrate to others that they were being underestimated. Juan Galarraga recalls being named a group director at Target, one of the youngest at the time. He started to hear people questioning his promotion as being the result of minority hiring policies rather than his capability. Instead of getting angry or defensive, he used the comments to further drive his performance and to show others that he had indeed earned—and deserved—the promotion.

For Lou Nieto, his ambition was fueled in part to quiet his critics:

> I've always had this compulsion to excel and do well because I've run into so many people in my life who try to diminish what you accomplish by saying, "You probably got into Harvard because you're Latino" or "You

probably got into University of Chicago because you're Latino." I always feel it's not good enough to be just as good as the people around me because somebody can try to diminish it. So I've always strived to be better than everybody around me.

Good enough is not enough

Our transformational leaders described how they mentor younger Latinos to also be ambitious. Myrna Soto tells her mentees to never be satisfied with good enough, and to always strive for more. Similarly, José Armario advises young Latinos to never back down, and to develop a *fire in the belly* for professional growth. He tells them about one of his secrets to success:

Number one was I never backed down from taking on a more difficult job or challenging project because I wanted to show my skills and to learn from the work accomplished. I never backed away, even though it meant more work. I always found that there was more to gain than to lose. My advice to young Latinos, "Take on more and challenge yourself."

Likewise, Monica Lozano shares this with Latino Millennials:

I'm a firm believer in raising your hand and your voice. It's important for others to know that you consider yourself prepared to take the next step. Leaders don't lean back, they lean in, and they stand up in order to be recognized for their work, their talent, and their contributions. It's important to demonstrate a desire to stretch, to expand networks, to learn new things and to be exposed to new situations.

The lesson for the next generation of Latino leaders is to not be afraid to think big, and to express your expectation of achieving great things. When Latinos hedge their ambitions and dreams because they want to be "realistic," they end up for the worse because of that hedging. Without a high sense of ambition, Latino professionals will achieve only modest growth. Without high ambition, people may eventually realize that their static career is self-imposed. They have taken only small steps up the career ladder because they sought nothing more. If being a CEO or C-suite executive seems like an alien idea, the reason may be that they haven't been sufficiently convinced to believe it's possible.

These transformational Latinos did not settle for what they *could have*, but rather pursued what they *wanted*. Their ambition helped them have a career based on the premise of pursuit; they took the offensive. They discovered that a conservative approach was not for them. In their upward mobility, they further validated that their ambition was crucial. Along the way they realized that the struggle gave them strength, much like the tempering of steel.

In the quest to fill the pipeline of future Latino leaders, we must acknowledge that ambition is a good thing and must be encouraged.

Risk-taking as a Catalyst for Growth and Getting Noticed

As we've described in earlier chapters, Latinos should not shoulder an additional burden of proof in workplace performance that non-Latinos don't. Latinos often work against a backdrop of flawed assumptions and negative stereotypes. They often live with the reality of facing harsher consequences for even small missteps. For these reasons, Latinos may feel exposed, vulnerable, and insecure throughout their careers. They worry that any mistake might make them look bad, so they can be prone to freeze up or take the safe route.

And yet, the Latino executives we interviewed taught us that without having the courage to take career chances, Latino professionals cannot expect to, as Price Cobb famously said, "crack the corporate code." What is clear from their stories is that Latino professionals have to give themselves permission to be pioneers and to explore career opportunities that may not have guarantees. They must be open to following a path without a clear roadmap. To be a transformative Latino leader requires being comfortable taking risks.

Next, we look at some of their tips for taking risks.

Taking risks means abandoning excuses to not take on opportunities that stretch us

Avoiding risks is impossible in a career; something is always at stake, so it's a matter of deciding which risks to take. Transformational leaders do not view risk-taking as a gamble, but rather as making a move on an opportunity they may have ignored in the past. We've learned from these executives that effective risk-taking means being able to abandon excuses and realize that often the only thing of significance standing in the way of upward career mobility is oneself.

For example, we noticed that transformational leaders have a unique perspective on *developmental job assignments*—those ad hoc projects that pop up out of organizational necessity. These may not necessarily be part of a job description, but they require a volunteer to complete the project. Taking on such assignments means the aspiring Latinos are seen as more valuable to the organization and provide a visible opportunity to test themselves and to be tested. These assignments allow volunteers to demonstrate their capabilities as decision makers, giving them the chance to make their mark and be noticed.

IHOP's Darren Rebelez took unconventional risks that accelerated his advancement. After successfully working in operations in the food service and restaurant industry, he took a developmental assignment in marketing and category management—areas he knew very little about. This broadened his skillset tremendously, giving him the opportunity to work with franchise owners. The franchise experience was instrumental in propelling him to the chief operating officer position at 7-Eleven, and ultimately to become the president of IHOP.

You have to be willing to explore some possibilities, try some new things, and put yourself in a position to potentially fail if you expect to succeed down the road. Not everything's going to be easy for you, so at a certain point you have to decide, "I'm going to take a chance," whether that chance is going to a new company or even trying different jobs within a company.

When I look at my career, I can't say that I had a linear career path. It was untraditional. I've seen so many times where people have had an opportunity to do something different that's a little bit out of their comfort zone, they say, "Yeah, that's not really the job I want; I want to do this other thing." I tell people, "That's OK, but you have to understand that when the decision-makers ask about who to put in the next advanced role, if you lack the experiences that the other candidates have, you're probably not going to get the job. You must recognize that if you're not willing to do some of those other jobs because you're afraid, that's your decision, but if you don't take that risk, you're not going to be as competitive for the roles that everybody's aspiring to."

Latino leaders must also recognize when career moves are too cautious. Beware of the trap when successive jobs do not move you beyond the zone of familiarity, security, and comfort. Cari Dominguez, the board director at ManpowerGroup, recalls early in her career being asked by one of her bosses to take a role that did not really stretch her skills or add new experiences in her preferred professional direction. She saw the potential risks this might have on her future career aspirations. Feeling she wasn't growing enough, she decided to leave the corporate sector for a political appointment position at the U.S. Department of Labor.

At first, the move seemed counterintuitive—leaving the corporate world for a political role when most individuals in political jobs are vying for corporate positions, which she already had. Political posts are full of uncertainties, reputational risks, and potential failure. However, she stacked those risks against the potential professional stagnation that she could have faced by accepting a role of limited growth and possibilities within the status quo. She saw that public policy-making offered her new opportunities to broaden her skills, gain new career credentials, and build new networks in a brand new field and, in the spirit of a transformational leader, she proceeded as if success was guaranteed. After successfully leading the department's Glass Ceiling Initiative, an initiative designed to remove artificial employment barriers affecting the advancement of women and minorities, Cari was appointed Assistant Secretary of Labor by President George H. W. Bush And having seen her work during his father's administration, President George W. Bush appointed Cari to serve as chair of the U.S. Equal Employment Opportunity Commission, one of his very first appointments. Both her private and public sector experiences ultimately provided the foundation she needed to become a corporate director. Clearly her risks paid off.

A willingness to take risks does not mean that Latinos can be careless about their career path. Sloppy, half-hearted job moves will benefit a career very little. Rather, successful Latino leaders view new jobs as a laboratory. They use each assignment to attempt new projects and to experience new environments. But more importantly, they realize that even if a particular position doesn't lead to advancement, each assignment contributes to their future success path. Experience is the ultimate teacher, and having great credentials as well as broad experiences are key to being noticed for promotion.

Accomplished Latino executives did not let the fear of failure consume them. They realized that doubt can do much damage in career moves. They did not give that doubt or fear of failure mental space. They also recognized that waiting until they were absolutely ready was simply a stall tactic. Even when not 100 percent ready, they took career risks and proceeded into new roles as if failure was inconceivable.

Taking risks leads to being noticed

Juan Galarraga's career may not have been possible without his taking some early risks. First, he came to the U.S. to go to college, even though he did not speak English. Later, he took another big risk: accepting an hourly wage job even though he had a college degree. He took a job unloading trucks at Target, beginning at 2 A.M. each day.

Juan continued to take risks with assignments throughout his career, which resulted in a meteoric rise up the ranks at Target Corporation. For example, after being an assistant manager for only a year, he was asked to fill in as a store manager for ninety days while the current manager was on leave. He realized that being asked to take this assignment meant that he was on the radar of top Target leaders. He didn't hesitate, and took the job even though he was not sure he was quite ready. When the manager decided not to return from leave, Juan took over as the store manager, even though he was only twenty-four years old. He recalls:

> Running that store felt incredibly intimidating. At a very young age, I was responsible for a $30 million store with close to 200 team members. All of my assistant managers were more experienced, potentially more qualified, older than me—and I had worked for several of them previously.

What we can learn from Juan's move into the store manager position is that taking risks isn't about *taking* a big chance, but rather *giving* oneself a big chance. Latinos can take heart in knowing they have been fielding similar challenges and overcoming them most of our lives.

Juan's next move involved turning around a store location that was considered to be underperforming. His willingness to take a gamble and move to a different city—even when he didn't always realize the full extent of an opportunity—enabled him to acquire additional skills and gain more confidence. He explains:

> After a year and a half of running a store, I get a phone call to move to Naples, Florida, to take over a high-volume, highly visible, broken store. It had years of struggling operationally, and low team morale. The phone call I got at the time: "Hey, we have this great opportunity where you can end up getting promoted or fired." Those were the type of things I applied for. I jumped on it! I felt like it was a great opportunity because I knew how to run a store; now I have the ability to turn a store around.

One morning Juan gathered everyone he managed at that store and had them write out their complaints, frustrations, and disappointments on pieces of paper. He then had them light a bonfire he'd set up behind the store and toss their pieces of paper into the flames. He explains:

> I called a mandatory all-team meeting with everyone at 6 A.M. Most team members did not know who I was at that time because the first few days I was there, I had been working overnight in the back room. But as they went to the back of the store, they saw this big bonfire. They looked at me with a look of "What's going on?" I asked everyone to write down a story of something that was going on at the store that they didn't like or that didn't make them feel good. Then everyone, one after the other, read what they had written. When we were done, I had them throw their pieces of paper in the bonfire and I said, "No more, it's a new day, a new life, let's have each other's back. Today, we start anew!" I had heard them, and they had heard each other. That day we began turning that store around to the point where it became one of the most successful ones in the region.

And so it was. From that point on, he kept taking leadership risks with that store and its team, and in a few months, Juan successfully turned the store around. Morale was up, as were sales and profitability.

Juan's performance, risk-taking, and confidence led to a rapid string of promotions. By age twenty-eight he was a group director running a $2 billion business unit with one hundred stores. His next move required him to relocate to Target's corporate headquarters in Minneapolis. He continued to excel, soon earning the title of vice president of healthcare operations. Then came another call asking him to take over a region. Not even thirty-five years old, he was now a leader of a $17 billion business with five hundred stores in seventeen states.

Juan's accelerated career trajectory did cause some adversity and increased scrutiny by others who thought he was too young for some of his roles. He is currently the senior vice president of store operations for Target, a position he credits in part to his willingness to take career risks. What other Latinos can learn from him is that a willingness to take risks early and throughout a career not only provides new skills, experiences, and increased visibility, but also helps build much-needed confidence to take on even greater challenges.

José Armario includes a willingness to relocate as accepting risk and shares this:

> I was one of the few people in my group who followed opportunity no matter where it went. I wasn't afraid to move, to take on the next job. A lot of my friends stayed and waited for the next job because they didn't want to relocate, and sometimes those next jobs never materialized.

George Herrera, the current board director at Wyndham Worldwide Corporation, believes that it is always better to try and then fail than to play it safe. People learn from mistakes, which helps them grow. He credits this approach to his willingness to take over the family business at a young age and growing it into a much larger company. He took this same approach when he was asked to become the first non-Mexican American to lead the U.S. Hispanic Chamber of Commerce as CEO.

Gilbert Casellas recalls the risk he took in leaving a well-paying job at a prestigious law firm for a judicial clerkship. It was a calculated risk, but one that eventually opened many more doors for him. It also helped him become a partner at his original law firm when he returned from the clerkship, which was faster than if he had played it safe and not taken the clerkship position.

Deeply Valuing Relationships

Transformational Latino leaders must also know how to cultivate relationships, both inside and outside their organization. Those we interviewed shared numerous stories where investing in and nurturing relationships helped them find people who would give them honest feedback, help them access critical information, and commit themselves to the interviewee's future success. In fact, cultivating relationships was so vital to all the executives interviewed that it is the topic in our research that generated the most content by a wide margin.

Paul Raines, CEO of GameStop, sums up the importance of relationships, which is one of his personal keys to success:

> You have to build relationships. They are so important because they carry you along the rest of your career. Those relationships you're building right now with that mid-level manager, or your boss, or your colleagues—those people will continue to grow, and they will carry you with them. So build solid relationships. Those can be Latino relationships, or they can be non-Latino relationships. They can be in professional societies or whatever relationships are available to you. Maximize them! Take advantage of them!

Investing in and nurturing relationships requires a variety of strategies. Let's explore what the executives had to share.

Relationships help overcome isolation or feeling like an outsider

Patricia Diaz Dennis, the current board director at MassMutual, recalls the important support her relationships provided when she was the first Latina at a major Los Angeles law firm:

> This is where it started becoming obvious to me that I was different. I joined the Mexican-American Bar Association because I needed support from people who were like me, who grew up in the way I did. It was such a wonderful camaraderie. I really needed networks of people with whom I didn't have to explain trivial things. I felt like it was home. We would be able to share about how hard law school was for most of us, how hard we had to work, how proud we made our parents, how we were still kind of isolated at our jobs, and how we needed to support each other.
>
> Exposing your vulnerability is really tough, especially when you're in your first job. You learn to call your buddies, somebody in another firm who's done something similar, and ask for advice. "How do I handle this without seeming stupid to the person I'm working with?" There's that anxiety in all of us. I'm sure this was true for all young people just starting out in their jobs, but it was heightened by the fact that most of us were among the very few Latinos and Latinas in our law firms or among the very few in our companies. We needed a safe place where we could ask questions.

Capitalize on the fact that senior executives are constantly on the lookout for new talent

In organizational settings, you don't find sponsors, sponsors find you. Getting yourself on the radar of senior executives or potential sponsors requires a reputation of performance excellence. Charlie Garcia, the former CEO of Sterling Financial Group and current head of ALPFA, has a story of how being noticed the first time generated a ricocheting effect. After excelling at the Air Force Academy and distinguishing himself as an intelligence officer in the military, Charlie was spotted by four-star General John Galvin. Charlie was soon traveling with Galvin to meet with other generals, dignitaries, and presidents of foreign countries, as well as conducting briefings for the Senate Armed Services Committee.

Based on the superior quality of his work for General Galvin, Charlie next caught the eye of Mort Zuckerman, owner of *U.S. News and World Report*. Zuckerman encouraged him to apply for the White House Fellows Program and wrote a letter of recommendation on his behalf. Soon Charlie was in the program, and his fellowship spanned parts of both the Reagan and George H. W. Bush administrations. During this time he established relationships with William Bennett, former Secretary of Education, and John Whitehead, Deputy Secretary of State and former Chairman of Goldman Sachs, both of whom became lifelong career advisors.

Build relationships outside your comfort zone— which means not just in Latino circles

While connecting with other Latinos has proven to be a successful way to leverage relationships, Latinos often make the mistake—particularly early in their careers—of cultivating relationships with only people who are similar to them or who are part of their peer group.

Transformational leaders look outside their immediate circle and develop relationships with people who are not like them: people who work at different companies, who have different skillsets, or who belong to different peer groups. George Herrera encourages young Latinos to build relationships outside their comfort zone:

> If you're looking to go up those rungs and enter the corporate boardroom, you're going to need to start socializing and gathering at events where those individuals are. Approximately 99.9 percent of those events are not exclusively Hispanic events. I know that in the Latino community we're very culturally attuned to each other because we love family and we want to be in a family. But if you're born and raised in Miami and that opportunity is in Boise, Idaho, you should choose to move. Then you should learn that you must get out of your comfort zone and network outside of groups that have Latino relevance.
>
> Developing relationships with non-Latinos doesn't mean that you give up your culture; it doesn't mean that you give up your pride. It means that you must learn that you need to circulate in the circles where your immediate boss and some of the potential board members may be socializing so they will begin to see you in their environment. I think that's something we really don't do often enough or well enough. We're scared and beat up with trepidation.

Monica Lozano recounts how her intention to get more involved and build relationships with community leaders outside of her day-to-day circles resulted in a sponsorship relationship that helped her career tremendously:

With regards to networking and relationship building, I was doing a lot of work with local, small nonprofit organizations and was asked to join the board of the YMCA for Greater Los Angeles. I accepted because I thought it would a great place for me to stay connected to community organizations and community leaders. Little did I know that these board members were the civic and business leaders of L.A. Through that experience I met the president of a regional bank, and over time he asked me to join his board of directors, my first such position. I recognize him to this day as being the person who gave me a start on corporate boards.

Monica's ability to cultivate relationships has been a critical component in her career success which includes serving as a board director for the Walt Disney Company, Bank of America, and Target Corporation, and as a member of the board of trustees for the University of Southern California, as well as on President Obama's Council on Jobs and Competitiveness.

Cari Dominguez also advises young Latinos to seek common ground with allies beyond the boundaries of race, ethnicity, class, gender, or age when establishing relationships:

By extending yourself you'll find meaningful relationships, and they will find you, often in surprising and unexpected places. It's great to be within your network, but the people who will most likely sponsor you and will support you and serve as references are those who are, for the most part, outside of that network. The people that have supported me and facilitated opportunities for advancement have not come from the Latino community. For example, the deputy assistant secretary of Labor was an American University graduate, so when he found out I was an A.U. graduate, he took an interest in my career. When I was at Bank of America, I found another connection. My boss came from IBM, and I happened to have had some good friends from IBM so we bonded through common friends. That relationship showed me that to get ahead I had to break grounds and try not to stay exclusively in the Latino circle of influence and support.

For Latino professionals like Charlie Garcia who grew up in Latin America, building relationships outside the family may be a new phenomenon:

I would say that I wasn't good at networking and had to change by asking for help and developing relationships outside of the family. In Latin America, you asked your immediate family for help if you needed it; help was in the family unit. You didn't network and ask questions and favors from people outside of the family. So networking was something that I had to learn to do, and it wasn't easy.

Trust is the foundation of relationships

Trust was cultivated by our transformational leaders by showing that they cared for others, were able to guard confidences, could keep promises, and had the best interest of others in mind. Darren Rebelez states:

I've always strived to build good relationships and trust with people. That doesn't always mean we're buddies, but you must establish trust with people.

George Herrera, recalls a time when as CEO of the Hispanic Chamber of Commerce, he was challenging a corporation's unfair practices in dealing with the Hispanic community. George had a great relationship with a Latino professional who also worked at the company. His friend was worried that the escalation of the situation could cause him to lose his job. George handled things skillfully, resulting in the company's taking a new approach to dealing with their Latino stakeholders. Equally important, George resolved the matter in a fashion where his friend not only kept his job, but also found his position at the company strengthened through the new policies. George has maintained a deep relationship with his friend because he established a foundation of trust.

Patricia Diaz Dennis advises young Latinos to seek out relationships based on trust and to be savvy about how they develop this trust:

Find somebody whose judgment you trust and who will respect your confidence. It's usually not somebody at work. This person should show good judgment, and you should feel you can discuss things with them without becoming too vulnerable. Going outside the organization is helpful because people at work can exploit your sharing too much, especially at big companies. Fellow workers can exploit your weakness because everybody is competing for a very few jobs at a certain level.

Relationships that Launched a TV Show

George Herrera recalls a time when his relationships helped him launch a TV show idea he had called *Hispanics Today* on NBC:

> I met with Orlando Padilla, who was at General Motors, and Rudy Beserra, who was at Coca-Cola. I knew Rudy from his days at the White House because I was a delegate to the Reagan-Bush campaign at the national convention, and then Rudy had gone to work for Reagan at the White House. I turned to them right away and said, "I'm trying to get a TV show," and they countered, "TV show?" Next I talked to Jamie Dimon, then the CEO of Bank One and now the CEO of JPMorgan Chase, about the show and he said, "If you get the TV show, we'd love to advertise on it."
>
> I then returned to NBC with the treatment *and* written sponsorship commitments from General Motors, Coca-Cola, and Bank One. I told the president of NBC New York, Dennis Swanson, "Here's the treatment, and by the way, I've sold all the advertising for the twelve shows if you put me on the air." He replied, "Well, you know what? I like your style, I like your idea, I'm going to put you on the air, and I'm going to put you on the first Sunday of every month after *Meet the Press*."
>
> In September 1998, *Hispanics Today* went on the air on twelve NBC-owned and affiliated stations throughout the country in the top twelve markets. It was seen by 12 million viewers every month.

Hispanics Today became a ratings success, so successful that NBC quickly changed it from a monthly to a weekly show. It highlighted Hispanic leaders like Linda Alvarado, owner of the Colorado Rockies baseball team and founder of a construction firm. The show had a great impact on the broader Latino community because it gave young Hispanics successful role models that they had not seen before on TV.

George's ability to rely on the professional relationships he had established was essential to the creation of *Hispanics Today*—which will be part of his legacy.

Some relationships will create sponsors

Establishing strong relationships makes it more likely that these people will become sponsors who will advocate for you, giving you exposure to other executives. They will fight to get you promoted by making sure you are considered for promising and challenging assignments. They will protect you from negative publicity, or help you avoid contact with damaging executives.

One of José Armario's sponsors was Jim Skinner, the former CEO of McDonald's. Jim encouraged José to seek a corporate director seat. When a retail bank approached José to serve on their board, Jim advised him that this might not be the best board to join. José listened and passed on that opportunity. However, he soon joined the board of USG in Chicago, and eventually the board of Avon Products. Based on his ability to build a relationship with the CEO of McDonald's, he encourages young professionals to build relationships with their superiors in the corporate structure.

Early in his career while working at a bank, Lou Nieto established a wonderful relationship with the senior vice president of commercial banking. When the SVP's credit analyst went on a two-week vacation, Lou was asked to fill in temporarily. Lou performed so well that the SVP decided to keep him in that position even after the other person came back from vacation. The person he had replaced had an MBA, while Lou had only completed his undergraduate degree and had just one year's work experience. This gave him an accelerated immersion into the world of commercial banking, and that early break was extremely useful when he later pursued his MBA at Harvard Business School. Most significant was the fact his experience validated the importance of caring about people. In fact, Lou mentions that when ex-employees and coworkers are asked to describe him, "They will say that I'm strategic and that I get results, but they always first say that I care about people."

In his book, *Good Is Not Enough*,[1] author Keith Wyche talks about the ability to get others to "wear your T-shirt." By this he means that when people walk around bragging about how wonderful they are and all the great things they can do, they are in essence wearing their own T-shirt, often leading to their being seen as braggarts. However, because Latinos and other minorities are less prone to call attention to their accomplishments, they rely more on others to advocate for them—they need others to wear their T-shirt. Through their ability to establish meaningful relationships, transformational Latino leaders got others to wear their T-shirt, and that elevated their chance of career success. Monica Lozano validates this idea:

> Relationships, either in work or outside as it relates to career advancement, are absolutely critical. I've always said your reputation is the one thing that follows you your entire life and those relationships not only become helpful to you but will also be, in many ways, those that speak for you. When somebody asks, "Can you tell me about so-and-so?" and receive the reply, "She's extraordinary," that's validation.

It's also important to stay in contact with mentors and sponsors, even after leaving a company. While some work relationships may be short, they have the potential to last if you continuously cultivate them. After Victor Arias was accepted into the business school at Stanford University, his bank president, Art Gonzáles, immediately put him in the company's

---

1   Wyche, Keith R., and Sonia Alleyne. *Good Is Not Enough: And Other Unwritten Rules for Minority Professionals*. New York: Portfolio, 2009.

management program so that he could gain relevant experience before leaving to study for his MBA. This was extremely valuable for Victor because it provided him with relevant business experience. Before leaving for Stanford, Victor submitted a letter of resignation. However, Art encouraged him to instead request a leave of absence, reminding Victor that he might want to return someday. Even though he had three other job offers after completing his MBA, Victor went back to Texas to work for Art. Victor says having Art as a sponsor was a "godsend." He further explains:

> I think that he saw something, and I was fortunate that he saw that something in me. He was one of those guardian angels you sometimes don't recognize.

When Art's daughter was later going to business school, Victor (who had helped establish the National Society for Hispanic MBAs) made a donation to the school's scholarship fund and allocated the scholarship to Art's daughter, thus further strengthening their relationship. Victor tells others that by building and sustaining relationships, "you find out who has your back."

Build mutually beneficial relationships

Another notable approach for building relationships is to establish a reciprocal situation. Our leaders did not seek relationships based on what they felt they could gain from the relationship, but with a willingness to give: investing time and energy in other people. They have mastered the art of building relationships because they tend to give as much as they can with no immediate expectation of return in mind. And they often gave more than they received. Patricia Diaz Dennis shares how her willingness to help others has resulted in career opportunities:

When I was a young lawyer, I took a younger lawyer under my wing. I felt sorry for him because he had nobody when he had moved from the East. He and I were in the same department, so I invited him over for dinner, making tacos every Friday night. He loved my tacos. He eventually gave my name to someone who then gave my name to presidential personnel, resulting in President Ronald Reagan appointing me to the National Labor Relations Board job. Every single job I've gotten has been because of a friend who recommended me or somebody who knew me.

For Gilbert Casellas, his ability to build and nurture mutually beneficial relationships has resulted in tremendous career opportunities. His relationship with a fellow trustee for the University of Pennsylvania helped him secure a spot on the board of directors at Prudential. Later, a friend he met while a member of the Hispanic Bar Association introduced him to the Clinton administration, leading to his first government appointment. His firsthand realization of the importance and value of building relationships is one reason his advice to younger Latinos is so helpful:

I had a partner in my firm in Philadelphia who said he thought I was a good trial lawyer after I told him the story of how I grew up and worked in a family business, a dry-cleaning business belonging to my dad's uncle. I managed the counter all day, dealing with people of all walks of life. My partner said, "That's why you're a good trial lawyer. You worked with people of all walks of life. They came in there, and you treated them well." I said, "Maybe that's what it is. I don't know if I can answer it any better." I do try to cultivate relationships. When I talk to people about networking, the one thing I say is, "Networking isn't just going to a meeting. It's really about building relationships. And in building relationships, people want to know that you're there to give, not just to take."

By nurturing their work relationships on a consistent and generous basis, these leaders avoided what is sometimes called "911 networking," people only reaching out to their network when they need help or want something. Those who practice 911 networking are seen as opportunistic and are quickly labeled as *takers*, not as *givers*. They're seen as manipulative, devious, or just plain selfish. People want to know that others in a network care about them as a person—not as a means to an end.

Some Latinos make the error of seeing relationship building as playing office politics, acting as if they're above it all. They believe that their hard work, knowledge, and skills are all that is required to move up. They lack leadership maturity and have yet to realize that transformational leaders are highly interdependent individuals who need strong relationships with bosses, direct reports, senior executives, customers, suppliers, and the broader community.

All bosses (the good, the bad and the ugly) are key people

One of the most important relationships any professional can build is with the immediate boss. That person evaluates performance, which has a long-lasting influence on career success. Patricia Diaz Dennis reminds others: "It is absolutely critical to maintain a strong relationship with one's boss." Jorge Figueredo, executive vice president at McKesson, also encourages those with a bad boss to still maintain a good relationship with them:

Even when you have a bad boss you can learn so much from them. First, you can learn what not to do when you become a boss. Second, rarely are bosses bad 100 percent of the time, so learn from them while you can because bad bosses don't tend to stick around too long.

Monica Lozano adds that another way of dealing with a bad boss is to simply excel at work. She states:

Create allies and find sponsors when you have a bad boss. Identify other sponsors in the organization but first demonstrate really high levels of performance. Never let yourself be put on your hind feet because you didn't perform at the very highest levels.

As we can see, the benefits of being able to manage relationships effectively are many and varied. The key distinction for our transformational Latino leaders is that relationship building was not considered additional work—it *was* the work.

From Being to Doing

These first three keys to success—embracing ambition, taking risks, and investing in relationships—are traits, dispositions of how to *be*. Transformative leaders demonstrate key differentiating competencies as well, which are the necessary action-oriented skills and behaviors. In the case of our Latino executives, these are being politically savvy about how to navigate corporate culture, establishing and shaping one's own leadership style, and paying it forward by giving back to the community—topics we turn to in the next chapter. ⋙

Building Latino Talent Inside and Outside the Organizational Walls

Lou Miramontes, a retired partner at KPMG, provides an excellent example of just how transformational leaders go about making a difference in the Latino community. Shortly after being named a partner, he recalls this scenario:

> When I returned to the U.S. practice after a foreign assignment in Latin America, I observed that there weren't a lot of Latino leaders in corporate America. You hear they don't have the skill or they don't have the contacts so they don't know how to navigate situations. I said to myself, and I told people, "You're absolutely nuts. I just spent five years in Latin America dealing with some of the most savvy, successful Hispanics, and they got it. They had good success, and they are thriving so it has nothing to do with the color of our skin or our last name. It has to do with opportunity, and it has to do with getting those folks to go into the mainstream.

Lou went on a mission to change KPMG, developing a strategy to bring in more Latinos. He convinced the CEO and the chairman of the business case for more Latino partners due to accelerating international and Latin-American business growth. After getting their buy-in, he developed an internal network with the handful of other Latino partners. Understanding that these Latinos needed guidance, he secured mentors and sponsors to teach them how the business really works, how decisions are made, how to secure budgets for initiatives—how the corporate culture operates. Over a ten-year period, they successfully recruited and promoted a record number of Latinos.

Lou's realization of the need for more Latinos had compelled him to make a positive impact. He also took his mission of growing Latino talent outside the firm's walls. He decided he wanted to help increase the overall number of Latinos going into the fields of accounting and finance. He became actively involved in the Latino nonprofit ALPFA. For years, he has helped to secure jobs for Latino graduates with big firms, helped raise scholarship funds for bright Latino students, and raised awareness within the larger Latino community of the benefits of working at accounting and finance firms.

Now a director on a corporate board, Lou is a member of the Latino Corporate Directors Association (LCDA), which helps to secure board seats for Latino executives. It's no surprise that he is joined as a member of the LCDA by other transformational Latino leaders highlighted in this book, including José Armario, Victor Arias, Gilbert Casellas, Patricia Diaz Dennis, Cari Dominguez, Charlie Garcia, Grace Lieblein, Monica Lozano, Lou Nieto, Darren Rebelez, and Luis Ubiñas—to name just a few.

CHAPTER 7

What to Do: Three Key Competencies of Transformational Leaders

"Cuestionar tu propio proceso es una necesidad.
Si no te cuestionas a ti mismo, es imposible mejorar."

To question your own process is a necessity. If you don't
question yourself, it's impossible to improve.

—Alejandro González Iñárritu, Mexican film director

We have delved into the three traits of becoming a transformative leader: embracing ambition as an honorable intent, taking risks as a catalyst for growth and getting noticed, and valuing relationships deeply. Now let's examine the three competencies, the skills and abilities that emerged as necessities.

- Political savvy about corporate culture
- Ability to establish and shape your own leadership style
- Giving back to the community

We believe that there is a developmental sequence to these three competencies.

First, individuals must learn to master the politics determining how to advance within the corporate culture. They cannot survive very long when trying to break into the leadership ranks without this skill. Yet there is a delicate balance here: authentic leaders will recognize the warning signs of nearing the danger zone of compromising their own uniqueness and of losing themselves by hewing too closely to corporate norms.

When credibility and relationships have been established within the system, transformative leaders don't just stay with the pack, they find ways to differentiate themselves from others. By doing so, they begin to formulate and shape their unique leadership style. Having mastered the cultural customs of the corporation, they know when and where to break the rules. The Latino executive who has done the foundational work of being authentically grounded in their cultural identity can now identify outlets through which their diverse views and behaviors can flow outward, and in that, differentiate their leadership.

Finally, after leaders have accumulated a followership, career accomplishments and recognition, and financial success, they are strategically placed to generously share their time, resources, and sponsorship.

Let's take a deeper dive into each of these competencies.

Political Savvy About Corporate Culture

When an ambitious person comes from a traditionally underrepresented group, any organization's unique corporate culture poses a formidable challenge to securing the top echelons. Why? As we saw in Chapter 4, Latino and corporate American cultures can clash in profound ways. Because corporate America was founded by European-American men who established their norms for business based on what worked best for them, it follows that this confers advantages for them and disadvantages for those who do not have the same cultural legacy.

Being able to decipher and follow a company's culture is an all-encompassing endeavor because the culture defines particular ways to think, speak, and act within the company. Those who don't follow established ways are seen as not fitting in. Those individuals who do break through by meeting their impact metrics tend to be successful and that success leads to greater leadership roles. Those leaders then reinforce the existing culture within which they have triumphed, through a variety of mechanisms such as allocating resources, giving rewards, and doling out punishments.

Transformative leaders go further to influence changes in the culture. For leaders and companies committed to becoming more diverse and inclusive, cultural changes are needed because the legacy culture norms actively reinforce the glass ceiling that few minorities can break. Before anyone can achieve a position with enough power to influence cultural changes, they must first have an intimate knowledge of the culture and become successful at navigating within it.

How to master corporate culture without losing your own sense of identity is the issue. Following are some of the leaders' insights:

Be a student of corporate culture

The former Bank of America executive Cari Dominguez told us:

> Understanding the unwritten rules at work is more valuable than the written rules. Everyone knows the official rules, but only a few really understand the unwritten ones.

Through keen observation of what was happening around them, the Latino leaders in our study figured out the unwritten rules. José Armario, the former McDonald's executive and Avon board member, explains how he picked up cues on how people advanced within McDonald's corporate structure:

> I carefully observed how some approached promotions. I liked how they did it in terms of a balanced, professional, fact-driven way, and I tried to emulate that. But I also saw the political ugliness of an executive team where some people are jockeying for time, always have something to say, and are "besties" with the boss (or try to be) in ways that can influence decisions along the way.
>
> If you observe, you pick up the good and try to emulate but stay wary of some of the other not-so-positive intentions that people may have. Some people move up the ladder because they've made the right connections; they hit it off with people. Their work has been okay, but they have the confidence of the person in charge. They survive, but eventually the cream does rise to the top. You do get exposed for who you really are the higher up you go. In the corporate culture, if you didn't know your stuff you got exposed quite easily. I saw some people fail when they got exposed, while those who were knowledgeable and fact-driven, and knew their responsibilities, typically not just survived, but thrived.

Even the most seasoned corporate executives are sometimes thrust into environments where they must quickly determine the corporate culture. Comcast Corporate SVP Myrna Soto tells how she learned this lesson very early in her career in a customer-service role, and it served her well as she made her way to the top:

Early in my career I was at this company with a very unique corporate culture: a privately owned family company, headquartered in Miami, but with roots in Norway and Eastern Europe. There I was, a Hispanic in Miami, and, I'll admit, a little loud and boisterous. I was initially not welcomed since I was not really what they wanted. While they wanted results, discipline, and hard work, they were very reserved. You talked when you were spoken to, so I learned what it would take to be able to navigate and grow within the company by respecting some of the corporate cultural norms. However, I still challenged procedures, asked many questions, and contributed ideas about how the call center was being run. Because of this combined approach, I quickly ascended to a management role.

At first Myrna's dual approach of playing by the corporate norms but still offering her break-the-mold ideas was rewarded by the culture because she achieved results. But soon enough she began to hear that her style had its limits and was not always appreciated by everyone within the company:

Because I was this young whippersnapper who had just graduated from college and was learning about their operations, I'm saying "God, we should be doing this and we should be doing that, and this and that and blah, blah, blah." There was a point in time where some of the leaders above me said "Hey, you know, settle down, because every time we have a meeting you're always kind of like… whatever (outspoken)." Even in a culture where my ideas weren't necessarily welcomed, it was impossible for me to restrain myself 100 percent. I think I learned over time how to better nuance my adaptation to the culture without losing my distinctive voice. I learned how to introduce my ideas and how to respectfully challenge the status quo by saying, "I hear what you say, but I believe that you should consider what I'm sharing with you."

And it worked. As I ascended to more senior roles, I was provided the platform and the opportunity to be able to take very distinct stances on certain topics and issues. If I look back and ask, "Would I have had as much courage as an entry-level worker in a particular place to take the stances I took later on as I ascended to more senior roles?" I'm not so sure.

Later, when she left that company to join American Express, Myrna discovered another cultural transition she needed to make:

I moved from wearing semi-casual, business casual in Miami, to the corporate power suit at American Express. These are rules that nobody explains to you, but when you enter the environment you quickly realize, "Oh, I'm not fitting in."

As much as there can be tensions between archetypal Latino and corporate American cultures, there are numerous individual Latino leaders who find that their personalities and inner drivers naturally gravitate toward the corporate culture. For example, Lou Miramontes's personal work style aligned perfectly with the culture at accounting firm KPMG. This not only helped him fit in, but also gave him a competitive advantage in the aggressive work environments of professional services firms where people are vying for a limited number of partnerships.

I learned the keys to success. The first was that you had to be willing to work crazy hours during busy seasons. But I was used to working long hours and getting up early. That was easy; my dad did it, rising at 4 A.M. to go to a factory. In contrast, I had the privilege of putting a suit on and going to an office. That ethic of work was with me, setting me apart from the pack. I was able to work and learn how to serve clients and develop relationships.

Later, Lou came to see the value of performance evaluations as another way to gain insights on how to be successful within the culture of KPMG:

Performance evaluations pointed out to me the tasks I did well. Those evaluations were also very blunt about what I did not do well. Having both sides of the table come at me in a constructive way was really helpful. Sometimes there were criticisms that were tough to hear: "Hey you're superficial; you didn't follow-up," or "You have to be more visible." Bottom line: you have to have a cultural learning component to your professional life.

Once you learn the corporate culture, use your leadership position to change it

Patricia Díaz Dennis recalls being on the National Labor Relations Board when she had her third child. Because of her role as a leader, Patricia felt it was important to shift the culture to be more supportive of parents, and to have family-friendly policies. She also saw that leaders needed to lead by example.

I realized I needed to be what I wanted the change to be. So I brought my newborn daughter Alicia to the office and I nursed her there. Then I let the women on my staff—I had a staff of twenty-one lawyers—know that if they needed time for family-related reasons or if they were going to come in late or leave early, it was all okay. When you're a professional, doing your work on a flexible schedule is acceptable; that you do get your work done is the important issue.

For some of our Latino executives, having key decision-making roles at their company helped them see how things really got done behind the curtain—including practices that were unfair. Cari Dominguez recalls being confronted with this reality when she had a leadership role in human resources at a major banking institution:

I was responsible for the care and feeding of the top two hundred executives—compensation, executive recruitment and benefits, developmental assignments, executive education—anything that had to do with the top executives. It was a one-stop shop so the executives wouldn't have to go through each other or go through any complicated processes. They would simply go through me. I had my own team who worked with the chairman and the vice chairman, making sure that these executives were well taken care of: bonuses, equity, different perks. But it became clear that there were really no criteria for who received the perks and who didn't. I kept wondering why did some get it, while these others didn't? It was quite the subjective process.

Not surprisingly, this led to her recognizing that the culture at this organization favored certain groups over others. Men enjoyed international assignments, executive education programs, and other opportunities for which others were not seriously considered—which gave them an edge when it came time for promotions and increased pay. Cari felt the culture needed to change.

As people moved up the ladder, they became part of a much more subjective process when being considered for the rewards, the transfers, the assignments. Since I felt very strongly about how these things were happening, I went to the chairman and said, "We've got issues. There are invisible barriers here concerning the advancement of people." The CEO was quite shocked because he was a very progressive individual who had three daughters. He said, "I want everyone to feel included, so let's do a study." He commissioned me to do an upward-mobility review, and I was able to brief him and the whole management committee about the findings. We made structural changes to the process after the conclusion of the study.

Having learned how the inner workings and company culture at an institution can limit upward mobility for women was pivotal for Cari, leading her to decide she needed a broader platform from which to heighten awareness of issues of disparity and inequity. She would soon be called upon by then Secretary of Labor Elizabeth Dole to take a role with her political team, and eventually become the Chair of the U.S. Equal Employment Opportunity Commission.

I wanted to use this platform for public policy making to really make companies accountable for the progression, the advancement, the inclusion, and the parity of treatment for all their employees. That's where the Glass Ceiling Initiative began. We developed a final project and met with the policy council and the White House. President George H. W. Bush at the time actually used talking points we had drafted in one of his presidential debates. It was a highly accepted initiative. To this day I have women coming up to me and saying that as a result of all that public policy-making work, they got an opportunity within the company to advance and to move into non-traditional areas.

Through a thorough understanding of how corporate culture works to the benefit of a privileged few and against most others, Cari was able to leverage that insight to make positive, transformational change—not just within a particular company but nationwide.

As Latinos strive for more C-suite roles, they have to be able to not only understand corporate culture, but to be able to change and shape it as well.

Ability to Establish and Shape Your Leadership Style

Our successful Latino executives' leadership styles were consistently shaped from values, character, and experiences forged in the crucible of their formative years where family, culture, institutions, and personality were all defining influences. Many characteristics of their leadership styles would have been apparent early in their careers, and likely were more generic: discipline, hard work, accomplishing tasks, and inspiring others to follow them.

But the characteristics of their differentiated leadership styles— those actions that may run counter to the corporate culture— often did not fully manifest until they had unraveled that culture and the politics behind it. In essence, culture grants grudging permission to be challenged after deference has been paid to it.

Let's first look at the power of the formative years in shaping leaders, and then at those moments of truth when the transformative leader breaks the existing paradigms.

The essence of the person becomes the essence of the leader

GameStop CEO Paul Raines acknowledges that his leadership style was deeply influenced by his upbringing in Costa Rica and close connection with his family:

> My Latin heritage plays a huge part in what I've done in my career and with my leadership style. As a leader and as an executive in any organization, I've approached things as a family more than I would have had I not had that experience of being born and raised in Costa Rica. Our motto here at GameStop is "Protect the family." That's how we define our reason for being.

By invoking a leadership style that creates a family environment, Paul's approach ripples far beyond the workplace. He told us, "I get letters and emails from people I've met twenty-five years ago, and they still remember me.

Another way that Paul's approach transcends normal workplace boundaries is his deep commitment to helping others be successful—which serves as another foundational component of his leadership style. He states:

> Maybe it relates to my Catholic upbringing. I have found that you get a lot further by helping people around you be successful than by always trying to stand out by yourself. And you'll find aiding others makes you successful over time.

Even though Paul describes his philosophy as being a servant leader, fiercely focused on helping others and rooted in family, that does not mean he has a soft approach. He relies on accountability and developing a reputation for excellence to round out his leadership style.

Looking in the mirror for accountability is extremely important. Bad leaders look in the mirror when things are going well and congratulate themselves, and good leaders look in the mirror and ask, "What am I going to do different today to try to make the situation better?" You have to develop a reputation for excellence in everything you do. There's no room for excuses. The last job I had to be interviewed for was my first job after coming out of school. Ever since then I've been pulled along by people I knew, people I met, and relationships I built. Excellence in everything you do is very important. You can't be mediocre.

Darren Rebelez, president of IHOP, says his leadership style was solidified by his experiences attending West Point, the U.S. Military Academy. He recalls West Point as being extremely challenging from an academic standpoint, but he loved the environment because of the esprit de corps and the sense of purpose. He describes what it was like:

You're there to go to school, but it wasn't just going to school. West Point is really a leadership school, cloaked in a college. You were there to train, to become a leader, and to be prepared to help defend the nation if called upon. I went there from '84 to '88. The Cold War was still in full swing, and the Soviet Union still existed. So we were training for a potentially very large, conventional war. My best friends in the world today are the people I went to school with there.

Darren tells how his leadership style was further defined by his military experience:

I was really excited about getting into the Army, and after four years of training and education, I became an infantry officer, a paratrooper, and an Army ranger. It was a really good experience. I was taught about leadership and practiced leadership by being placed in charge of people. When I think about the level of responsibility that I had as new lieutenant who's twenty-two or twenty-three years old, it's quite a staggering thought. My first job was as a platoon leader where I had forty men I was responsible for. Then shortly after being promoted, my unit was deployed to the Gulf War. I was twenty-five years old, leading 120 soldiers, and responsible for millions of dollars in vehicles and equipment. I had to take them halfway around the world for a fight. The level of responsibility I was given and the leadership challenges I faced were not like anything I would get in corporate America, certainly at that stage of my career.

When asked how his West Point education and military career impacted his leadership style, Darren stated:

My military career is central to how I approach things. I learned that 80 percent of leadership is showing up. You just can't mail it in if you're going to be a leader. You have to be there, on the ground, with your people. In the infantry, we have a saying that you have to lead from the front, especially when things get a little dicey and the soldiers are looking for you to show them what to do. So I've always viewed leadership as a hands-on exercise.

Even today, in my job as president of IHOP, I get out and visit restaurants and visit our franchisees. It never ceases to amaze me that people are so impressed that I, as president of the company, actually show up and sit down to have conversations with the people who work there. It's such a simple thing, but it means so much to people and builds confidence in them and trust between them and their leaders. They should expect more out of a leader than just showing up, but that's the way it is.

Another principle that I learned at West Point is doing the harder right versus the easier wrong. That's actually something that's in the cadet prayer. I always think about this because it's simple to take the easy way out. But as leaders we're held to a higher standard, and that oftentimes means making difficult decisions. The only way anybody's ever going to follow you is if they trust you, and the only way to build that trust is through demonstrating character and integrity.

When Darren decided to leave the military and pursue a corporate career, he relied heavily on his military leadership experience. He recalls interviewing with PepsiCo during this transition.

I said, "Look, I don't know much about this business, but the one thing I do know is if you give me a group of people I can get stuff done." They said, "OK, we've got a job like that in our restaurant business."

True to his word, this leadership style eventually took Darren all the way to becoming the president of a restaurant chain.

Target's Juan Galarraga feels that two very different aspects of his life greatly influenced his leadership style: being an immigrant, which instilled in him a relentless work ethic, and realizing he wasn't as great at soccer as he had thought he was. He explains that as a youth growing up in Venezuela, he excelled at soccer, oftentimes being the best player on the team. But when he came to college in the U.S. on a soccer scholarship, he soon realized he was no longer one of the best players on the team. This required him to shift his playing style to focus more on teamwork and team success as opposed to personal success. He credits this emphasis on establishing high-performing teams as a key to his career success.

US Hispanic Media Group's Monica Lozano says her approach to leadership was shaped by a variety of experiences growing up, including being an activist as a student at the University of Oregon:

> I joined in the Cesar Chavez boycotts in solidarity with the United Farm Workers. We were boycotting the student union because they were serving non-union lettuce. We'd get up at five in the morning and make sandwiches to sell in front of the student union. UFW were boycotting Safeway stores, so we would choose a store to picket. There was also a big vote on campus to divest from investments in South Africa to protest apartheid there. It was the first time I had been a part of student activism. They were issues I could relate to on a personal level.

Those days of activism chartered Monica on a path to becoming the publisher of *La Opinión*, the largest Spanish-language newspaper in the U.S., providing a daily platform to the needs, wants, and aspirations of the Latino community.

Seizing the moments of truth to forge a differentiated leadership style

Here are two moment-of-truth stories from leaders we interviewed. For each one of them, it would be a watershed moment—a milestone in the forging of their leadership styles.

Monica Lozano tells the first story. She clearly remembers a very difficult moment of truth that went a long way in defining her leadership style. The family-owned newspaper she was leading was facing an existential crisis. Given many social, economic, and media trends, the Latino newspaper needed to (ironically, given many of the themes in this book), change from a familial culture to a more professional one in order to remain relevant. Media segmentation was completely transforming the media landscape. After sixty years of having a great brand in a region where Spanish-language television and radio were quite parochial—and not much competition—suddenly there was competition everywhere, including from emerging power-houses such as Telemundo and Univision. She explains how they rose to the challenge in spite of great personal anguish:

> As much as we valued the deep personal relation-ships, we needed to shift the culture of the company. We were repositioning *La Opinión* from being a Lati-no-owned business to being an American institution and to demand our rightful place in U.S. society. We had to demand excellence from everybody, and drive accountability throughout the organization. We went through a significant process of articulating a vision and evaluating where we stood against that vision, building our internal competencies, and developing the kind of external relationships that are required to succeed in this business. At the end of the day we needed to monetize all of this to have a revenue stream that was going to support our dreams.

In the end, Monica helped to successfully elevate the organiza-tion to the next level. But it took strong leadership to do it. As she describes, when transformational leaders chart the course for others and for the organization, they bring culture change while still finding ways to retain cultural elements that could carry over to the new reality:

> My orientation toward leadership is very collaborative. I really believe in empowering teams; I believe in delegating. You get the best and the brightest around you, and then successfully communicate the passion and the possibility of what can be. The responsibility can't be the responsibility of just one person. It has to include the entire organization.

> You can only win if you can create a culture that empowers a company and all of the people who work there to want to win with you. I'm very hands on, very much about managing by walking around and getting to know the people on the team. I would try to meet every new employee, "Come in and let me tell you why we want you here, what I'm expecting of you. If you ever need me, I'm here." I don't know if that's a Latino style or just my style. I learned it from my dad. He was very accessible. You don't want to lose the essence of the spirit of the business.

Charlie Garcia tells the second story. In addition to the numerous leadership roles he's held, he has written two books related to leadership. In 2003, he wrote *A Message from Garcia: Yes, You Can Succeed*. He tells the following moment-of-truth story which involves the Supreme Court, Colin Powell, Governor Jeb Bush, and President George W. Bush.

> When I was on the Board of Education in Florida, the issue of affirmative action at the University of Michigan had come before the Supreme Court. Colin Powell issued a short press release saying that

he strongly supported affirmative action. Both President George W. Bush and Governor Jeb Bush submitted briefs against the University of Michigan. I found out a group of Fortune 500 CEOs were submitting a brief to the U.S. Supreme Court in support of affirmative action, and I decided to join that brief. When I called the lawyer handling the brief, he said, "Hell, who are you? You've got this small company, and this is a Fortune 500 brief." Then they found out I was on the State Board of Education and working for the president on the Air Force Academy board, so I became a signatory to that brief. Well, my action really upset the governor who I was working for in Florida, Jeb Bush.

I was also in the doghouse with the president of the United States and his staff. The Supreme Court decision came out in favor of affirmative action, with Sandra Day O'Connor writing the majority opinion. I went to see the president at an event in Crawford, Texas. I said, "Mr. President, I hope you remember what Ronald Reagan said." "What's that?" "When someone is your friend 80 percent of the time, they're your friend." He laughed. As I was about to leave, he put his hand on my shoulder, turned me around, and I remember thinking, "Wow, he's pretty strong for an old guy." But he stuck out his hand and said, "Charlie, I want to thank you for serving my administration and thank you for standing up for what you believe in."

The very next week an important White House policy giving special consideration to Latinos was being discussed, but before they announced the new policy, they wanted my input—which had never happened before.

Giving Back to the Community

Giving back to the community requires the trait of a generous spirit, combined with the competence to do it well. The arc of the transformative Latino executive is not complete until the accomplishments of executives have elevated and inspired them into bettering the lives and prospects of individuals and groups outside their corporate world. In contrast to the business world's reciprocal transactional nature of exchanging many tangible, extrinsic benefits, giving back to the community is more an act of generosity that does not expect nor demand anything in return.

Those who have accumulated power, wealth, and influence can then use these assets as leverage on behalf of others who may need an extra lift to seize opportunities just beyond their reach. Transformational Latino leaders also realize that if they don't become involved in the process of making a difference and clearing the way for more Latinos to come through, they can't complain about the lack of a Latino pipeline.

The Latino executive also carries an additional burden to give back since there are so few Latino corporate executives who can be tapped for help. They are constantly being called on to support Latino and other diversity initiatives. For the executives we interviewed, it was a call they all have responded to. In many cases they were the first wave of Latinos at their corporations, and they labored alone for much of their careers to disprove stereotypes. They had to learn how to read unspoken messages, spot danger signals, and solve overcoming obstacles. They were ready for the hard work of being the first or the only Latino in the company. They knew that their successes and failures would be considered as representative of their Hispanic ethnicity. Because of this labeling, they are determined that the next generation of Latino leaders will not be as alone as they were. The need is so great that many expressed anxiety about not being able to do enough.

Myrna Soto believes wholeheartedly that this giving back is a key responsibility of transformational Latino leaders:

> All my Latino brothers and sisters out there with similar stature as me need to help other Latinos. I also believe in HITEC's (Hispanic IT Executive Council) vision and mission, which is that we need to push and pull each other up to higher levels every time we have an opportunity.

Juan Galarraga recalls that an obligation to help others was always part of his leadership style, but the seriousness of it really kicked in when he was promoted to a vice president position at a very young age:

> There was a point in time when I started to realize that I needed to be part of something bigger than myself. That's when I started to fall in love with the idea of paving the way for others, specifically Hispanics, and not just at Target, but within the broader Hispanic community. I realized that I would have never been given those chances if I didn't have the right mentors, and/or sponsors throughout my career, and I realized that I was being looked up to as a role model by a lot of team members.
>
> For years I've been very involved with the Hispanic Association for Corporate Responsibility [HACR], which is where I started the Hispanic Executive Forum. Then I was blessed to join the board of the

Hispanic Scholarship Fund, an organization that builds the foundations toward education for the Hispanic community. I am passionate about this work and would not feel complete as a leader if I did not give back this way.

While giving back with maximum power and influence becomes easier as leaders achieve the highest levels, the discipline and practice of giving back should begin early in Latino leaders' careers. For example, Gilbert Casellas's commitment to making a difference began early in his life, deeply rooted in his family's history with the mutual aid societies and social clubs back in Tampa.

Gilbert, the current board director at Prudential Insurance, started making an impact while an undergrad student at Yale University. Noticing the relatively few Latino students at Yale, he first established a successful Latino student organization. Next he secured funds from a foundation to establish the first Puerto Rican cultural center on campus. Eventually he became involved in demonstrations against the ineffective ways that Yale was recruiting Latino students. Soon Gilbert was meeting with the president of the university. He eventually helped Yale establish a better Latino recruiting strategy, resulting in a substantial increase of Latino students. That set the stage for a lifetime of lifting up Latino talent throughout his career at law firms, law schools, in government, the military, and in corporate America. Each time he did so at a greater scale and with more sustainable results.

Across the country at Stanford, Victor Arias was playing a similar role. After building a strong connection with Dr. Jerry Porras, one of the authors of the book, *Built to Last: Successful Habits of Visionary Companies,* Victor started Latino business student organizations which ultimately led to his becoming one of the founding members of the National Society of Hispanic MBAs.

For Lisa Garcia Quiroz, the Harvard alum, her role in making a difference included helping other Latino students be accepted into Harvard. She was actively involved in the undergraduate minority student recruitment program, working in the admissions office for three years advocating for Latino students. She was so involved and made such an impact, *The Harvard Crimson* published a profile of her, calling her "the Godmother to her Community." Today she remains actively involved, helping Latino students by serving as the chair for the national Hispanic Scholarship Fund.

Luis Ubiñas also began making a difference early in his career. He joined his first nonprofit board in Boston when he was only in his mid-twenties. Then, after a successful nineteen-year career at consulting firm McKinsey & Company, he left and joined Ford Foundation as its president so he could give back at a significantly larger scale.

José Armario felt it was his obligation to increase the number of Latino leaders at McDonald's:

> I was fortunate that McDonald's already had a strong commitment to diversity, but we were tasked to find the time and ways to strengthen the Latino networks at the corporation, to put together plans to present to the head of HR or the COO or CEO, plans of how to help grow Hispanic succession and pipelines. There were constant discussions about these initiatives. As I rose in influence, I also became more influential in accelerating and strengthening the pipeline of Latino leaders at McDonald's. I always tell people I mentor: "Somebody did you a favor along the way. You now have to do the same. You need to pay it forward because if it stops with you, then we all lose."

These transformational Latino leaders who understand the power and obligation of giving back, and who are skilled at doing so, do not hesitate to ask other Latinos in positions of authority, "What has your contribution to Latino advancement been?" Their answers will speak volumes.

Purpose-driven Leadership

As we wrap up these two chapters of the three key traits and the three key competencies of transformational Latino leaders, there is one final characteristic that pulls these elements together and that is being a purpose-driven leader. AT&T's Patricia Díaz Dennis believes this strongly—that having a purpose provides a compass for a person's actions and career decisions:

> Most people think that leadership is something positional, such as being a CEO or a CFO or general counsel. For me, ultimately, it's about something very different. It's about leading your life with purpose. Think about where you want to go, what you want to accomplish, what impact you want to have in the world, and then devise a plan and ultimately follow that plan. Don't get cast about—take control.

When asked to describe her purpose, Patricia doesn't hesitate:

> My purpose is to inspire, serve, and connect others to achieve extraordinary things. I want to make life better for the people who are with me on this journey, as well as the people who come after.

Inspired? Hopefully you are. In our next chapter, we'll tackle one more leadership topic, one that many Latino professionals tend to struggle with: power. ❧

CHAPTER 8

Power Ambivalence:
The Achilles Heel

"Lavarse las manos del conflicto entre los medios poderosos y los impotentes al lado de los poderosos, no es ser neutral."

Washing one's hands of the conflict between the powerful and the powerless means to side with the powerful, not to be neutral.

—Paulo Freire, Brazilian educator and philosopher

So far our exploration of Latino executive success has been a story of onward and upward. The leaders we interviewed have been inspirational. They have overcome a myriad of societal and organizational biases by optimizing their resilience, hard work, and ambition, as well as coming to terms with their cultural identity.

However, in our research we saw a consistent uncomfortable theme that could be one of the root causes of why Latino presence in executive leadership in corporate America has been stuck at 4 percent for too many years. While we have documented various root causes anchored in systemic discrimination, unconscious biases, and inflexible corporate cultures, there is at least one cause within Latino culture that could be at play as well: a deep-seated ambivalence toward the concept, practice, and pursuit of power.

Clearly, Latinos have power in numbers. Being the largest ethnic minority in the U.S. at 17 percent of the population, they have an annual purchasing power of $1.7 trillion, which is growing around $100 billion a year. They have political power too, with an ability to tip elections as they did during Barack Obama's victories in 2008 and 2012. This kind of impact proves that this once-marginalized minority is on a path to demographic relevance.

Yet it is a sub-optimized power. In the 2016 presidential election, many assumed Donald Trump's vitriolic rhetoric against Latinos would unleash a bang of Latino electoral resistance. Instead, Latino power ended in a whimper, as they were not able to play a decisive role in the outcome by turning up to vote as much as they needed to. True before Trump's election—and even truer afterward—Latino social, educational, and health needs remain near the bottom of government priorities. What these shortcomings show is that even though Latinos are in a demographic boom and have more money to spend, their ability as a collective force to wield power and gain influence is still somewhat meek and muted.

This sub-optimization of power also plays out among Latinos in their careers. Though we interviewed twenty of perhaps the most powerful Latinos in corporate America, we had difficulty finding a compelling or well-defined approach on how Latinos can individually and collectively increase their power in their work environments. We detected a consistent desire to pivot to another subject when the topic was broached, and an ambivalence in their remarks when it came to the topic of power.

Our Latino executives' relationship with power seemed to be ancillary. For example, several commented that power resulted only after the pursuit of something more positive. For Jorge Figueredo, the executive vice president for HR at McKesson, gaining power takes an indirect route. He describes it this way, "I don't make having more power the goal. I focus on other issues and power will come." Similarly, when asked about power, Korn Ferry's Victor Arias shared, "I have a negative connotation of power only because power suggests that rather than trying to influence others to do the right thing, you are trying to force them to do the right thing."

Southwest Airlines board member Grace Lieblein had a very successful career in corporate America yet she had this to say about her relationship to power:

> I probably gave away more power than I tried to take. Power to me was not something I had to go grab. I always felt like the more power you give away, the more it comes back to you at some point. Sounds like a Zen philosopher, I know. I'm really not a power player. It goes back to my not being political. Instead I have a position. I ran GM Mexico, I ran GM Brazil. I used power as a part of those jobs but used it appropriately. I just never thought in the vein of having to gain more power, of having to attain a bigger position, or get more, more, more. That's just not who I am.

GameStop's Paul Raines observed:

> When it comes to power, I'm a contrarian. I don't see the word power as a real word that I use and talk about very much. There's definitely power in organizations, and I'm often confused when I read about concentration of power in case studies or in publications such as the *Wall Street Journal*. I just don't see the world that way.
>
> I'm trying to have more of a servant-leadership mentality than the other way around. Maybe I think that power comes from the base and it's an inverse pyramid. I see my relationship with power as more of being a servant to the power of the customer than anything else. I've always believed that if you do a great job on what you're working on today and establish a reputation for excellence, the power issue takes care of itself.

This hesitancy to speak directly about power and their relationship with it seemed significant to us. So we decided to compare how our Latino leaders discussed the topic of power against the discourse of a group of executives from another racial/ethnic minority group: African-Americans.

In the philosophy that from a diversity of backgrounds, experiences, and culture there are lessons to be learned that can benefit other groups, what can Latinos learn from the Black approach to power? As you will see, the contrast is stark. It surfaces questions of whether Latinos are leaving some power on the table due to their ambivalence, and if so, how they can optimize power and yet stay true to a Latino ethos?

One final caveat: clearly the Latino executives we interviewed are high achievers and successful leaders with exemplary track records—all characteristics of using the power of their positions, of being able to articulate a vision, of developing a followership, and achieving results. However, it's the ambivalence toward this power that intrigued us. In a world with massive forces holding back broader Latino achievement, is there a deeper reservoir of power that Latino leaders could be tapping into to exponentially amplify the positive impact they are already displaying?

Compare and Contrast, a Case Study: African-American Executives and Power

Authors Price Cobbs and Judith Turnock provide a comprehensive examination of the relationship that successful African-American executives have with power in the workplace. Their book, *Cracking the Corporate Code*,[1] is based on stories from thirty-two Black corporate executives, and declares that if African-Americans do not grasp the essence of power's importance, they will never have real power in corporations. In our own review of their relationship with power, we found that not only are African-American executives more comfortable than Latino executives discussing power, they are more comfortable actively pursuing it.

Cobbs and Turnock describe four key realities that exist in corporate life that African-American leaders have come to understand. First, they agree that within an organizational context, power involves conflict and disagreement. Second, for those who aspire to positions of influence, a critical personal attribute is the willingness to engage in conflict with others. Third,

---

1   Cobbs, Price M. and Turnock, Judith. *Cracking the Corporate Code: The Revealing Success Stories of 32 African-American Executives.* AMACOM Publishing. New York. 2003.

that African- Americans recognize that whether stated openly or not, every organizational transaction is a statement of who has and who does not have power. Finally, there's an acknowledgment that unless African-American executives know what to do with power when they have it, they will squander it.

The acceptance of these four realities clearly demonstrates a strong embrace of power, as well as a level of comfort with the conflict associated with it. What has led African-Americans in the U.S. to this very different relationship to power compared to Latinos? The answers lie in comparing and contrasting how the different contours of the Black and Latino experiences led to different philosophies about interacting with power, different leadership role models, and different institutional responses— all of which have led to different outcomes.

By looking at Black and Latino experiences through three lenses we can distill why these two communities emerged with different points of view around power. The three lenses are these:

- Affinity through experience
- Faith and religion
- Educational, not-for-profit, and political institutions

Affinity through experience

Both Blacks and Latinos in the U.S. have suffered greatly from prejudice and discrimination. Oppression, pain, and death were often delivered by similar means. Other dimensions of the violence against these two groups was manifested differently due to different historical circumstances. European Americans brought Black slaves by force to the Americas. Mexicans were driven from their own land after the Mexican-American War. Blacks faced slavery. Latinos faced indentured servitude. Blacks were brought in chains; Latinos even today are deported in chains.

However, there are fundamental differences in the systems of oppression that Blacks and Latinos endured. These differences had a distinctive impact on how both groups came to understand the power of affinity through skin color and a shared experience.

While Latino subjugation was fragmented across the U.S., Black subjugation was systemic. The institution of slavery was part of a massive, cohesive economic system dependent on unpaid labor that powered the American South. Southern society was structured around slavery and its ancillary repercussions. It lasted more than 200 years, and to demolish it required a civil war in which more than 620,000 Americans died.

Given this systemic nature, Blacks had a more uniform history of oppression compared to Latinos, whose tyranny varied depending on where in the U.S. it happened, the socioeconomics of the populace, and their immigration status. By its very nature, the crucible of slavery, and after that, Jim Crow laws, made a deep and broad shared experience—and therefore a strong affinity among Blacks—inevitable.

In contrast, there has not been one massive oppressive unifying experience for all Latinos as there was for Blacks through slavery. They also have more of a choice in the matter than Blacks about whether they are willing to affiliate or not. As we pointed out in Chapter 2, depending on skin color, accent, or other behavioral choices, many Latinos can choose to pass on the fact they are Latino and can escape the claws of racism. The Latino community is experientially, racially, and economically diverse: they come from different countries, have different levels of Spanish-speaking ability, and grew up with different levels of a Hispanic embrace. While they have many elements of shared communal affinity, they have to work harder embracing that affinity.

This difference between Blacks and Latinos in the nature, depth, and extent of the shared experience then sets up a different context for a sense of collective power or powerlessness. Blacks have more of a shared understanding that power dynamics are a major factor affecting their lives; therefore, they tend to have a greater sense of commitment to prioritize the confrontation of this make-it-or-break-it reality.

Faith and religion

In the absence of any form of recourse outside the slave system, Blacks turned to the church as a way to survive. The Christianity forced on their slaves by white slave owners was a form deeply distorted to provide a rationale for slavery. The owners believed that converting their slaves to this religion would lead them to accept their fate. Instead, Blacks appropriated the Christianity of their owners and made it their own. They recognized that the Bible was a story of liberation from slavery, that the plantation owner was Pharaoh, and that the Jewish slaves of the Old Testament were the Black slaves of their time. Their leaders such as Frederic Douglass, Harriet Tubman—and in the post-slavery era, Malcolm X, Dr. Martin Luther King, Jr., and others—were their Moses.

The Black churches helped to solidify spiritual and communal strength within the African-American community. Over the centuries these churches evolved with countless acts of faith and resistance, piety, and protest. The churches were—and remain—sustained and animated by the idea of freedom and liberation. This strength makes it easy to comprehend how Black churches have served as the foundation for organizations such as the Southern Christian Leadership Conference and, of course, the civil rights movement. With the support of their churches, African-Americans developed a long history of engaging in peaceful marches and participating in non-violent movements to demand what they envisioned as just and righteous.

In contrast, the Latino collective psyche is grounded in Catholicism, even for those Latinos who have converted to Protestantism. Devout Catholics often point to the religious vows of poverty, chastity, and obedience. When Spain colonized Latin America, the Catholic church played a key role. Its priests gave sermons on the virtues of being obedient and subservient, having a "God willing" mentality, and accepting one's place in life. White slave owners failed to instill a mindset of subservience in their Black slaves through Christianity. In contrast, the subjugated populations in Latin America accepted this message of passivity. That Latinos developed less of a willingness to engage in conflict, therefore, is understandable.

Educational, not-for-profit, and political institutions

As the shackles of slavery were broken, and out of the ferment of Black liberation after the Civil War, the historically Black colleges and universities (HBCUs) emerged. HBCUs such as Spelman College, Howard University, Morehouse College, and 104 more, are a source of great pride for the Black community because of the lengthy and significant role they have played in educating young African-American men and women. Some of these schools are over one hundred years old and have long lists of accomplished alumni. The experience of attending an HBCU further solidifies shared communal responsibility and emboldens African-Americans to pursue power for the benefit of the greater good.

In contrast, there are the Hispanic-serving institutions (HSIs), which have only been designated as such since 1992. According to the nonprofit national educational organization called the Hispanic Association of Colleges and Universities (HACU), there are 470 HSIs enrolling two-thirds of all Hispanic college students. These institutions have not yet reached the stature of the HBCUs, though during the Obama era, they began to strengthen their structural foundations and grow through increased governmental and individual donor contributions. But they are still early in their journey compared to the much more established HBCUs.

In politics, look no further than the Congressional Black Caucus, a much larger, and many would agree, more powerful and vocal group than the Congressional Hispanic Caucus. Also consider the impact of African-American advocacy organizations such as the National Association for Advancement of Colored People (NAACP), the National Urban League (NUL), and the People United to Save Humanity (Rainbow PUSH Coalition).

Latinos also have powerful platforms such as the United Farm Workers (UFW)—with its heyday being the 1970s under César Chávez—the National Council for la Raza (renamed UnidosUS in 2017), the League of United Latin American Citizens (LULAC), the Mexican American Legal Defense and Educational Fund (MALDEF), and similar organizations. But in contrast to the Black organizations, they are not as deeply embedded in the power dynamics with American institutions and government.

The Black institutions and organizations created platforms from which a long list of leaders championing the cause of African-American rights emerged, in addition to those mentioned earlier: Frederick Douglass, W.E.B. Du Bois, Sojourner Truth, Harriet Tubman, Rosa Parks, Malcolm X, Reverend Jesse Jackson, and President Barack Obama. Latinos can proudly point to César Chávez, former San Antonio mayor Henry Cisneros, and Supreme Court Justice Sonia Sotomayor, but their list of household-known names runs much shorter than that of the African-American community.

Comparing Responses to Power

Now we layer in the cultural elements that also have influenced African-American responses to power dynamics. What we've learned through our analysis of power and the African-American experience is that theirs is a community with a much more developed understanding of—and appreciation for—what it takes to obtain more influence in corporate settings. Their familiarity with power, gained through a sustained, cohesive, and long history of struggle for equality through conflict, enables them to be more comfortable with the discord and tension brought by that pursuit of power. Most importantly, they've learned to leverage their shared responsibility as the rationale and the source of strength to engage in the struggle.

The shared responsibility is carried over into the workplace by African-American executives. There they may stand up more boldly on issues that may not impact them just as individuals, but as African -Americans as a whole. They may say, "I'm not doing this so much for me, but I'm willing to fight this fight for our community." What we've learned is that this collective responsibility is so prevalent that accomplished African-American CEO and author of the book, *Click: Ten Truths for Building Extraordinary Relationships*,[2] George Fraser wrote, "African-Americans of means who

---

2   Fraser, George C. Click: *Ten Truths for Building Extraordinary Relationships*. New York: McGraw-Hill, 2009.

do not reach down and lift up their own, and are not philanthropic at some level, should be socially isolated and ostracized."

So why were African-Americans in the Cobbs and Turnock book so expressive in their views on power, yet our Latino executives more subdued? Our premise is that Latino executives seem less willing to invite disturbance, which means they are less willing to joust for position and advantage when it comes to acquiring and wielding power.

Part of this uneasiness with conflict likely comes from the strong Latino cultural trait known as *simpatía*, a Spanish word that refers to a general tendency to avoid personal conflict and emphasize positive relationships with others. In their 1991 study on Latino behavior, Marín and Marín[3] found that because of *simpatía*, Latinos tend to suppress behaviors that are considered forceful or overly aggressive. Similarly, in 2003, author Norma Carr-Ruffino[4] found that Latinos are more likely to avoid aggressive stances on subjects because they want others to think well of them.

Consequently, Latinos often enter corporate America with conflicting thoughts and feelings about obtaining, maintaining, or using power. Non-Latinos often observe that Hispanics are not as successful chasing power because deep down they think power is objectionable, or even illicit. Thus, they develop a proclivity to stand back and respond passively. This lack of aggressiveness in the pursuit of power may partly explain the dearth of Latino executives in the C-suites. George Herrera says:

> I don't think that we fight for power well. We don't unite
> to pursue power like African-Americans do. I think that

---

3 Marín, Gerardo, and Vanoss Marín, Barbara. *Research with Hispanic Populations.* Applied Social Research Methods Series. 23. Thousand Oaks, CA. Sage Publications, 1991.

4 Carr-Ruffino, Norma. *Managing Diversity. People skills for a multicultural workplace* (6ᵗʰ ed). Boston, MA: Pearson Publishing. 2003.

one of the problems is that Latinos continue to have this feeling of vulnerability, of just feeling scared—and that's unfortunate. We don't have the willingness to go out there and really rattle the cages.

An executive coach who works with many Latino and Black leaders reinforces this point, sharing that his Latino clients are excessively concerned with how they are perceived by others. He cited several examples of Latinos who didn't want to press certain issues because they felt others would consider them too aggressive. On the subject of advocating for Latino causes, the coach described many who didn't want to be perceived as forcefully pushing the Latino agenda. By comparison, his African-American clients are much less worried about how others perceive them or about being considered too aggressive. More importantly, they feel an obligation to advocate for African-American issues regardless of what others may think.

Latinos Must Forge Their Own Path to Greater Power

To be clear, we are not saying that style-wise there is a right or wrong way to interact with power. Nor are we saying that Latinos are not capable of engaging in displays of power that involve conflict. What we are advocating for is that Latinos engage in the dual process of being less ambivalent about power while at the same time changing their approach to it in a way that is grounded in, but does not conflict with, Latino sensitivities and ethos.

Resolving power ambivalence

When as consultants we see the need for culture change in our work, rather than proposing the adoption of another group's culture values and preferences, we seek to learn from others' experiences, and then look for things within the culture that can actually be tapped to motivate the change.

For example, the values of *familia* (family), *comunidad* (community), and *simpatía* (solidarity/affection) for Latinos are elements that can contribute significantly to creating and nurturing an environment of high involvement—characteristics we don't want to lose. However, as we saw in Chapter 4, cultural virtues can also have a shadow side, and in the case of Latinos, even these positive cultural attributes have served to undermine our ability to be as powerful as we can in corporate America and have sub-optimized the collective impact we can offer in the advancement of Latinos into managerial and leadership roles.

What is it within our culture we can tap into to motivate a change in behavior when it would seem to contradict our deeply cherished notions of how to interact with others? In this case we believe it has to be an appeal to our having fallen short of fully living up to our communal values.

How is this true? One of the big contradictions in Latino culture in the U.S. is that for all our love for *la familia* and our self-image of being a communal people, we are actually allowing our differences within the Latino community to create divisions (as we saw in Chapter 3). These divisions are fundamental reasons for our inability to mobilize collective action with a power commensurate to our total numbers.

By failing to fully display our values of *comunidad*, we are not only contributing to exclusion in a world rife with people being discriminated against because of their differences, we are actually hurting our collective ability to advance—and that of individual Latinos to rise to their full potential. Thus we further lessen the impact Latinos can demonstrate in enhancing the performance of corporations—and the impact we can have on the U.S. society and economy as a whole. Knowing how we hurt ourselves should give us greater *coraje* (courage) to speak truth to power more frequently—not just in a pleading or polite way, but in an assertive and powerful way.

While greater courage is needed, we have the tools at our disposal to summon it. We possess assets within our own culture to celebrate and to be proud of. These assets are potential sources of greater Latino power. As we leverage them, we can construct a distinctive Latino response to optimizing power.

Latino Cultural Assets as Power Differentiators

What are these cultural assets we can leverage more powerfully? In Chapter 4 we outlined various ways corporate America can benefit from Latino culture. Now we offer three cultural assets Latinos can tap within themselves to become more powerful.

The power of biography

In a vastly diverse world posing both threats and opportunities to business, having employees with book knowledge and finely honed skills and competencies will not be enough. The systemic disruption taking place in every industry requires alternative ways of seeing, interpreting, and of devising responses.

Latino biographies, in all their complexity and richness, when embraced and understood, can be mined by the individuals themselves to offer a different perspective. Latinos who have worked through their cultural identity are also well positioned to better understand the similar journeys customers and coworkers face as they seek products, services, and meaningful work.

To utilize their backgrounds powerfully, Latinos must consistently engage in cultural reflection and soul searching as it relates to Latino biography. Doing so enables Latino leaders to lead in a centered way from their differentiated biographies to take bolder stands.

And because, as a community, the average age is younger that it is for most other ethnic/racial groups, our power comes from hope for a better tomorrow and lies in the talent, biography, and the possibilities associated with youth.

The power of a global and bicultural perspective

Latinos are not always bilingual, but they are almost always bicultural. That means they are adept at moving effectively in varied cultural environments and have leveraged this skill to be accepted. But what is the impact when they introduce new cultural values, behaviors, and skills into an environment unaccustomed to diversity? McKesson's Jorge Figueredo observes:

> My bicultural background absolutely helped me with my career. I was able to not only recognize I was different but that there could be various ways of looking at the same thing. That not only gave me greater insight, it also helped me to more effectively recognize that there were multiple points of view that needed to be heard and addressed in any room.

Victor Arias leverages his bicultural identity to be able to transcend many lines that often are kept separate in society:

> There's a switch in my head and I always keep it on. While I spend a lot of time with executives in my board and executive search work, I go out of the way to talk to and connect with the housekeeper at the hotel as well.

I also pay attention to how people, including executive candidates, treat other people not like them, and that's a really big filter for me.

When Lou Miramontes was offered an expat assignment in Mexico, he found the situation ironic:

My *abuelita* (grandmother) who lived across the street from me, said, "Why are you going to Mexico? Do you know how hard it was for your grandfather to get here and now you're going back?!" I talked to the chairman about her concern and he told me "They think you're one of them in Latin America, but we also know you're one of us in the United States. You have to be crosscultural, multilingual. You have to be able to play in all those buckets." I learned how to be bicultural, resulting in great effect on those around me, on emerging Latino talent, and for my career.

Because ours is a history shaped by twenty-seven different nations, Latinos epitomize what it means to be global. We can provide the ideal archetype to corporate America of what a global leader must be. Ours is a community with a rich history of bringing globally diverse groups together to construct a collective identity, a unique gift offered by Latinos.

The power of sacrifice

Millions of Latinos are in the U.S. because of huge risks their great-grandparents, grandparents, or parents took in uprooting themselves from their homeland to seek a better life in *El Norte* (The North) for their children and their children's children.

For nearly 60 million Latinos, the massive migration has—for the most part—paid off, and now U.S. Latinos are the seventh largest economy in the world. As a people, this ability to do a large-scale relocation and, in that, positively influence another culture and economy means that we have operated with transformational power in the past. We can do so again today by flexing the power of our numbers and love for this country to counteract rising anti-immigrant attitudes and policies.

Juana Bordas said it best in her book, *The Power of Latino Leadership*,[5] "Latino power is rooted in history and tradition, an understanding that the past is the rich soil that nourishes tomorrow. Latinos owe a great debt to the leaders who have paved the way for our community to blossom."

Latino power thus dictates that supporting the greater Latino community is not an option, but rather an obligation. Luis Ubiñas states, "Anything less is a dishonor" to those who paved the way. We believe Latinos will continue to advance as a community because we see our ties to others as a series of mutual obligations and privileges connecting us to our past, connecting us now, and connecting us into our shared future. If we teach Latino Millennials and Gen Xers to build on the legacy of those who paved the way, our community will continue to more powerfully inject corporate America with the many benefits associated with Hispanic heritage.

Sandra Rivera, senior vice president and general manager at Intel Corporation, and member of the company's Hispanic Leadership Council, elaborates on the responsibility that Latino executives have to be more successful in giving back to the Latino community, especially when it has served as a foundation for their personal success.

I realized that all of the ways that I was being successful in my career and all of the contributions that I

---

5   Bordas, Juana. *The Power of Latino Leadership: 10 Principles of Inclusion, Community, and Contribution*. San Francisco, CA: Berrett-Koehler, 2013.

was making are very much rooted in these Latin heritage values that I grew up with. As I became more aware of that, I started to feel the responsibility to pay it forward and to advocate for the broader Latino community. Because I'm actually the highest-ranking Hispanic leader at Intel now, I feel even more responsibility to make sure that I am supporting Latinos.

This type of sacrifice amplifies Latino power.

The Latino Collective Can Ground Our Relationship to Power

By leveraging our uniquely Latino assets, we can now claim our own approach to power, one that comes from a goal of advancing the collective. We see power stemming from the community for the greater good. Given our proclivity toward *simpatía*, our attitude toward power is grounded in our relational approach to leadership.

The Latino approach to power is desperately needed by today's hyperpolarized society. We are well suited to build bridges of understanding and cooperation. We can no longer afford to stand idly by and let others walk over *our* bridges on their own march for more power and influence.

Sandra Rivera describes why Latino executive advocacy is so important:

> Other Latino executives at Intel and I feel we need to create a community of support to identify young Latino leaders we want to nurture, and to make sure we are attracting, retaining, and growing Hispanic talent. We are dedicated to our Latino employee population that might otherwise not be supported. Through our

positions of authority, we give them support and the self-confidence they need to achieve greater levels of success.

But that nurturing needs to be a very directed effort. It isn't going to happen by chance. It was this realization that if we want to have a vibrant Latin community that is contributing to Intel, we have to make a specific effort. Our Latino executive community is really very committed from a leadership perspective to pay it forward, and we must bring our Latino community along. We have a deep level of commitment to provide support, advocacy, and visibility. Because if we are not nurturing our Latino talent, they may never really achieve everything they are capable of.

With great power comes great responsibility so I do feel that sense of responsibility, especially as a Latina. We take care of our brothers, our sisters, our parents, our grandparents, and our community. That's what we do.

George Herrera takes seriously the responsibility that comes with greater power. He shares a story of an experience when he was CEO of the U.S. Hispanic Chamber of Commerce. The situation involved an internal and biased policy at a major corporation that adversely impacted the Latino business community. George took an approach that unequivocally leveraged power. He didn't let the issue go unnoticed and made the corporation aware that he knew of the internal policy. He was willing to address the issue with the seniormost executives at the company including the CEO and board chair. He didn't let the company off the hook when they offered to simply write a big check for the USHCC. He didn't succumb to peer pressure by other Latinos suggesting he should back off. And finally, he conveyed a willingness to expose the unfair practice to the broader community.

The end result was a favorable solution by the company that led to tremendous benefits for Hispanic business owners, as well as to the corporation that was able to reap the rewards of greater market expansion due to resolving the impasse—all in response to George's power moves.

While George's example showcases that Latinos can also play the power game, we are still left with the cultural ambivalence that many Latinos show about wielding more power. So how can Latinos move past these mixed feelings about power, in ways that are congruent with our cultural values? We offer the following guidelines:

- Power will come when forged through collaboration, because it leverages our strength in building relationships. Yet we must accept that we won't always maintain *simpatía* with others when we are advocating for the advancement of the Latino talent agenda. We have to learn to accept and live with uncomfortable power dynamics instead of perpetuating our acquiescence.

- We must acknowledge that no one will just give us power, so we must always be in the pursuit of it. Furthermore, we must recognize that when we withdraw from the power game, it's not about being nice, but rather it's abdication.

- We must speak truth to those in power (the majority culture) about the corporate 4 Percent Shame and about how corporations need to put action behind their words of valuing diversity. Those words are meaningless if executives of the majority are not willing to lead the change. We also need to speak truth to those leaders *within* our Latino community who aren't doing enough and celebrating those whose actions advance diversity.

• Our concern for the collective good of the Latino community obligates us to challenge injustices imposed on Latinos. Whenever we feel personal unease in advocating for Latino issues, we can gain strength, courage, and resolve by leveraging our existing mindset where the needs of the Latino community supersede any one of our individual needs.

This Latino-grounded approach to power can manifest itself in the workplace in a variety of impactful ways. It can be on display whenever Latino executives sponsor or strongly advocate for other worthy Latinos during talent reviews. We strengthen our communal position whenever the top Hispanics within a company push to establish, for example, an internal Latino Officer Caucus to advocate for internal Latino talent. The broader Latino community benefits whenever there is robust advocacy for, and participation in, Hispanic nonprofits and professional associations by visible Latinos from the C-suites.

We gain awareness and perspective when there is full throttle support to bring in external Latino thought leaders, authors, and consultants. We build collective strength when we gather the resources to send young professionals to Latino leadership development programs offered by academia and nonprofits. We win respect when our Latino leaders protest the massive deportations happening under the Trump presidency in the same manner as African-American executives have done in response to the Black

Lives Matter movement. And we can all rejoice when every Latino executive has a ready answer when asked, "What have you contributed to the greater Latino collective?"

Y allí está. (And there it is.) Ready to seize the day? ❧

CHAPTER *9*

The Next Generation of Latino Leaders: Latinx Learns, Challenges, and Rises

"Preferiría ser la cola de un león que la cabeza de un ratón."

I would rather be the tail of a lion than the head of a mouse.

—Daddy Yankee

The personal and professional biographies of the executives we interviewed—with stories of struggle and triumph, lessons learned, new paths forged—generated insight and wisdom we have sought to capture as a definitive guide to Latino career success.

Given that the Boomer Latino executives grew up and then prospered in an earlier time, how relevant are their experiences and their choices climbing the rungs of the corporate ladder to Latinos one or two generations later, the ones for whom this manifesto is primarily intended?

To find out how much these different generations do or do not have in common when facing and resolving the challenges of assimilation pressures and cultural identity as they sought career success, we conducted research to compare the generational experiences to see how many of the lessons learned were transferable. Where do Latino Gen Xers and Millennials face the same or different dynamics? How are their responses similar or different? Do they have blind spots where the perspective of the generation before them could open their eyes?

The research included:

- Five separate focus groups consisting of Latino Millennials and Generation Xers to capture regional and family national origin diversity. We conducted one group each in Dallas, New York, and Los Angeles, and two in Chicago. Each group had between 5 and 10 young, upwardly mobile Latino professionals working in corporate America, with a total of 38 participants.

- An online survey of young Latino professionals conducted during June and July 2017. In total, 302 Latino professionals completed the survey, answering questions related to their identity, education, and aspects of Hispanic heritage they found helpful or detrimental to their career success.

- One-on-one interviews with four young Latinos who have been identified as rising stars within their organizations, and are actively involved in their community. By exploring more deeply some of their aspirations, experiences, and thoughts on a variety of topics, we wanted to learn what challenges they were facing, and whether they were performing and behaving differently than their predecessors had.

- Multiple large group dialogues we have facilitated with up-and-coming Latino talent in a range of corporations and universities.

- Many formal conversations with young Latinos we have mentored, as well as informal conversations in our daily personal and professional lives.

Before we delve into our findings, let's have a look at the demographic realities of younger Latinos.

Youth is a defining characteristic of the nation's Latino population. A review of the 2016 Pew Research Center study titled, "The Nation's Latino Population is Defined by Its Youth"[1] reaffirms that Hispanics are the youngest major racial or ethnic group in the U.S. With an average age of twenty-eight, Latino youthfulness is making an important contribution in countering the challenges presented by the aging of the U.S. population, especially when compared to similar economies such as China and Japan. With the youngest population among all ethnicities and races in the country, Latinos represent the core of the future of American society.

Nearly six in ten Hispanics are Millennials or younger

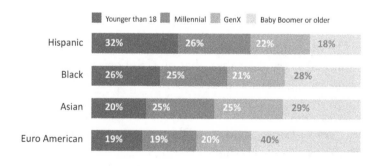

---

1   Patten, Eileen. "The Nation's Latino Population Is Defined by Its Youth." Pew Research Center's Hispanic Trends Project, Pew Hispanic, 20 Apr. 2016, www.pewhispanic.org/2016/04/20/the-nations-latino-population-is-defined-by-its-youth/.

Key findings from the Pew Research Center study, "The Nation's Latino Population is Defined by Its Youth"

- About one-third of the nation's Hispanic population is younger than 18, and about a quarter of all Hispanics are Millennials. Altogether, nearly six in ten Hispanics are Millennials or younger.

- The median age of Hispanics—28 years—is well below that of the major racial groups. For example, the median age among European Americans is 43. For Asians, the median age is 36. For Blacks, the median age is 33.

- Among the nation's Millennials, Hispanics have a greater share than all American adults. Hispanics make up 21 percent of all U.S. Millennials versus 15 percent of all adults.

- Hispanic Millennials are much less likely to be immigrants and are more likely to speak English proficiently. They are also more likely than older generations to be of Mexican origin.

- Nearly half (47 percent) of U.S.-born Latinos are younger than 18. By comparison, just 27 percent of U.S.-born Blacks and 20 percent of U.S.-born European Americans are younger than 18.

- The median age among foreign-born Latinos is more than 20 years older than that of U.S.-born Latinos (41 and 19 years, respectively).

This new generation of Latinos is also starting to rebrand themselves as Latinx, and so in this chapter we too will begin to make this transition when referring to Latino Gen Xers and Millennials (see sidebar for the whys of the rebranding).

Why Latinx?

Increasingly, this younger generation of Latinos is claiming the label of *Latinx*. There are various reasons:

It is not sexist. The genderized terms Latino and Latina use the male form "Latino" grammatically as the generic when referring to both men and women.

It does not reinforce a binary view of gender. Therefore, it allows for the full spectrum of gender identity and expression.

It's cool. It fits current trend of x-factor as being a contemporary differentiated, wild card.

There is still a lively debate in the Latino, Latina, Latinx community about this term, but it is clearly gaining more traction.

What did we find out about Latinx under age forty? As with every generation they have their own set of assets and liabilities. Among their assets, we discovered that Latinx are:

- asserting their Latinx-American bicultural identity in the workplace with more confidence than any generation before

- approaching their career development and advancement in an organized and sophisticated way

- being adamant about not receiving advantages just because they are Latinx

- seeking power more comfortably and explicitly

Among their liabilities, Latinx professionals face some unique challenges and potential blind spots:

- an individualism that can undermine serving the community

- diminished Spanish-language and Latino culture fluency and knowledge

- relocation reticence

- lack of Latino role models

Let's now explore these cultural assets and liabilities in more detail.

Latinx Assets

Woven throughout the pages of this book is a driving assumption that Latino heritage is a trove of cultural riches that must be mined to add value to personal identity, as well as to quality of leadership. But there are generational shifts within ethnic cultures, and Latinx professionals' cultural and generational assets manifest in some distinct ways compared to Boomer Latinos.

A bicultural identity

The most important aspect of the Pew Research Center study was its declaration that Latinx professionals have a strong connection to both their Hispanic and American cultures: "Latino Millennials and Generation Xers are bilingual Americans who are assimilated into American society but still value the emotional connection to their Hispanic heritage—they are bicultural."

This finding reinforces our observations from Chapter 3 that one of the most powerful ways for Latinos to overcome our intra-Latino divides is to embrace a pan-Latino and American mainstream bicultural identity. Latinx are leading the way in this pursuit, and in this respect their story is not following the total assimilation arc of previous immigrant groups who came to the U.S.

When most immigrants arrive in a new country, they tend to take a relentless, linear path toward assimilation. Each successive generation in the new country undergoes a further process of assimilation and dilution of cultural identity. This assimilation usually takes hold across three main components:

- Immigrants tend to adopt English as their primary language.

- Immigrants embrace the American work ethic of being self-reliant and hard working.

- Immigrants are expected to take pride in their homogenized American identity.

We learned in our discussions with Latinx that many are moving away from the melting pot mythology of straight assimilation into American culture. Though they faced pressures to assimilate, Latinx as a group are choosing to retain their Hispanic identity instead of becoming fully assimilated, which would have been predicted based on the trends of earlier immigrants. We were heartened to see that Latinx are not losing their sense of differentiated identity. As one New York focus group participant stated:

I'm *ambicultural*. I listen to Coldplay and Mark Anthony. I embrace my dual identity.

Seeing it as a worthwhile struggle, Latinx are choosing to fight to maintain their Hispanic identity. Our online survey results indicate that they are so grounded in their sense of identity that an astounding 69 percent of respondents said they have never held back or hidden any part of their Latino ethnicity in the workplace.

In essence, they see their Latino-ness as an asset and differentiator, adopting a bicultural identity in which they still embrace their Americanness. They celebrate and accept their Latino identity as another dimension of who they are. This is not to say that the Latino identity is not a complex issue for Latinx; however, we are saying that Latinx are more unambiguously willing to lean into their identity.

A Latina focus group participant in Los Angeles talked about authenticity and identity, saying:

> The more you hide your Latino background, you become less like yourself. You can be as successful as you want to be; however, when you're not being authentic, are you really successful? That's not really who you are."

We found several reasons for this bicultural acceptance. The sheer size and continued rapid growth of the Hispanic population in the U.S. makes it easier to maintain a connection to Hispanic heritage. Latinx have a plethora of choices if they want to hear Spanish radio, watch Spanish-language TV, hear Spanish music, or eat at Latin restaurants. Because they are surrounded by Hispanic cultural elements, Latinx are finding it easier to maintain the connection to their heritage than did previous generations. A New York focus group participant shared this perspective:

I arrived in this country back in 2002. Then more people would look at you differently if you had an accent. Now I think there are a lot more Latinos in the United States as a whole. I remember when I first arrived in Missouri, there was like nobody that looked like us, my sisters and me. Now you see Latinos everywhere, even in a place like Missouri."

Latinx see their biculturalism as a competitive advantage in the workplace. Unlike some of our Latino executives who entered organizations at a time when their Hispanic heritage was seen as a disadvantage, today's Latinx are manifesting their biculturalism as part of their career strategy, seeing it as something that will serve them well in business.

Viewing their biculturalism as an asset emboldens them to highlight it in the workplace. A Latina in the Dallas focus group boldly asserted:

I see my ethnicity as an asset. Being bicultural opens up more doors for me. I am who I am. I have my culture, and it's important to me, *whether people accept it or not.*

In our survey, nearly two-thirds (64 percent) of young Latinos felt that the fact they were either bilingual or bicultural was one of the main reasons for their professional success.

Words of Wisdom from Latinx Leaders

José Padilla, 29, Finance Manager, Facebook

José is the son of Mexican immigrants. He grew up in the neighborhood of Bell Gardens, just outside East Los Angeles. After earning a bachelor's degree in 2010 from the University of California, Berkeley, he began his career as an auditor at Deloitte. He joined Facebook in 2013, and today is an R&D finance manager and serves as the president of Facebook's Latino employee resource group (ERG) called Latin@fb. José shared these insights:

Embracing Latino identity at work

I often speak to a lot of Latinos who don't want to embrace their Hispanic heritage because they worry they will be viewed as a token Latino, or others may think they only got hired because of a quota. It's as if identifying as Latino diminishes their credibility and merit. When I have conversations with Latinos who believe that, I advise them that there will eventually come a time when they will be comfortable to say, "Yes, I'm Latino, and this is part of me. I want to bring this part of me to work every day. But I want my own actions and own merits to speak for themselves." And once they do that, they will have more of a willingness and openness to embrace their diversity and leverage it as an asset in the workplace.

On being a role model

Often when thinking about the lack of diverse leaders in corporate America, people cite that "You can't be who you can't see"—meaning you can't be a leader unless you see people in leadership positions who are Latinos. More and more this inspires me to try to be that leader. Why can't I be the person—the Latino leader—that's at the top and serve as a role model?

On Latino leadership development programs

I have no doubt that Latino leadership programs are necessary and that companies should continue to invest in them. There are a lot of things specific to our Hispanic culture and our ethnicity that affects how we engage in certain situations and in our leadership approach. In fact, the Latino Facebook ERG is working on its first Latino Leadership Day for all U.S.-based Facebook Latinos at our headquarters this fall.

Helping this phenomenon is that for the past 20 years, corporate America has amplified its efforts to create more diverse and inclusive work environments, encouraging employees to "bring their full selves" to work. Many Latinx have accepted this invitation, feeling they can more readily express their biculturalism because corporate America is creating a safe place, or sanctuary, for them. One Dallas group participant told us:

> One of the things that I really like about being bicultural is that it is Latinos who can bridge the cultures and be mediators to the two sides in the workplace.

By comparison, Latino Baby Boomers faced more pressure to assimilate. They were surrounded by more prejudice, more resistance, and a general lack of knowledge about Hispanic heritage. Today there is greater emphasis on inclusion, of knowing the difference between right and wrong when it comes to discrimination and unconscious bias. All this further confirms that being Hispanic in the workplace has benefits. This creates more eagerness and increased motivation for Latinx to say, "Wait a minute. Not only do I not have to hide my Latino identity, it's actually a good thing to be unapologetic about it. Why not embrace the Latino thing?"

As corporate America creates conditions that nurture biculturalism as they look to build their pipelines for future Latino leaders, companies are opening more job opportunities for Latinos who stay connected to their roots, and in some cases are actually pressuring them to *not* lose their unique voice and biculturalism. Latinx are noticing this demand for Latino talent.

One focus group participant in Los Angeles even warned that corporations should continue to encourage young Latinos to be themselves at work, or else the Latinos will leave. She stated:

The advice I would give corporations and CEOs is let us be ourselves. Let us be authentic and really tap into that talent. Really nurture our talent because our talent is who we are; it comes from within. If corporations try to change who we are and change how we see the world, then they're just keeping us in a box where we're not going to be happy. We're not going to excel to our fullest potential if they're trying to change who we are or our values. I'm not going to let anyone change who I am, and I don't care how much money they pay me, I will leave if they won't embrace my talent. I'll walk out that door. I'm always going to stay true to my values, and one of my values is just being authentic and Latino 100 percent of the time.

Millennial Latinos Influencing Cultures Worldwide

The Latinx cultural influence transcends national and racial ethnic lines. Within a mere six months after its release date in 2017, the hit Latin song "Despacito" (Slowly) made history for being the most-streamed track of all time, at 4.6 billion plays globally according to Universal Music Latin Entertainment.

The song by Puerto Rican singer Luis Fonsi and reggaeton star Daddy Yankee, and its accompanying remix featuring Justin Bieber, has young Latinos and non-Latinos in the U.S. and around the world singing and dancing.

Recently, Andrés was riding in the car with one of his closest friends Jason Douglas, who is African-American. Jason's teenage son, Mikey, and eight-year-old son, Ethan were in the back seat. They had all just left a music festival where salsa artist Gilberto Santa Rosa had performed, and Mikey not only danced salsa, but danced it authentically. On the way home, "Despacito" came on and Ethan was singing along to the Spanish lyrics—not just mouthing the words, but in a way that was clearly internalized. "Despacito" had become his song as well.

A third reason Latinx are embracing their ethnicity unapologetically is that Millennials as a group are more open about race and ethnicity. Their greater acceptance of difference makes it easier for Latinx to remain connected to their heritage. A focus group participant in Los Angeles describes the Millennial mindset this way:

> While Millennials tend to be more judgmental about what your values are and who you are as a person they are much more open and accepting about other cultures.

Sophisticated career strategy

The older Latino executives we interviewed were ambitious and willing to take risks. In many cases they were pioneers because they were the first, or the only, Latinos in their environments. They have had career trajectories that are quite impressive. In most cases, however, their careers unfolded as opportunities arose. They followed their instincts and took a somewhat ad hoc approach to their career.

By comparison, our discussions with young Latinx professionals showed they have a clearer outlook, greater maturity, and a much more sophisticated approach to their careers. They conveyed a heightened sense of organizational savvy and a more refined career mindfulness. A Latina focus group participant in Los Angeles described her thought-out plan for her career:

> When I'm thinking about my career trajectory, I must have a career plan and I'm calculated about having that plan. I'm always weighing pros and cons, pros and cons, and making sure that each move I make is the right one. But if I fail, that's OK too, as long as I get back on track.

Latinx are also taking a more thoughtful approach to their careers at a much earlier age. Another Los Angeles participant said:

> I'm serving on the advisory board of USC, but my long-term goal is to serve on a corporate board. There's so much to do between now and then, but I'm telling people now.

Robert spoke at the University of Chicago for a Hispanic Scholarship Fund Youth Leadership Summit held in July 2017. The summit brought in 150 of arguably some of the brightest event high school juniors in the country. They all had well-constructed plans for their future. They knew where they wanted to go, not just for their undergrad degrees, but for graduate school as well. Most already knew what type of career they wanted to pursue, and several already had plans to become entrepreneurs. Robert doesn't recall thinking this way when he was a high school junior. This further validates our finding that young Latinos are taking more ownership of their future, and dismissing the *Si Dios quiere* (God willing) mentality of earlier generations.

I'm no victim

While our young Latinx professionals embraced the benefits that come with being bilingual and bicultural, we noticed that they are especially sensitive about programs and initiatives that appear to give them preferential treatment based on their Hispanic heritage. They want to be given opportunities because of the skills and perspectives they bring to the workplace, not because of their ethnic background. A focus group participant in New York told us:

> I don't want to be like, "Oh poor little Latina." No. I don't want pity from anyone.

Words of Wisdom from Latinx Leaders

Julissa Ramirez, 31, Commercial Drones Technical Program Manager, Intel Corporation

Julissa was born in the Dominican Republic, the oldest of four, and raised by a single mother. She moved to the Bronx in New York when she was nine, and grew up there. She earned Bachelor's and Master's degrees in engineering, both from the Rochester Institute of Technology. In 2012, she joined Intel, where today she leads large, global cross-functional programs and projects. She is also a leader in Intel's Latino employee resource group. She shared these insights with us:

On the value of Latino employee resource groups

The Intel Latino Network (ILN) has given me the opportunity to progress with my Latino self, and I've flourished because of that. I feel more connected to who I am because of those ERG experiences and the opportunities that have been given in the corporate world through the ERG. The ERG also helped me find a community of peers, as well as a professional network and development group that has taken me to heights that I never would have imagined.

On the importance of giving back to the Latino community

To me, giving back to our communities is our duty. The only way we're going to move forward as a community is if we, the ones who have some level of success, go back and reach out and pull others up. It's the only way. We've got to push up and pull up. This is part of my DNA; I have to do it. I can't really say that I care about my community, and just sit back and do nothing. How will that help the next generation do better?

On her relationship with power

When you said "power," the first word that came to my mind was confidence. "Power" is not a negative word; it means that you have the ability to influence others and that you can affect change. Because I wear my differences on my skin, it can be intimidating to be the only Latina, woman, or person of color in the room. Once you walk in you can do one of two things: you can be affected by it negatively, or you can take the opportunity and show the value you bring to the table because of your differences. I don't see power as an individual thing, I see power as a community/shared thing. Power is not something I can take from someone. I can have my own light and others can shine just as bright. No one can take the power that I have from me. I see it as something we can build together.

For them, receiving such preferential treatment was the equivalent of others believing that they had the misfortune of being Hispanic and because of this they needed extra care. Our young Latinos rejected this notion outright.

A Dallas focus group participant described it this way:

> I've always been against minority contracting. I want to compete based on what I do, not where I'm from.

We believe that part of this attitude of rejecting preferential treatment stems from rejection of any notion that being Latino means in some way you are less than someone else. Considering their Latino-ness as an asset, Latinx don't feel the need for any added protection or special consideration. One of the Latinas in our Los Angeles group described it this way:

> Rule number one: never play the victim card. That rule is always something that's very key to me.

It's difficult to determine where this strong resentment against handouts and preferential treatment comes from. One theory is that these Latinx professionals grew up with stories about how their grandparents and great-grandparents attended segregated schools, had to drink from different water fountains, or had to flee Cuba to avoid imprisonment. When confronted with these stories, Latinx see examples of triumph and perseverance. Yet they fear that non-Latinos will hear these stories of discrimination and plight, causing them to feel sorry for Hispanics because of the endured hardships of past generations.

What this means for corporate America is that programs targeting Latinx, as they become more and more prevalent, should be positioned to convey the message of leveraging strengths, as opposed to being offered to remedy a perceived deficiency in the Latino community. Instead of positioning such programs as a way to *fix* Latinos or to provide them the tools they *lack*, they should be positioned as efforts to enable Latinos to leverage the strengths their ethnicity and their unique skills and talents provide.

Willing to play the power game

The Latinx we spoke to also seemed more willing to embrace power. When asked about their relationship with power, our focus group participants were crystal clear that they passionately pursued power, making these types of comments:

I want that power, I want that influence, and I rather feel like I'm now seeking that power, or that influence, more than ever before.

I do seek out power because I've been at places where the culture is not good. I want to have that level of influence to say, "I determine the culture of this organization, or I determine the culture of this team." Therefore, I'm much more of a power seeker.

Yes, I compete for power! I really put my name out there where my superiors know that I want to be recognized as a powerful influence. It feels good knowing that I have that within me.

I'm actively seeking power as part of my long-term plan. I want a seat at the table because I feel like we all deserve to be there.

I want that power, and I've always wanted that power.

When I think about power from a family perspective, I remember growing up with a very family atmosphere where my grandmother was the matriarch; the women were very powerful. Thinking about power in a professional way is not a concept that most women in my family consider. But I would like to change that. I would like power.

These comments reflect a trend that seeking power is a positive attribute. In our online survey, only 17 percent of Latinx felt that having ambivalence toward power had a negative impact on their career. This attitude will serve the Latino community well as younger generations strive to increase Latino influence and impact.

Latinx Liabilities

At times we did notice that young Latinos struggled with aspects of their culture: attitudes that they felt were not positive that they chose not to embrace. For example, a Latina focus group participant in Chicago shared:

I recall being at home with my mom and my great-aunt while I was in college. My great-aunt offered her opinion, "What's the point of going to school? You just need to get married." I looked at my mom, letting her know I was furious. My mom looked at me and said in a consoling tone, "Just let it be; it's an older way of thinking."

Another focus group participant shared a similar feeling:

I embrace my culture because that's what makes me unique. But there are pieces of my culture that I don't like, like having to dress conservatively, or that women can't leave home until they are married. Those are the pieces that I don't embrace. I'll embrace the food, I'll embrace the celebrations, I'll embrace the things I'm proud of, but the other stuff, I just let it bypass me because it's not part of who I am.

Having heard some state dislikes of their own culture, here are our observations of Latinx liabilities.

Individualism

While we were proud to see that Latinx are more bicultural and are retaining their bicultural identity, we sensed that they have embraced the more European-American values of individualism, displaying a significant focus on personal achievement. We suspect that part of this desire to excel is to repay past generations for the sacrifices they made to provide them with greater opportunities. As mentioned earlier in the book, anything short of success would be a dishonor to those ancestors who paved the way.

However, it was troubling that there was not an equally vibrant stance on leveraging individual achievement to help others. We did not hear many stories about having an obligation to support the broader Latino community. While they wished to be connected to the Latino collective and saw their Hispanic heritage as an asset, the communal aspects of Latino culture seem to have been replaced by European-American individualism. In fact, embracing a Latino identity in some ways was seen more so as an advantage for *each individual* rather than as an advantage for the community as a whole.

Our hope is that as these Latinx professionals mature and accumulate the trappings of individual achievement, they will discover the definition of excellence that encompasses a responsibility to help the larger Latino community to succeed. We are hopeful that Latinx will continue to embrace the vibrant components of their Latin heritage—the salsa, the food, the history and the culture. Embracing Latino heritage doesn't mean leveraging it simply for personal benefit; doing so also includes having that shared responsibility for the success of the broader Latino community.

Language and culture

An embrace of Latino identity is also connected to Spanish-speaking ability. If Latinx are to be the future stewards of Hispanic heritage in the U.S., they must master the language to better connect with all the richness that being Latino entails. From a practical perspective, being able to read, write, and speak Spanish fluently further enables Latinx to utilize their ethnicity as an asset.

Those who retain their Spanish-speaking ability see being bilingual as an asset in the workplace. A participant in our Dallas group who has his own business outlined the benefit:

> Being bilingual and bicultural helps my business get access to a wider client base, and I'm able to better service the growing Latino market. Many of my competitors can't do that, which benefits me greatly.

Besides connecting to Latino values through language, learning about Latin-American culture will serve Latinx well. Studying the history and learning the cultural nuances and national identities of Latin-American countries and their people better enables Latinos to gain a more global perspective. This knowledge strengthens bonds within the Latino community and minimizes the ethnic divides that may prevent us from understanding our shared roots.

Relocation

Corporations who wish to hire and promote more Latinos often speak of a general lack of willingness of Latinos to relocate for career opportunities. We wanted to know how Latinx felt about this perception, and their responses seemed to confirm that moving away from family is still a big issue. This is not surprising when you consider that in our online survey, when participants were asked to describe what aspect of Hispanic heritage had contributed the most to their personal and professional success, 82 percent answered, "Family."

Several of our focus group participants mentioned that while they themselves may be willing to relocate, the reaction from their immediate families would be mostly negative. "Why are you leaving us?" "Who is going to take care of us now?" "What are we supposed to do now?" and "You're choosing career over family" were all responses they said they would expect to hear if they told their family they were moving for their work.

Several participants did notice a paradox in that their parents or great-grandparents found the courage to leave their families and home countries to come all the way to the U.S., often with very little money or English-speaking ability. And yet these same family members struggled when their children expressed a desire to move away. A Chicago participant said:

> I like being around my family. That's my culture. What is interesting is that my mom is far away from her family, for they're all still in Mexico. They moved away! They adjusted! Yet they don't want us to move away from them. It's a little bit of hypocrisy.

Words of Wisdom from Latinx Leaders
Jeffrey Martínez, 34, Retail Market Executive, PNC Bank

Jeffrey was born in North Bergen, New Jersey, the son of a Colombian mother and a Cuban exile father. He earned a bachelor's degree from Rutgers in New Jersey. He's a military veteran, having served for nine years in the U.S. Army National Guard, where he did tours of duty in Iraq and Kuwait. After starting his professional career at JPMorgan Chase, Jeffrey joined PNC in 2014. Active in the company's Latino employee resource group, he shared these insights:

On being authentic

I remember speaking to Pablo Sánchez, who ran the retail banks for Chase. One of the pieces of advice he offered was this: "Look, I am who I am. And so I align who I am with the companies that find value in who I am." It was probably one of the first times I heard, "Be who you are! There's a company out there who's going to value you."

On travel as a means to connect with Latino ethnicity

I love to travel and I've found that it helps to reignite that passion around my heritage. Next week I'll be back in Cuba for the fourth time, and I'd say I've probably been to maybe 70 percent of Latin America. Through travel I experience Latin culture and music. I love seeing it live, being in Argentina, for example, where it's the tango. That has made me proud of my heritage, a passion that was a silent when I was a teenager. Whether it's spending time in Lima, Machu Picchu, Colombia, Ecuador, Brazil, Central America, or the Islands, there's something to be really proud of. Today I have no problem going to a tower and screaming out my heritage and my family's story.

On challenging ourselves to give back

It's tough trying to figure out how to reach a point where we can really give back. We all come from humble means so we must put our own oxygen mask on first before we can help the other person. As we grow into senior managers and executives, giving back has to be top on our minds, and we must have a strategy for it. But first we must advance to that top spot!

These sentiments raise the probability that Latinos may be more inclined to turn down career opportunities that require relocation. Results indicated that nearly one-third (30 percent) of our survey participants said that an unwillingness to relocate has had a negative impact on their career.

Yet we did see that several of our focus group participants realized the importance of relocation, and not just from a career perspective. Some indicated that Latinos need to get out of their safe zone and be ambitious when it comes to relocation. A Los Angeles participant shared:

> I feel like Latinos need to leave California in the sense that they need to open their wings and build their networks. If Latinos are concentrated in just California, we're not going to be able to show people what we can do. If we're not willing to leave California and go work for a company some other person is. It's important to me that we're open-minded and that we really spread our wings, exploring other cultures and communities. For many of us, California remains a safety net.

Another Los Angeles participant added that a willingness by current leaders to relocate helps even younger Latinos to be more open to relocation. She shared:

> My little brother is my everything so when I was considering going to New York, I wondered, "If I move, what am I showing?" I wanted him to go to an East Coast university and get that exposure, but if I was not willing to relocate, how can I tell him, "Go experience something else." I thought I'd be hurting him more if I didn't expose my own self to relocation. He could

retaliate by saying "Well, you stayed in California. I want to go to UCLA." I insisted, "No, no, let's try the East Coast. Let's go!"

Lack of Latino role models

Our Latinx professionals collectively felt that older, more successful Latinos are not providing much help or mentoring. One reason for this is that there were very few or no Latinos for them to look up to in their organizations. This idea was expressed by a Dallas focus group participant who said:

> There aren't too many role models or mentors or anyone who can help me get to the next level.

Our survey results confirm this is a real issue in the community: 67 percent of the respondents said that a lack of Latino role models was one of the main hurdles to their career success.

Without role models, Latinos may struggle to advance in their careers and can have difficulty navigating corporate America. Another Dallas participant said:

> I wish I would've had mentors when I was younger, and I wish I had had somebody pushing me harder, telling me how to do things. Without role models, Latinos have to learn how to climb the corporate ladder the hard way.

Some expressed exasperation with Latinos who had succeeded in the workplace but then failed to help them. Even worse, several shared that successful Latinos were, in fact, making advancement more difficult for the next generation. A Chicago participant expressed exactly this sentiment when he shared:

My experience has been that as soon as Latinos reach a certain level, they forget about everyone else. And it's weird because if there's a ceiling or roadblock, and they make a crack, they then go back and seal it so everybody else has to struggle to break it again.

In Los Angeles, a Latina participant shared a similar perspective:

Latinas have probably been their worst enemy by not wanting to help other Latinas. Even in a Latino organization, that has been my experience.

Unfortunately, we found a similar feeling within our New York focus group as well when one of them told us:

White sponsors are not threatened because as they're moving up the ranks, they have been more than willing to sponsor me. When Latinos help out, there's a lot of back talk such as this: "I helped you and you should be grateful." As Latinas, we hear that a lot, "Well, you're not grateful for what I did for you." There's a sense of this attitude: "I will do so much for you, but I will not take that hurdle to then sponsor you to the next level."

Our survey data confirms that what these participants described is a reality for many Latinx. Only 13 percent of our respondents said that their most important mentors have been Latino. Even more troubling, our data indicates that young Latinos are starting to model the behaviors of Latinos who have made it to the top but then fail to mentor younger Latinos. While young Latinos lament the lack of Latino role models and Latino mentors, when asked if they mentor young Latinos, almost two-thirds (65 percent) indicated they do not!

Words of Wisdom from Latinx Leaders
Patricia Mota, 33, President,
Hispanic Alliance for Career Enhancement (HACE)

Patricia grew up in East Chicago, Indiana. She is Mexican-American and the daughter of hard-working parents. She earned bachelor's and master's degrees from Indiana University. She was recently appointed as a member of the Illinois Treasurer's Latino Advisory Council and the Indiana University Latino Alumni Association Board. In 2015, she was named by Negocios Now as one of Chicago's Top 40 Hispanics Under 40. Patricia shared these insights:*

On the responsibility of successful Latino professionals
We have to ensure that we are courageous and fearless about achieving our highest potential. We have a huge responsibility to ensure that we're out and visible in our communities, whether it's serving on nonprofit boards, speaking engagements, or volunteering. We must be involved in making decisions when it comes to economics, government, nonprofits, education, and workforce development. We need to make sure that we're aligning what we best bring to the table in terms of our capabilities and our own strengths to keep the community moving forward.

On what corporations need to do
Companies need to invest more in their Latino employees and make sure that they provide them with holistic programming. One of the biggest areas to become an effective leader, no matter who you are, is to understand yourself and understand what is it that you bring to the table. And part of that is understanding your culture and your background. A lot of corporations may have their own internal programming or coaching. That's great, but for corporations to accelerate the advancement of Latinos within the organization they need to look for culturally relevant programming.

On how Hispanic heritage impacts her career
It directly translates to what I have the opportunity to do today, which is to lead a national nonprofit organization. We spend a lot of time emphasizing the worth of traditional Latino values. Specifically, being able to connect to the community and learning about young professionals' experiences to connect and help them achieve their highest potential is a priority. A big part of my role is building relationships, and that's important for me in terms of the family values that I grew up with. We must continue to ensure that Latinos are taking care of each other.

Percentage of professionals who mentor younger Latinos

Latinos and Mentoring

In our surveys, two-thirds of both Latino executives and Latino professionals indicated that non-Hispanics have been their most important mentors. This finding is not too surprising given the lower number of Latinos in more senior roles who could serve as influential mentors.

What is surprising, and very concerning, is how much Latino-on-Latino mentoring is occurring. 89 percent of our Latino executives, who are mostly Baby Boomers, indicate that they mentor younger Latinos. But our data suggests that while these Latino execs are actively mentoring, there simply aren't enough of them to mentor the next generation of Latino leaders.

Because a large number of Latinx professionals are not receiving mentoring from Latino leaders, they do not see the value nor learn for themselves how to mentor younger Hispanics. The result is that only 34 percent of Latinx professionals reported they are currently mentoring younger Hispanics. This lack of Latino-on-Latino mentoring has a negative impact on Latino career advancement.

The Way Forward for Latinx

Youth has spoken. They are ready to stand on the shoulders of the pioneering Latino and Latina executives who broke new ground and paved the way. But are the entities around them—the government, the schools, the not-for-profits, the corporations—ready to fully capitalize on this rising Latino talent force? We worry that they are not.

In our conclusion that follows we present what needs to be done to channel the energy, ambition, and vision of Latinx professionals as they seek their rightful place as leaders in their organizations and society. Following the conclusion we summarize the entirety of our case through our ten-point Latino Executive Manifesto.

Adelante! Forward! ❧

CONCLUSION

Without More Latino Leaders, Companies Will Suffer

*"Cuando estas convencido que una causa
es justa, continua luchando."*

When you are convinced a cause is just, keep fighting.

—Rigoberta Menchu, Guatemalan human rights activist
1992 Nobel Peace Prize

We have come to the end of the journey of laying out a guide to Latino career success. We saw that leadership requires education, know how, and specialized skills. It requires ambition, hard work, risk-taking, and determination. These are, however, universal truths about requirements for leadership in general. This Latino Executive Manifesto also sought out the Latino differentiator. Was there anything unique about the career journeys and the leadership qualities of the 20 executives we interviewed because of their Latino heritage?

The answer is an unequivocal yes.

We have seen that for the Latino executives we interviewed, the foundation of their success was their ability and commitment to be *auténtico* (authentic). For these Latinos and Latinas this cultivation of being people of good character demanded they also come to terms with the implications of their Latino heritage. This journey of self-discovery led them to prove the promise of diversity: that having a diverse leadership, management, and talent pool with different experiences, backgrounds, and styles provides corporations with a competitive advantage.

We delved into the specifics of how the Latino differential can be revealed in the workplaces and the C-suites of the leaders whose stories we heard. This is not to say that leaders must manifest their Latino identity to be leaders, as is true for the many Invisible Latinos out there. Our quest was to seek out those leaders who specifically saw their cultural identity as key to being a transformative leader. Hence, our claim that this is a *Latino Executive Manifesto*. For those Latinos who seek executive leadership and at the same time embrace their culture or fear shedding it in their quest to the top, the messages in the book have been for you.

After having put the focus on Latinos and what we need to do (that is in our power) to get ahead, we now turn to the outside forces who also have a responsibility, the ability, and the resources to accelerate the advancement of Latino leaders in corporate America. As we brought to light in this book, without more Latinos in the executive ranks, not only will the Latino community suffer; so will corporations if they don't reflect at all levels of the organization a nation that will consist of one-third Latinos by 2050.

The best practices to accomplish Latino leadership goals are well known and have been well documented. Here are five actions that government, universities, not-for-profits, and corporations each must do to truly contribute to the rise of a meaningful number of Latino leaders.

What Government Needs to Do

1. Resolve the status of undocumented young people who grew up in the U.S. and put them on the path to citizenship.

2. Create parity in the funding of Hispanic-serving institutions (HSIs). Currently HSIs are underfunded to the tune of 66 cents for every federal dollar per student going to the rest of higher education annually.

3. Voters must hold politicians accountable for their hostility to education in communities of color.

4. Diversify government leadership and pipeline ranks with Latinos from the emerging talent pool.

5. Publicly challenge corporations to increase their Latino talent pipelines and Latinos in leadership, and withhold contracts unless certain goals are met.

What Universities Need to Do

1. Help Latino parents who did not graduate from college understand the value of a university degree, and in the process help them access and navigate the many financial and advisory resources available.

2. Aggressively source and attract Latino faculty and administrators to better attract Latino students.

3. Hold faculty and administrators accountable for the graduation rates of Latino students. Too many Latino students make it into college, only to drop out at disproportionately higher rates.

4. Develop an endowment with contributions not only from traditional donors, but also from the Latino community to help finance the education of Latino students.

5. Insert into the core curriculum more content on Latino history, societal contributions, and cultural influences.

What Not-for-profits Need to Do

1. Prioritize helping Latino students learn how to navigate the college application process and college life socialization.

2. Partner with government and corporations to provide meaningful forward-looking internships with real life work experience coupled with a mentor.

3. Change the mindset that it's a zero-sum game of competing for slices of the funding pie to one where the collective pie gets exponentially larger through collaboration.

4. Hold their corporate sponsors accountable when they fall short in advancing Latino talent.

5. Be exceptionally clear to corporations about their most unique and effective impact on Latino talent development and be ready to refer requests that don't match this sweet spot to other Latino not-for-profits.

What Corporations Need to Do

1. Become knowledgeable of Latino culture and values and stop pressing Latinos to assimilate and instead create conditions that nurture Latino professional success. Incorporate some Latino culture into their corporate culture and stop trying to "fix" Latinos.

2. Aggressively accelerate Latino leadership development holistically through internal and/or external leadership development programs, mentorship and sponsorship, but most importantly, through pilot stretch assignments.

3. Differentiate among the various Latino talent pools and segmented markets in ways that are as rigorous and sophisticated as marketing campaigns. There is no single Latino talent force in the same way there is no single Latino market.

4. Encourage their highest-ranking Latino leaders and executives to work together to advance the Latino talent agenda through a Latino officer caucus or roundtable.

5. Provide opportunities for Latinos to influence major corporate and commercial strategic initiatives.

Intel Case Study: Corporate Latino Talent Best Practice

Every January, global technology companies gather in Las Vegas to attend the Consumer Electronics Show (CES) to showcase their latest innovations and technology related to consumer electronics. In 2015, Intel Corporation CEO Bryan Krzanich chose CES to not only highlight Intel's technology advancements; he announced the company's investment of $300 million to increase diversity in its workforce. It is still the largest diversity investment by a technology company, and supports a pledge that by the year 2020, Intel's U.S. workforce would mirror the talent available in the country.

While the $300 million investment caught the attention of many corporations, it is Intel's long history of successful internal Hispanic initiatives that have long been admired and applauded by the Latino community and has served as best practices for other companies to emulate regarding world-class Latino initiatives.

Intel's Top 6 Hispanic Initiatives include:

1. The Hispanic Initiative Program (HIP). Formed in 2006, HIP provides development and retention programs targeted toward Intel's current Hispanic employees, and forges partnerships that position Intel as an employer of choice in the Hispanic community. Under this initiative, Intel offers leadership training, skills development, and networking opportunities to build enthusiasm among Intel's Hispanic employees.

2. Intel Latino Network (ILN). ILN is a chartered strategic employee resource group with chapters located at Intel's U.S. sites. Though ILN's membership is inclusive, their charter is to provide leadership, professional development, and networking opportunities to members, and help Latinos advance their careers. ILN is called upon to help in the recruitment, development, and retention of Latinos.

3. Hispanic 1st Year TouchPoint Program. Connects Hispanic employees in their first year at Intel with more experienced peers. The program facilitates integration for recent hires by providing them with resources and assisting them with the creation of their Intel network. When first launched, this program immediately contributed to reducing turnover of first year Hispanics.

4. Intel Hispanic Leadership Council (IHLC). Dedicated to the advocacy and sponsorship of Hispanics at Intel. Members of the IHLC are the company's most senior Hispanic leaders. They serve as role models of leadership and champions of the company's Hispanic employees, Hispanic talent, and leadership pipeline initiatives.

5. Blueprint for Extraordinary Performance. An internal leadership development series created to address the challenges of isolation, this program leverages a cohort learning model. Latino participants develop tools and skills needed to effectively navigate their careers at Intel, connect with each other, build more effective relationships with their managers and peers, and drive their own development. The program, which ran from 2009 through 2015, was sunset recently with over 1,000 alumni.

6. Hispanic Inspire Conference. Its purpose is to strengthen leadership and business acumen. Featuring executive speakers, workshops, and networking sessions, the conference connects employees to important development content and a network of influential peers.

These programs do indeed make a difference. Hispanics who have participated in these various programs and initiatives are retained—and are receiving promotions —at a higher rate than non-participants.

HACE Case Study: Not-for-Profit Latino Talent Best Practice

One way companies can increase the number of Latino leaders is to have them participate in Latino leadership development programs offered by not-for-profits.

To uncover the key elements of a successful program, we conducted a focus group of seven Latinas who had completed the Mujeres de HACE (Women of HACE) Leadership Program. The program is run by the Hispanic Alliance for Career Enhancement (HACE) and consists of Latinas participating as a cohort through seven modules delivered over a three-month period.

Through the women's stories of what they had gained from the program, we identified four key beneficial outcomes that helped these women further advance in their careers:

Increased conviction to demonstrate personal resilience to face the challenges of being a leader

By discussing real-life issues, the program helped participants identify triggers, ways of coping, and more productive ways of thinking, feeling and behaving to maximize their effectiveness. Sample quotes:

> *I no longer feel intimidated when I'm the only women or minority leader in the room.*

> *I'm better able to leverage my talents to move up within my company. Not just lateral moves, but moving up to senior roles.*

Deeper connection to the Latino community

Participants developed deep friendships and family-like bonds due to the in-depth conversations and shared experiences. Each participant felt they were a teacher *and* a learner during the program. Sample quotes:

I now have this incredible network of people I can reach out to for support and guidance. The network is tremendous.

It's incredible to connect with Latinas who have experienced similar struggles.

I've built bonds and relationships that I will hold forever. I don't feel isolated as a Hispanic any longer.

Increased confidence

Participants felt better prepared to overcome personal barriers and obstacles that may have diminished their faith in their ability in the past. Sample quotes:

Because I'm much more confident, I applied for a job I never would have applied to before.

I've been promoted twice since I completed this program and now I want to be a vice president someday. I didn't have that aspiration before.

Greater clarity of their Hispanic heritage

By looking at issues and behaviors from a cultural lens, participants were able to look at their own cultural identity challenges from the perspective of their Latina-ness being an asset rather than a liability. They felt better prepared to join more senior level ranks within their company, while remaining authentic to their Hispanic heritage. Sample quotes:

Now I feel better prepared to become a leader while I'm still being myself and being a Latina.

Since I was born in Latin America, the program has helped me better understand U.S. culture and how my heritage can serve as an asset.

The program is definitely making an impact. Forty percent of participants report a promotion or salary increase within six months of completing the program.

The Legacy of Today's Latino Executives

Llegamos! We got to the end of this book. But this book journey was intended to be just the start of a new era. Building off the legacy of the Latino and Latina executives of a previous generation as exemplified by the twenty executives we interviewed for the book, it's time to address Latino leadership advancement in a new and disruptive way. One that engages identity rather than buries it, that is authentic rather than imposed, one that treats women and men fully as equals, one that seeks out Latino cultural influences to integrate into the fabric of organizations, and one that looks to the new generation of Latinx to change how we view work, society and the world.

Latinx—les toca. Latinx—it's your turn. ❧

"*Merece lo que sueñas.*"

Deserve what you dream.

—Octavio Paz

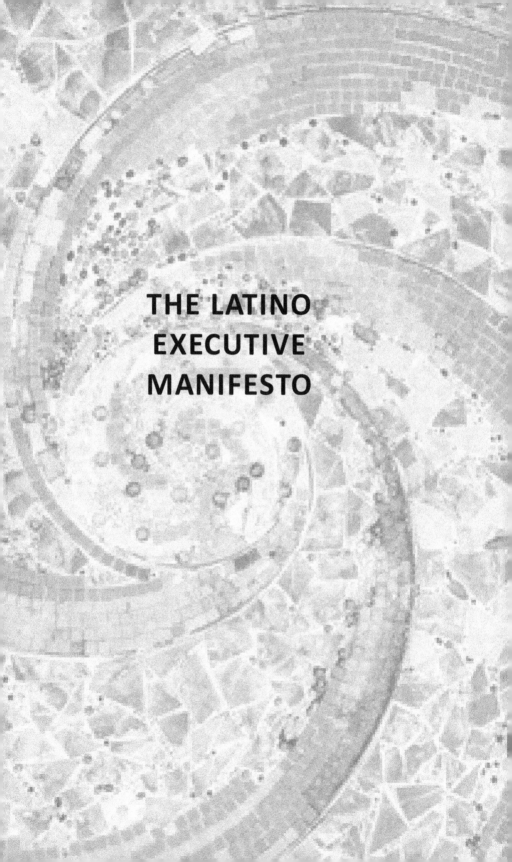

THE LATINO
EXECUTIVE
MANIFESTO

1.
Corporations have failed to become true meritocracies.

They must shed the self-image that they are color-blind, and instead proactively address the conscious and unconscious biases that have kept Latinos from rising to the height of our potential.

2.
Latino leaders must engage with and resolve their own cultural identity.

Conclusions will vary for each leader about what it means for them, so we must allow for variances. But it can't be ignored and the sooner it can be addressed, the more effective Latino leaders will be.

3.
Latinos must reclaim our communal spirit to overcome intra-Latino divides.

Focusing on our national, socioeconomic, and regional rivalries leads to a lack of unity and weakens the power of our numbers, our institutions, and our leadership.

4.
Corporations must be willing to adapt to and capitalize on the differences that Latinos bring to corporate culture.

Embracing Latino culture will create more inclusive environments for Latino talent and equip companies to better serve Latino consumers and clients. Non-Latinos will benefit from Latino cultural assets in same way Latinos have been enriched by other cultures.

5.
Latinos need to double down on the relentless pursuit of higher education and rally behind it as a civil rights issue.

Latino college attendance is trending upward and we need to accelerate this trend significantly by any means necessary in the face of massive budget cutbacks. Education is the greatest bulwark against hostility and biases, and for achieving the highest levels of leadership.

6.
Latinos must embrace ambition as an honorable intent.
While maintaining humility, we also must not be naïve. No one is going to hand us opportunities if we are not openly seeking them. The community should celebrate those who demonstrate this ambition because we all benefit.

7.
Latino leaders must give back to the community.
True excellence requires leveraging high personal achievement reached to help others achieve success. The journey of the Latino executive is incomplete if they don't give back to others.

8.
Latinos need to get over our ambivalence about power by claiming more of it and redefining it on our own terms.
Where ambition is personal, power is collective. The impact of Latino power in corporations, government, and society is incongruent with our massive numbers. Yet, even as we operate with more power we must contribute a differentiated way of wielding it.

9.
The next generation of Latino leaders can be more powerful by pursuing the path of a bicultural identity.
Resist assimilation. Instead develop a differentiating American-Latino identity that embraces and celebrates the multiple influences of mainstream American culture and that of one's specific Latino heritage(s).

10.
Master the rules of corporate culture so you can break them when the right time comes.
Master the rules of your own culture as well, and in the crucible of being a successful Latino in corporate America, find ways to have both cultures shape and influence each other. In this, create the conditions for greater creativity, innovation, and transformation.

An Invitation

We want to hear from you. Go to www.thelatinxinstitute.com and share with us and the community what the Latino Executive Manifesto means to you. What challenges you the most? Excites you? Makes you think?

Comment on it. Refine it. Share it. Print it. Post it.

We are a rising power in corporate America. Be authentic, be ambitious, be excellent! The Latino community, the broader society, and the corporations you currently serve—or will serve in the future—need more authentic and successful Latino leaders so they can survive and thrive in the twenty-first century.

Now go back into the public square and manifest yourself as a Latino executive.

BIOGRAPHIES

LATINO EXECUTIVE
MANIFESTO LEADERS

Victor Arias, Jr.

Senior Client Partner, Korn Ferry
Board Member, Popeye's Louisiana Kitchen

Victor Arias, Jr. is a senior client partner in the Dallas office of Korn Ferry. He is a core member of the CEO/Board Services practice and is also the Global Leader of Diversity & Inclusion for the firm.

Since 2001, Arias served on the Board of Directors of Popeye's Louisiana Kitchen and recently retired after fifteen years of service. He is a trustee emeritus for the Stanford University board of trustees, a prior member of the Stanford GSB Advisory Council, a current member of the UTEP Leadership Council, and a past White House Fellows Commissioner.

He is also past national president and co-founder of the National Society of Hispanic MBAs, a prior member of the Notre Dame Institute of Latino Studies board, and a founding board member of the recently formed Latino Corporate Directors Association (LCDA). He recently became chairman of the board of the Latino Business Action Network (LBAN), the key collaborator and driver for the Stanford Latino Entrepreneurship Initiative (SLEI) with Stanford University.

Arias earned his MBA from Stanford University and BBA from University of Texas at El Paso, where he was named a Distinguished Alum in 2009.

José Armario

CEO, Armario Enterprises, LLC
Board Director, USG Corporation and
Avon Products, Inc.

Born in Havana, Cuba, José Armario is a dynamic C-Suite executive with over twenty-five years of senior level leadership experience. He holds a master's degree from the University of Miami and was inducted into the Alumni Hall of Fame at Miami-Dade Community College.

He is currently the CEO of Armario Enterprises, LLC a firm specializing in management consulting and corporate acquisitions. He spent twenty years at McDonald's Corporation, including roles as general manager of McDonald's Chile, president of McDonald's Latin America and Canada, and retired as executive vice president of supply chain, sustainability, development, and franchising. He previously held leadership roles at Luxottica Group and Burger King Corporation.

Armario currently serves on the corporate board of directors for USG Corporation and Avon Products Inc. He also serves on the boards of Good Samaritan Hospital, the President's Council for the University of Miami, and the Greg Olsen Foundation.

Gilbert Casellas

Non-Executive Chairman,
Omnitru Technologies, LLC
Board Director, Prudential Financial

Born and raised in the Ybor City section of Tampa, Florida, Gilbert Casellas received his BA from Yale University and his JD from University of Pennsylvania Law School. He served as law clerk on the U.S. Court of Appeals. He began his career with the firm of Montgomery McCracken, becoming a partner and a member of the Management Committee.

He was appointed by President Clinton as General Counsel of the U.S. Department of the Air Force, and again appointed by President Clinton to serve as the chairman of the Equal Employment Opportunity Commission. He also served as co-chairman of the U.S. 2000 Census Monitoring Board. During the Obama administration, he was appointed to serve as a civilian member of the Military Leadership Diversity Commission.

He currently serves as non-executive chairman of Omnitru Technologies, LLC, a Washington, DC-based consulting and investment firm. Previously, he was chief diversity officer for Dell Inc. and previously served as president of the Swarthmore Group.

He is a board director for Prudential Financial, a trustee of the University of Pennsylvania and a member of the Council on Foreign Relations and the American Law Institute. He is a former President of the Hispanic National Bar Association and chairman of the board of the Hispanic Federation. He is a recipient of the "Spirit of Excellence" award from the American Bar Association, the U.S. Department of the Air Force's Decoration for Exceptional Civilian Service and Latino Justice/PRLDEF's Lucero Award. In November 2017 he will be awarded the Alumni Award of Merit of the University of Pennsylvania.

Patricia Diaz Dennis

Former Senior Vice President, AT&T
Board Member, Entravision Communications
Corporation and U.S. Steel

Patricia Diaz Dennis was born in Santa Rita, New Mexico. President Reagan appointed her to the National Labor Relations Board in 1983 and to the Federal Communications Commission. President George H. W. Bush appointed her as Assistant Secretary of State for Human Rights and Humanitarian Affairs in 1992.

She was previously SVP and assistant general counsel for AT&T. Patricia is the former chair of the national Board of Directors of the Girl Scouts USA and served on the World Bank Sanctions Board and NPR Board of Directors. She served on the Board of Directors of Massachusetts Mutual Life Insurance Company from 1996 to 2017. She is currently a director of Entravision Communications Corporation and U.S. Steel.

She received the Hispanic National Bar Association Latina Commission Primera Award (2016), Texas State Bar Association Women Lawyers of Achievement Award (2012) and the Association of Fundraising Professionals Award (2007).

She holds a BA from UCLA and a JD from Loyola University School of Law.

The Honorable Cari Dominguez

Principal, Dominguez & Associates
Board Member, ManpowerGroup Inc.,
Triple-S Management Corporation,
The Calvert Funds

Cari Dominguez was born in Havana, Cuba. Today, she serves on the boards of ManpowerGroup Inc., Triple-S Management Corporation, and the Calvert Funds. She is principal of Dominguez & Associates, a management consulting firm.

A former Chair of the U.S. Equal Employment Opportunity Commission (EEOC), her public service includes two presidential appointments. She served in the U.S. Department of Labor, where she launched the Labor Department's Glass Ceiling Initiative, designed to remove invisible barriers from the workplace.

Dominguez's experience includes senior positions at Bank of America and partnerships at two executive search firms. She serves on the board of the National Association of Corporate Directors. She is a founding member of the Latino Corporate Directors Association and active supporter of HACR. *Hispanic Business* magazine recognized her as one of the Elite Hispanic Women and one of the Most Influential Hispanics.

Dominguez holds BA and MA degrees from the American University. She is also a Fellow of the Advanced Study Program in Public Management of MIT. In 2003, she was conferred the honorary degree of Doctor of Humanitarian Service by Loma Linda University.

Jorge Figueredo

Executive Vice President, Human Resources
McKesson Corporation

Jorge Figueredo is Executive Vice President of Human Resources for McKesson Corporation. He is a member of McKesson's Executive Committee (EC) and serves as the top advisor to the CEO and board of directors. Previously, he served as Senior Vice President of HR at Dow Jones Inc. and spent twenty-two years at Liz Claiborne, concluding his tenure as president of its international division.

As a Cuban immigrant, Figueredo brings a unique perspective to the leadership table. He has been recognized in *Human Resource Executive* as a top HR leader and as one of the 100 most influential Hispanics by *Hispanic Business* magazine. He has been a member of the board of directors at St. Anthony Foundation, a nonprofit organization providing essential support to San Franciscans living in poverty.

Figueredo is an advisor at the University of South Carolina, a member of the Corporate Executive Board's CHRO Roundtable, and advisor to Cornell University's CAHRS program for HR graduate students.

Juan Galarraga

Senior Vice President, Store Operations,
Target Corporation

Juan Galarraga is senior vice president, store operations for Target Corporation, and is responsible for overseeing all operational processes of more than 1,800 stores and 320,000 team members. In his fifteen years at Target, he has held multiple senior leadership positions in stores, supply chain, healthcare and compliance where he led the company through various new initiatives to meet guests' evolving demands and expectations. As senior vice president of stores, he oversees the total operations of more than 450 stores in the Midwest, North, and Northwest regions.

Gallaraga, a native of Caracas, Venezuela, also plays an active role in helping the company define strategies to hire, retain, and develop future Hispanic leaders, as well as making a positive impact in the community and business place. He served as the executive sponsor for the Hispanic Business Council. He also serves on the Board of Directors for the Hispanic Scholarship Fund.

Charles P. Garcia

CEO, ALPFA
Former CEO, Sterling Group of Companies
Former Board Director, Winn Dixie Stores (Fortune 500)
Board Member, Junior Achievement USA
Board Member, Girl Scouts USA

Charles "Charlie" Garcia is the CEO of the Association of Latino Professionals for America (ALPFA). He serves on the board of Junior Achievement. Previously, Charlie was the founder and CEO of Sterling Financial Group, named by *Inc.* magazine as the #8 fastest-growing privately held company. He has been named "Entrepreneur of the Year" by three national organizations. He served for six years on the Board of Directors of Winn-Dixie Stores. Garcia was Advisory Board chairman for Aetna Inc. and chairman of the board of Empire Avenue Inc.

President Reagan awarded him a White House Fellowship. President George H. W. Bush chose him for the White House Initiative on Educational Excellence for Hispanics. Both President Barack Obama and President Bush asked him to serve on the Board of Visitors of the U.S. Air Force Academy. For his leadership, Air Force Secretary Michael Donley awarded him the Distinguished Public Service Medal.

He is a highly decorated military officer and was chosen by NBC/ Telemundo as a military analyst during the U.S. invasion of Iraq. He appears frequently on CNN, Fox News, and Univision. He has authored two leadership books, *A Message from Garcia* and *Leadership Lessons of the White House Fellows.*

Garcia has a JD from Columbia Law School, an MA from University of Oklahoma and a BS from the U.S. Air Force Academy.

Yvonne Garcia
Senior Vice President and Global Head of
Client Solutions and PMO,
State Street Corporation

Born in New York City, Yvonne Garcia is senior vice president and global head of client solutions and PMO at State Street Corporation. Prior to that role, she served as vice president for mass affluent marketing for Bank of America and as vice president for their China Construction Bank Strategic Assistance Program. She is a fully certified Six Sigma Black Belt.

Garcia serves as the chairwoman for the largest Latino professional organization in the country, ALPFA. Yvonne also serves as the chair of the Hispanic Scholarship Fund for Boston, and is the co-founding chair of Milagros para Niños, an initiative at Children's Hospital in Boston. Garcia was selected as one of the Top 5 Latina Executives in the country by *Latina Style* Magazine. Most recently, she was selected as one of the Top 22 Most Influential Women in Massachusetts by the *Boston Business Journal*, and was featured in *Fortune* magazine as one of the Top 50 Most Powerful Latinas in the United States.

Garcia holds an MBA from Boston University and a BA from SUNY Albany. She is also a graduate of the Army R.O.T.C. program at Siena College in Loudonville, New York, and holds a certificate in economics and culture from La Sorbonne in Paris.

Lisa Garcia Quiroz

President, Time Warner Foundation
Senior Vice President, Chief Diversity Officer,
Time Warner, Inc.

Lisa Garcia Quiroz is president of the Time Warner Foundation and senior vice president, chief diversity officer of Time Warner Inc. During her tenure, she has forged new and innovative initiatives that develop and support diverse storytellers and leaders, and has had an indelible impact on the media industry.

She previously launched two businesses at Time Inc.: *People en Español,* the best-selling Hispanic magazine in the U.S., and *Time for Kids,* an award-winning children's news publication. She currently serves as chairperson of the Hispanic Scholarship Fund, and is a director of the Public Theater and the Apollo Theater Foundation.

An active civic leader, Garcia Quiroz is the former chairperson of the Corporation for National and Community Service Board, a post to which she was appointed by President Obama, and she served as founding co-chair of the NYC Latin Media and Entertainment Commission under Mayor Michael Bloomberg. She is a graduate of Harvard College and Harvard Business School, and is a proud and native New Yorker.

George Herrera

Former President & CEO,
U.S. Hispanic Chamber of Commerce
Independent Director, Board of Directors,
Wyndham Worldwide Corporation

George Herrera is currently an independent director of the Board of Directors of Wyndham Worldwide Corporation. Previously he served on the Board of Directors of the Cendant Corporation. From 1998 thru 2004, he served as president and CEO of the U.S. Hispanic Chamber of Commerce. During his tenure, Herrera created a $100 million private equity fund, named Hispania Capital Partners.

From 1978 to 1998, Herrera served as president of Burgos and Associates, Inc., the country's leading Hispanic woman-owned management and financial consulting firm. He was the creator of the nationally syndicated television show "Hispanics Today," which was viewed by more than 30 million viewers on NBC, CBS, and ABC networks. In 2016, he was honored with the Lifetime Business Achievement Award by the Hispanic Heritage Awards.

In 2002, Herrera was named a Fellow for the Wharton School, University of Pennsylvania.

Grace Lieblein

Retired Vice President Global Quality,
General Motors
Board Director, Honeywell
Board Member, Southwest Airlines,
American Tower

Born in Lynwood, California, Grace Lieblein earned a bachelor's degree in industrial engineering from General Motors Institute (now Kettering University), and an MBA from Michigan State University.

Lieblein retired as vice president Global Quality of General Motors in 2015, at the time the highest-ranking Latina in the auto industry. She was the first woman to be named as president and managing director of GM Mexico, and she was president and managing director of GM Brazil. Prior she was GM's vice president of global purchasing and supply chain.

Leiblein has been a director on the board of Honeywell since 2012, and joined the board of Southwest Airlines in January 2016. She joined the American Tower Board in 2017 and has served on boards of the Karmanos Cancer institute and the U.S. Chamber of Commerce in Mexico.

Lieblein has been recognized numerous times for her business and technical achievements, including the Michigan Women's Foundation Women of Achievement and Courage award, the Engineer of the Year by Great Minds in STEM, and *Fortune* magazine's 10 Most Powerful Women in Automotive.

Monica C. Lozano

Former Chairman and CEO,
U.S. Hispanic Media, Inc.

Chairman, Aspen Institute Latinos and Society Program

Monica Lozano began her career in 1985 with the Spanish-language daily newspaper *La Opinión* and become publisher in 2004. In 2010, she was named chairman and CEO of the parent company, ImpreMedia and US Hispanic Media. She stepped away from the firm in 2016 and joined the Aspen Institute to chair the newly created Latinos and Society Program. Effective December 2017, she becomes President and CEO of the College Futures Foundation.

Lozano is on the board of directors of Target Corporation, Bank of America, the Rockefeller Foundation, and the University of California Board of Regents. She previously served on the Board of the Walt Disney Company and as a trustee of the University of Southern California.

She was appointed by President Obama to the Council on Jobs and Competitiveness and the President's Economic Recovery Advisory Board. She is a member of the Council on Foreign Relations and the Inter-American Dialogue.

Lou Miramontes

Senior Partner (retired) KPMG
Board Member and Audit Chair
OPORTUN Financial Corporation, Inc.
Board Member, Brown and Caldwell, Inc.

Born in Alameda, California, Lou Miramontes is a senior financial and audit executive with forty years of experience. He worked for thirty-eight years at KPMG where he held various roles, including senior audit partner, managing partner for the KPMG San Francisco office and senior partner for the Latin America region. He has served in operational, leadership, and client service delivery roles throughout his career in the U.S. and internationally.

Miramontes previously served on the corporate advisory council for the Association of Latino Professionals for America (ALPFA), and is currently an Educational Foundation Trustee at California State University, East Bay.

Miramontes has extensive experience supporting board of directors and C-Level executives on governance, compliance, financial reporting, and key operational matters. He is a member of the Board of Directors and Audit Committee chair of OPORTUN Financial Corporation, Inc., and Brown and Caldwell, Inc.

Luis (Lou) P. Nieto, Jr.

President, Nieto Advisory, LLC
President (retired), ConAgra Consumer Foods

Lou Nieto is president of Nieto Advisory LLC, an advisory firm for small and mid-cap consumer foods companies. He retired in 2009 as president of ConAgra's Consumer Foods business. He was previously president of ConAgra Meats, and president/CEO of the Federated Group. He was also a group president and corporate officer of Dean Foods. Early in his career he worked at Mission Foods, Kraft Foods, and Quaker Oats.

Nieto serves on the board of directors for Ryder and Auto Zone. He also serves as board chair of Fresh & Ready Foods, a private equity owned business.

He served as the founding chairman of Cristo Rey Jesuit High School's board of trustees. He was a member of the University of Chicago's College Visiting Committee. He also served as an elected village park district commissioner. He is currently on the Saint Ignatius College Prep board of trustees, the Chicago Community Trust board, and the Academy for Urban School Leadership board.

Nieto earned an MBA at Harvard University and was president of the Latino Association. He earned a BA from the University of Chicago and was elected to the Maroon Key Honorary Society.

Paul Raines

CEO, GameStop Corporation
Board Member, J.C. Penney Company

Paul Raines is the CEO of GameStop Corporation, a global video game retailer operating in fourteen countries that is a Fortune 300 company employing 40,000 people. Prior to joining GameStop, Raines spent eight years with the Home Depot including serving as executive vice president for U.S. stores. Prior to the Home Depot, he worked in global sourcing for L.L. Bean and with Kurt Salmon Associates.

Besides serving on the board of GameStop, he serves on the board of J.C. Penney Company and previously served on the board of Advanced Auto Parts. He is also on the board of Georgia Tech Foundation and on the national board of the Boy Scouts of America.

He has received numerous awards including being name one of the 100 Most Influential Latinos, a Maestro Award and the Distinguished Alumnus Award by the Georgia Tech College of Engineering.

Born in Costa Rica, Raines graduated with a bachelor's degree in industrial and systems engineering from the Georgia Institute of Technology.

Darren Rebelez

President, International House of Pancakes (IHOP)
Board Member, Torchmark Corporation

Darren Rebelez currently serves as president of the iconic International House of Pancakes (IHOP) restaurant brand. He also serves on the Board of Directors of Torchmark Corporation, where he is the chair of the compensation committee.

Rebelez, a retailing and restaurant industry veteran, is the former EVP and COO for 7-Eleven, Inc. He also held leadership positions at Exxon-Mobil Corporation.

Prior to his civilian career, Rebelez was an Army Ranger and Gulf War veteran. A native of San Diego, he is a graduate of the U.S. Military Academy at West Point, where he earned a bachelor of science degree in foreign area studies. He went on to also earn an MBA from the University of Houston.

Outside of work, Rebelez is on the advisory board of the Children of Fallen Patriots organization, which provides college scholarships to children who have lost a parent in the War on Terror.

Sandra Rivera

Senior Vice President and General Manager
Network Platforms Group, Intel Corporation

Sandra L. Rivera is senior vice president and general manager of the Network Platforms Group at Intel Corporation. She is also Intel's 5G executive sponsor and is responsible for guiding Intel's strategy, commitments, and deliverables for 5G.

Rivera joined Intel in 2000. During her Intel career, she has held various marketing and business development roles. In 2015, Intel recognized Rivera with its highest honor, the Intel Achievement Award, for helping to transform the telecommunications industry with Intel architecture technologies and network functions virtualization (NFV). Rivera is also a member of the Intel Hispanic Leadership Council, which consists of Intel's senior most Hispanic executives.

Before joining Intel, Rivera co-founded and served as president of the CTI Authority, a computer telephony distributor; and served as president of the computer telephony division at Catalyst Telecom. She also spent seven years at Dialogic. She started her career as an engineer at Westinghouse Electric Corporation.

Myrna Soto

Corporate Senior Vice President &
Global Chief Information Security Officer, Comcast
Board Member, CMS Energy, Consumers Energy,
Spirit Airlines

Born in Miami, Myrna Soto is corporate SVP and global chief informa-tion security officer at Comcast. Her scope of responsibility includes over fifty business lines within the Comcast portfolio. She is also the executive champion for the Hispanic affinity group at Comcast, "Unidos."

Prior to joining Comcast, Soto served as CISO and vice president of Information Technology Governance for MGM Resorts. She previous-ly held leadership positions with American Express, Royal Caribbean International, Norwegian Cruise Lines and Kemper Insurance.

Soto holds a bachelor's degree from Florida International University, a master of science degree in jndustrial psychology, and a master of business administration degree from Nova Southeastern University. CNET named her one of the top 20 Most Influential Technology Latinos in 2014. She was recognized by *SC* Magazine as one of the Top 10 Power Players for Women in Security in 2015, and named to the Top 100 CISOs list by Hottopics. Most recently she was named to *Fortune* Magazine's List of 50 Most Powerful Latinas and recognized by Multi Channel News as a 2017 Wonder Woman.

Soto is a corporate board director for CMS Energy and Consumers Energy and on the Board for Spirit Airlines. She is an Executive Management Committee board member of the Hispanic IT Execu-tive Council (HITEC).

Luis Ubiñas

President, Board of Trustees,
Pan American Development Foundation
Lead Director, Electronic Arts,
Board Member, CommerceHub, GFR Media,
Shorelight Education

Luis Ubiñas was born in New York City. He is currently president of the Board of Trustees of the Pan American Development Foundation. Ubiñas also serves on the Advisory Board of the United Nations Fund for International Partnerships and the Advisory Committee for the Export Import Bank of the United States. He is a trustee of the New York Public Library, and vice chairman of the Statue of Liberty-Ellis Island Foundation.

Ubiñas is lead director at Electronic Arts, and serves on the Boards of CommerceHub, the publically traded ecommerce backbone company, GFR Media, the largest media company in Puerto Rico, and Shorelight Education.

He served as president of the Ford Foundation from 2008 through 2013. Prior to leading the Ford Foundation, Ubiñas was a director at McKinsey & Company, leading the firm's media practice on the West Coast.

Ubiñas is a graduate of Harvard College, where he graduated magna cum laude and was named a Truman Scholar, and Harvard Business School, where he was a Baker Scholar, graduating with highest honors. He is a Fellow of the American Academy of Arts and Sciences and a member of the Council on Foreign Relations.

LISTINGS

LATINO
LEADERSHIP DEVELOPMENT
PROGRAMS

MANAGEMENT LEADERSHIP DEVELOPMENT: ACCELERATING GROWTH IN YOUR CAREER
Association of Latino Professionals for America (ALPFA)

www.alpfa.org

We have designed two days of intense sessions, through a Hispanic cultural lens, where participants are challenged by the facilitators and each other. We created a highly participatory program where Hispanic middle managers feel engaged and inspired by their newly discovered potential. They are also motivated to apply the freshly developed skills back at work to achieve higher levels of success and grow their careers.

Program Objectives

- Develop critical managerial and leadership skills
- Increase confidence in delivering results
- Become better candidates for internal pipelines into executive positions
- Highlight differences between being a Hispanic manager and being a manager who happens to be Hispanic

Participant Output

- Develop an action plan that will hone their leadership skills
- Follow-up conversation with manager to share the actions committed to as a result of the program and discuss how they will support them in their development
- Refined understanding of their leadership point of view and how it relates to leading
- Established strategy to engage their direct reports to share and infuse the content provided within their teams

MUJERES DE HACE PROGRAM
Hispanic Alliance for Career Enhancement (HACE)

www.haceonline.org

Mujeres de HACE is a leadership program geared to empower high-potential Latina professionals, at manager level or above, to succeed professionally and thrive personally by providing insight, access, and professional development in an effective manner: individualized, culturally relevant and via collaborative, mentoring, and powerful relationships that continue beyond completion of the program.

Key Program Components

- Discovering leadership style and strategic planning
- Developing your personal brand
- Building effective partnerships and networks
- Utilizing financial planning tips and tools
- Practicing negotiation and influence

Participant Benefits

- Deepen your professional network
- Become deeply engaged in the community
- Develop a career plan
- Individualized assessment and executive coaching

HACE LEADERSHIP ACADEMY
Hispanic Alliance for Career Enhancement (HACE)

www.haceonline.org

The HACE Leadership Academy is a dynamic and intensive Action Learning Experience that will transform high-potential Latino professionals into high-performing leaders, by developing the skills necessary to promote immediate and sustainable results for themselves and organizations they serve. The program is designed to address cultural values and challenges.

Key Program Components

- Exclusive access to alumni hosted roundtable discussions
- A robust leadership framework based on sound instructional design and practical application
- Application of tools and techniques to an Impact Project relevant to participating organizations
- A personalized leadership assessment
- One-on-one executive coaching
- Peer-to-peer coaching and facilitated project check-ins and web-based learning

Participant Benefits

- Broaden and deepen your professional network locally and nationally
- Develop essential leadership skills
- Learn best business practices for managing and engaging with teams
- Connect with a mentor upon program completion
- Individualized assessment and executive coaching

THE LATINA GLOBAL EXECUTIVE LEADERSHIP INSTITUTE

Contact Dr. Yasmin Davidds at Yasmin@latinaleadershipacademy.org

The Latina Global Executive Leadership Institute's mission is to mobilize the transformation of Latina mid to senior level managers to executive ranks by:

- Providing high-performing Latina managers with the knowledge, skills and tools to accelerate their development into the executive ranks.
- Providing culturally relevant strategies that allow executive Latina participants to step into leadership roles and promote the value of a bicultural influence.
- Empowering Latina managers to become influential change agent leaders who can align their organization's business initiatives with social responsibility participation.

Program Objectives

- Enable Latinas to understand their leadership journeys by reflecting upon and framing their life stories and experiences.
- Participate fully in open, intimate small-group discussions.
- Understand why leaders lose their way and the self-awareness needed to avoid derailment.
- Gain clarity about leadership principles, values, and ethical boundaries, and how they will respond under pressure when challenged.
- Explore how to build support teams and lead an integrated life.
- Understand the purpose of their leadership and empower other leaders, while they are optimizing their leadership effectiveness.
- Create personal leadership development plans to guide them throughout their lives.

ASCENDER PROGRAM
PepsiCo

www.pepsico.com/company/Diversity-and-Engagement

In 2013 PepsiCo North America Beverages launched Ascender, a yearlong development program for Hispanic talent that enables career growth. Ascender participants who complete the program have a 86 percent promotion rate.

Program Objectives

- Build capability through developmental discussions and interaction with senior Hispanic leaders
- Establish strong networks between peers and senior leadership
- Provide a chance to "give back" by providing insights on Hispanic business opportunities

Key Program Components/Participant Benefits

- Career development
- Two-day development conference
- Executive presence for Latino leaders
- DISC style assessment
- Panel discussion with executive sponsors
- Mentor pod kickoff
- Skill building
- Professional development workshops
- Networking
- Mentor pod action learning project
- Business leaders support
- Touch points and support from business leaders
- Executive leadership exposure
- Relationship building with senior Hispanic executives
- Action learning project team report out to senior leadership team

THE CENTER OF EXCELLENCE FOR LATINO LEADERSHIP
Southern Methodist University (SMU)

SMULLI@smu.edu, or call 214-768-8232

Located in Dallas, the center offers proven leadership development experiences that prepare high achieving Latinos for success in their current managerial positions and equip them for higher career levels.

The Rising Latino Leaders Program (RLLP) prepares individual contributors, supervisors, and first line managers for success in mid-level management. Over five days, practical interactive learning experiences, assessments, exposure to experienced Latino senior managers, and participation in a network of Latino peers enable participants to:

- Transition from individual contributors and supervisors to high potential leaders
- Develop critical business and leadership skills
- Gain awareness of how aspects of Latino culture affect performance and achievement
- Acquire tools to address cultural issues without losing authenticity

SMU also partnered with the National Hispanic Corporate Council to develop and offer the Corporate Executive Development Program.

THE CORPORATE EXECUTIVE DEVELOPMENT PROGRAM (CEDP)
The National Hispanic Corporate Council (NHCC)

www.nhcchq.org

The CEDP, designed and offered in partnership with Southern Methodist University's Cox School of Business, is intended to accelerate Hispanic executive and management careers by producing high potential leaders equipped with the knowledge, skills and tools to succeed. The program is offered in three phases delivered over nine months.

Core program elements:

Phase 1: Leading with Authenticity
Devoted to developing 'self' and understanding the power of culture in executive development.

Phase 2: Leading High-Performance Teams
Participants learn to leverage cultural diversity in others to maximize the performance of work units and teams and to work effectively across borders.

Phase 3: Becoming a Corporate Leader
Participants learn to apply heightened cultural awareness and develop social capital needed to lead strategic thinking, innovation, and change at enterprise levels.

Assessment
Each participant undergoes an assessment of individual competencies based on those identified with successful executive leadership.

Project
Participants work in small teams where they use their newly acquired knowledge to develop a business project in social entrepreneurship.

HISPANIC IT EXECUTIVE COUNCIL (HITEC)
Emerging Executive Program

www.hitecglobal.org

The Emerging Executive Program (EEP) develops emerging Hispanic IT leaders with the highest potential and desire to become the next generation of Hispanic IT Executive leaders. A critical component of HITEC's success is our Emerging Executive Program, which is a cornerstone of our core mission: to develop future Hispanic IT and business leaders.

EEP is more than mentoring. It's a fundamental shift in the approach towards developing a core executive skill set. EEP provides:

- A model to cultivate Hispanic IT expertise
- Exposure and interaction with high-level IT executives and business leaders
- A trusted and non-biased relationship with senior-IT executive (including HITEC Board Members)
- Guidance on career-related issues, which are unique to Hispanics in leadership
- Deeper understanding on how the CXOs develop their organizations in terms of core IT competencies and performance metrics
- An opportunity to elevate leadership through insightful executive coaching
- Webinars that will reinforce the skills needed to execute as an Emerging Leader

LIDERAMOS

www.lideramos.org

Launched in 2015, LIDERAMOS is an organization whose core mission is to improve and ignite leadership in the Latino community. LIDERAMOS will enhance and develop Latino Leadership Programs to strengthen a nation of diverse leaders who are culturally aware, civically engaged and community-serving, providing effective leadership for a multicultural society.

LIDERAMOS was formed to enhance existing programs and initiative programs in areas where none exist. LIDERAMOS has created a Latino Leadership Program Directory that lists existing programs in the Latino community.

LIDERAMOS aims to triple the number of leadership programs serving Latinos by 2022. America's future well-being is closely tied to the preparation and deployment of a critical mass of Latino leaders. LIDERAMOS is run by a Leadership Council composed of prominent thought leaders, leadership practitioners and experts who are committed to advancing the leadership capacity of the Latino community.

THE LATINO LEADERSHIP INSTITUTE
University of Denver

info@latinoslead.org

The Latino Leadership Institute (LLI) at the University of Denver (DU) is a premier professional development program advancing an elite network of Latino leaders. Through its exceptional Fellowship Program, the Institute prepares Latino leaders for the highest levels of influence in the business, education, government, and nonprofit sectors.

With the context that Latinos have contributed significantly to the U.S. for centuries, the LLI believes that all organizations innovate the most when their leadership reflects the diverse population of our country. We also believe in having a long-term measurable impact on the lives of Fellows, and the communities in which they work. To foster this impact, the LLI provides Fellows with the networks and knowledge to maximize the civic, economic, and political potential of the growing Latino community.

The Institute offers a rigorous nine-month certificate program that incorporates ninety-eight hours of course sessions focused on personal and professional development, board service, corporate finance, economics, nonprofit management, and public policy. The initial session is an outdoor Challenge Course that offers Fellows an inspiring opportunity for personal and professional growth while enhancing group interaction.

THE LATINO LEADERSHIP INTENSIVE
A Rigorous Two-Day Latino-Centric Leadership Development Experience

Contact Dr. Robert Rodriguez at Robert@drradvisors.com or Angel Gomez at Angel@angelgomez.co

The demand for capable, "Ready Now" Latino talent continues to grow. However, companies needing more Latino leaders are finding they lack the internal and external resources to build that talent pool quickly. That is why Dr. Robert Rodriguez and Angel Gomez have created the Latino Leadership Intensive—a concentrated two-day program to develop mid-career Latino professionals.

The Latino Leadership Intensive delivers cutting-edge content through a concentrated and sound instructional design based on Dr. Rodriguez's research on Latino development needs and Gomez's innovative adult learning methodology. The purpose of the Intensive is to provide Hispanic professionals with a rigorous learning experience focused on applying practical skills and techniques all through a Hispanic leadership lens.

Key concepts covered:

- Challenges faced by Latino and Latina leaders
- Applying collaboration skills
- Emotional intelligence and organizational awareness
- Making inclusive decisions
- Active listening as a leadership practice
- Acting strategically in problem solving
- Giving and receiving feedback
- Coaching and developing others
- Managing conflict and leveraging your influence
- Manifesting as a Latino leader

EFFICACY FOR LATINO PROFESSIONALS
Korn Ferry

www.kornferry.com/diversity

Efficacy, defined simply, is the ability to achieve the desired results. For Latinos and Latinas there often have been too few leaders that look like them to achieve this in corporate settings. In addition, there are multiple social and corporate culture barriers that create headwinds for Latinos and Latinas to be able to rise to the fullness of their potential.

Efficacy training helps Latinos and Latinas gain the skills and strategies needed to accelerate professional development by enhancing personal effectiveness by becoming clear about their life and career ambitions and then setting out strategies and action plans to achieve them.

The two, two-day programs are delivered approximately one month apart by one Korn Ferry facilitator, or a company's own trainer, certified through a train-the trainer program. Multiple post-program coaching options are also available.

On completing the course, Efficacy participants will be able to:

- Understand the headwinds they face in the workplace as Latinos and Latinas
- Create a plan for ongoing professional development.
- Demonstrate high levels of confidence and skills in the intellectual, influential, and relational arenas.
- Sustain high performance and increase promotional opportunities through continuous skill development.
- Develop a strategic problem-solving approach to managing personal and organizational obstacles.
- Reach an understanding with managers on perceived value of their contribution.

HISPANIC ASSOCIATION ON CORPORATE RESPONSIBILITY

www.hacr.org

The HACR Corporate Directors Summit™ brings together seasoned Hispanic leaders serving on publicly-traded companies and large private enterprises boards, to share best governance practices for effective corporate board service.

Key Program Components:

• Strategic board practices
• Trends in corporate boards
• By invitation only

The HACR Corporate Executives Forum™ was created to provide the most senior Hispanic corporate executives at Fortune 500 companies with a forum to discuss business issues, challenges, and solutions.

Key Program Components:

• Corporate board readiness coaching
• Employee resource groups best practices
• By invitation only

The HACR Corporate Achievers Summit™ program was developed to motivate, empower, and reconnect past HACR Young Hispanic Corporate Achievers™ participants.

Key Program Components:

• Leadership development
• Personal branding
• HACR YHCA Alumni only

The HACR Young Hispanic Corporate Achievers™ program was developed as a way to recognize the outstanding achievements of young Hispanic professionals in Corporate America.

Key Program Components:

• Trajectory to future executive ascension
• Cultural foundations of leadership
• By nomination only

The HACR Leadership Pipeline Program provides companies with a forum to develop their Hispanic employee resource group leaders, as well as mid and upper level Hispanic corporate leaders.

Key Program Components:

• Develop leadership and managerial skills
• Personal branding

SURVEY RESULTS

We conducted two separate online surveys to capture the beliefs, sentiments, and experiences of Latino executives and Latinx professionals. The Latino Executive Survey was fielded between March and April 2017 and received twenty responses. The Latinx Professional Survey was fielded between April and May 2017 and received 302 responses. Here are some of the most interesting answers. Specific findings from the overall results have been used throughout the book to support various observations.

Where were you born?

Executives

Gen X/Millennials

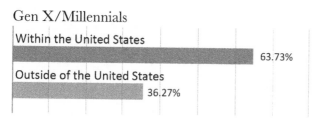

Where were you mostly raised?

Executives

Mostly, or entirely, in the United States
75%

Mostly, or entirely, outside of the United States
20%

Raised equally inside the U.S. and outside the U.S.
5%

Gen X/Millennials

Mostly, or entirely, in the United States
75.4%

Mostly, or entirely, outside of the United States
19.09%

Raised equally inside the U.S. and outside the U.S.
5.05%

From a language speaking perspective, are you...

Executives

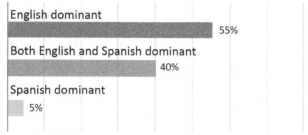

English dominant
55%

Both English and Spanish dominant
40%

Spanish dominant
5%

Gen X/Millennials

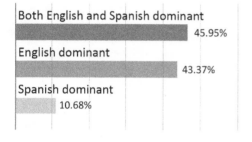

Both English and Spanish dominant
45.95%

English dominant
43.37%

Spanish dominant
10.68%

Was Spanish your first language?

Executives

Yes
50%

No
40%

Learned Spanish and English at the same time
10%

Gen X/Millennials

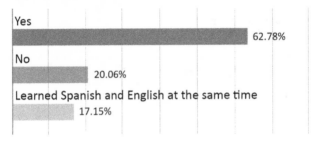

Yes
62.78%

No
20.06%

Learned Spanish and English at the same time
17.15%

Please identify the five most positive aspects of Hispanic heritage that have contributed to your personal and career success:

Executives

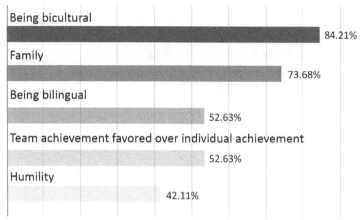

Being bicultural — 84.21%
Family — 73.68%
Being bilingual — 52.63%
Team achievement favored over individual achievement — 52.63%
Humility — 42.11%

Gen X/Millennials

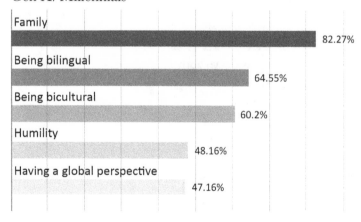

Family — 82.27%
Being bilingual — 64.55%
Being bicultural — 60.2%
Humility — 48.16%
Having a global perspective — 47.16%

Please identify the five biggest hurdles, as experienced in the workplace, of your Hispanic heritage that have negatively impacted your career:

Executives

Gen X/Millennials

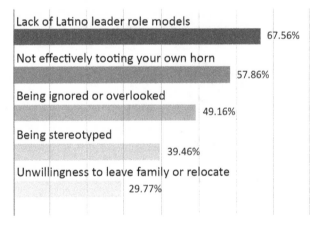

Regarding your Latino heritage, how much have you chosen to show in the workplace?

Executives

I have not held back or hidden any part of my Latino identity

57.89%

I have had to hide or downplay some parts of my Latino identity

31.58%

I identify as Latino in my personal life, but not in the workplace

5.26%

I don't identify as Latino in my personal life or in the workplace

0%

Gen X/Millennials

I have not held back or hidden any part of my Latino identity

69.26%

I have had to hide or downplay some parts of my Latino identity

22.64%

I identify as Latino in my personal life, but not in the workplace

4.05%

I don't identify as Latino in my personal life or in the workplace

1.01%

In the settings when you were in the minority in the workplace, how did it make you feel? (Check all that apply)

Executives

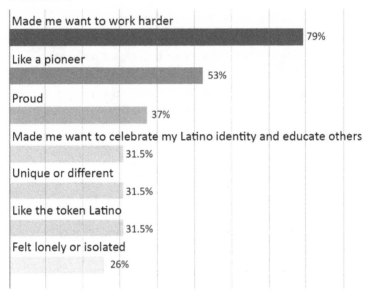

Made me want to work harder — 79%

Like a pioneer — 53%

Proud — 37%

Made me want to celebrate my Latino identity and educate others — 31.5%

Unique or different — 31.5%

Like the token Latino — 31.5%

Felt lonely or isolated — 26%

Gen X/Millennials

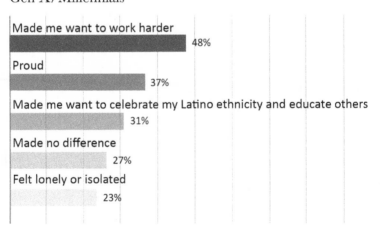

Made me want to work harder — 48%

Proud — 37%

Made me want to celebrate my Latino ethnicity and educate others — 31%

Made no difference — 27%

Felt lonely or isolated — 23%

In addition to having the right skills and achieving results, what do you consider the top five keys to your career success? Rank order the top five:

Executives

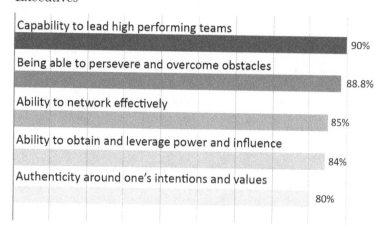

Capability to lead high performing teams	90%
Being able to persevere and overcome obstacles	88.8%
Ability to network effectively	85%
Ability to obtain and leverage power and influence	84%
Authenticity around one's intentions and values	80%

Gen X/Millennials

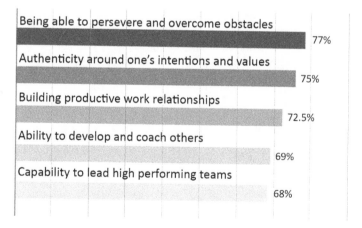

Being able to persevere and overcome obstacles	77%
Authenticity around one's intentions and values	75%
Building productive work relationships	72.5%
Ability to develop and coach others	69%
Capability to lead high performing teams	68%

Have your most important mentors been:

Executives

Gen X/Millennials

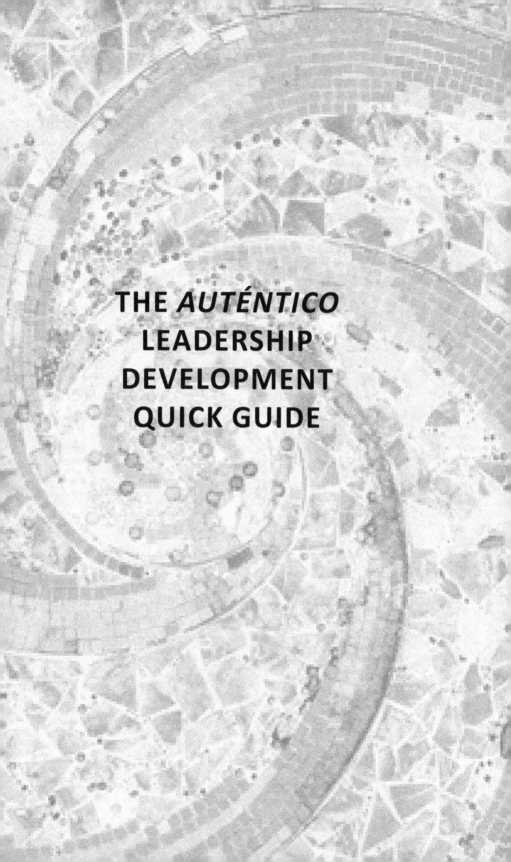

THE *AUTÉNTICO* LEADERSHIP DEVELOPMENT QUICK GUIDE

Throughout the book we have presented leadership concepts, dilemmas, challenges, and opportunities through the stories of Latino executives and rising Latinx talent. To help you with tactics to further your leadership development, we have created this *Auténtico Leadership Development Quick Guide*. It contains the following:

Summary of the key points discussed in each chapter of the book.

These are meant to allow a revisiting at a quick glance of each chapter's key findings and messages.

Reflection questions for each chapter.

These are intended to enable personal discovery of how best to link the chapter content to one's own experiences and reality. These questions can also be used for group discussion in book clubs, training, or employee resource group activities.

Developmental activities and actions.

These are intended to further guide you in steps you can take to gain skills and mastery of the concepts explored throughout the book.

Keep in mind that this development quick guide is intended to be a supplement to standard professional growth and leadership development. Latino professionals still need to gain proficiency in leadership concepts such as business acumen, decision making, conflict resolution, strategic planning, execution, financial management, etc. In addition, Latinos must still perform well in their roles and deliver results to advance.

The developmental activities outlined below will further complement and enhance your professional growth, emotional intelligence, and connection with your Latino heritage to set you on a path toward transformational Latino leadership.

Take flight. ✎⤙

PART 1
OUTER FORCES:
THE CHALLENGE OF BEING LATINO IN CORPORATE AMERICA

"Welcome. We love your differences—now just be like us."

Chapter 1
The Myths of Meritocracy and Color-Blind Corporate Cultures

Chapter Summary Points

- The tenets of meritocracy put work environments on a path that is supposed to be color-blind and gender neutral.

- Non merit factors suppress, neutralize, or even negate the effects of merit, creating barriers to individual Hispanic mobility in corporate America.

- Only 4 percent of executive officer positions in Fortune 500 firms are held by Hispanics.

- Latinos face both conscious and unconscious biases. These realities of Latinos experiencing discrimination and bias in the workplace undermine the promise of meritocracy.

- Making it even more difficult to overcome the myth of meritocracy is the current sociocultural environment in the U.S. leading to the rise of anti-immigrant sentiments and policies.

- Organizational leaders must move from mere awareness that these biases exist and additionally take proactive steps to provide Latino talent with exposure to other leaders and opportunities for stretch assignments.

Reflection Questions

- How diverse is the organization you work with and what is the Latino/Latina representation within that diversity?

- What is your organization's current state of including minorities, and in particular, the Latino dimensions of that inclusion?

- How do unconscious biases toward Latinos and other groups manifest in your organization?

- What are you doing now to help shed light on these realities?

- What could you be doing that you are not doing now to further make the organization aware of the gaps between their aspiration for a meritocracy and the reality?

Developmental Activities

❏ Seek out information related to your company's high potential and leadership development programs and initiatives.

❏ Determine what percentage of your organization's top leadership are Hispanic.

❏ Attend a workshop on unconscious bias to become more familiar with how bias manifests itself in the workplace and to gain greater understanding of your own biases.

❏ Study the leadership competencies valued and endorsed by your company. Seek out ways to enhance your proficiency in these areas.

❏ Become intimately familiar with your company's performance management systems and how they identity future leaders. Find your human resource representative to become acquainted with the process and then discuss your potential with your manager.

❏ Become more familiar with current immigration policy and legislation. Identity potential ways you can support initiatives aimed at fighting for immigrant rights.

❏ Support politicians who are strong advocates for immigration and for DREAMers initiatives.

Chapter 2
Identity Crisis: Assimilate, Opt Out, or Double Down?

Chapter Summary Points

- Latino identity relies heavily on how individuals choose to deal with their cultural surroundings.

- Unapologetic Latinos are leaders who all along have fully embraced their Latino identity and chosen not to cover any of it, even in the most non-Latino of environments.

- Equivocal Latinos are leaders who have some boundaries about their sense of Latino identity because of European-American values they were heavily exposed to in their formative years and in their educational and career formation.

- Retro Latinos are leaders who may have grown up as Equivocal Latinos but who for a variety of reasons in adulthood have gone back to their Latino roots to discover or rediscover those elements of a distant or submerged heritage and culture.

- Invisible Latinos are ones who have fully denied and disowned any connection to Latino culture deliberately, whether they grew up in a Latino environment or not.

Reflection Questions

- Which of the four Latino identity archetypes (Unapologetic, Equivocal, Retro, or Invisible) do you most relate with? Why?

- What insight have you gained about how you have managed your Latino identity in the past?

- Are you content with your current sense of Latino identity, or do you feel you have more internal exploration and changes to do before you will feel centered and at peace with your cultural Latino identity?

- If needed, what steps do you want to take to resolve your uncertainty about your Latino identity?

- How will you involve other Latinos and non-Latinos in your search for cultural identity process?

Developmental Activities

❏ Read the essay by Bernardo Ferdman and Plácida Gallegos titled "Racial Identity Development and Latinos in the United States." Determine where you fall on their continuum of Latino identity.

❏ Meet with someone you would categorize as an Unapologetic Latino and ask where they get the courage and resolve to connect with their Hispanic heritage so actively and visibly.

❏ Mentor a Latino high school student and discuss their relationship with their Hispanic identity. Answer their questions and raise their awareness about identity.

❏ Because we are not aware of their full story and their journey, commit to not judge any Invisible Latinos you meet. We have no right to pass judgment on how others choose to connect, or not connect, with their Hispanic heritage.

Chapter 3
Intra-Latino Divides: Truth or Consequences

Chapter Summary Points

- In the US the most divisive differences among Latinos are the ones around national heritage. These nationalistic fissures are the most debilitating in terms of Latinos gaining collective power commensurate to their rising numbers.

- The Latino community also carries a legacy of classism that is more powerful than racism in Latin culture. This creates socioeconomic differences that often overlap with the national identities divide.

- Latinos can also carry biases against people of different races. Latinos are not exempt from expressions of racism toward those with darker skin.

- Latinos can also be judged by other Latinos for their accented Spanish or English, or for not speaking Spanish at all.

- There are apparent divides among Latinos who grew up in Latin America and those Latinos who grew up in the U.S..

- Latinos are beginning to connect with the reality that their growing numbers will only translate into greater power and influence if there is a greater sense of common Pan-Latino purpose and unity.

- Successful Latino executives often learn to not view Latino identity as an either/or dilemma but as a both/and celebration. Their key to not being lost in the cultural identity maze is to embrace a bicultural identity.

Reflection Questions

- In the part of the region where you live and work, do you see and experience evidence of intra-Latino divides? If so, what are they?

- What are the divides that you experience most personally—both on the receiving end and on the reinforcing end?

- What, if anything, are individuals and organizations doing in your region to bridge intra-Latino divides?

- What are you doing currently to bridge the divides?

- What could you be doing that you are not doing now to bridge the divides?

Developmental Activities

❏ If you are not fluent in Spanish, enroll in a program to gain proficiency in the Spanish language.

❏ When meeting with Latin American friends, commit to practicing and speaking more Spanish to enhance fluency.

❏ Subscribe to Hispanic publications such as *Hispanic Executive* magazine, *LATINO* magazine or *Latino Leaders* magazine. Read the profiles of successful Hispanic leaders and gain insights from their diverse backgrounds.

❏ Visit a Latin American country to learn more about its culture, history, politics, and economy.

❏ Visit Latino enclaves in the U.S. you have not previously visited.

❏ Become more knowledgeable about current Latino research and demographic statistics. Start with reading current research from Pew Research Center—Hispanic Trends (www.pewhispanic.org).

❏ Commit to learn more about at least one different Latin American country each year.

❏ Read more Hispanic American and Latin American literature. Start by checking out the authors who we quoted at the opening of various chapters. Other Hispanic and Latin American authors just to get you started: Julia Alvarez, Richard Rodriguez, Junot Díaz, Mario Vargas Llosa, and Isabel Allende.

❏ Assess your own viewpoints and feelings toward Latinos from other nationalities.

❏ Seek out more information about the experience of Afro-Latinos in the U.S.

❏ Refrain from criticizing Hispanics who date or marry non-Hispanics.

❏ Write a letter to yourself that outlines an action plan of tactics you can implement in the next six months to further embrace your Latino identity. Seal the letter and give to someone to mail to you in six months. Hold
yourself accountable if you haven't completed the items in your letter.

❏ Along with supporting the U.S., support Latin American teams in the next World Cup. Attend viewing parties.

Chapter 4
Culture Clash: Can Corporate Cultures and Latino Cultures Be Reconciled?

Chapter Summary Points

- For too long the burden has been put on Latinos to assimilate to the norms of the dominant culture. Not only can this be detrimental to Latinos' own sense of personal identity and empowerment, but corporations then lose out on benefiting from the differences in perspectives and backgrounds that Latinos bring to the workplace.

- Cultures have differing beliefs about whether they can control the environment around them or not. Internal control cultures are those who believe they can, and external control cultures believe they cannot. European- American culture, and by extension, corporate America, tends to believe the former, and Hispanic American culture the latter.

- Latinos can tend to be hierarchical compared to the egalitarian European- American approach. This tendency can cut both ways in terms of emerging Latino talent acting with insufficient self-agency and Latino leaders acting with too much directedness.

- The all-in enveloping nature of *familia* in the Latino ethos comes from a sense of communal identity—who I am is defined by whom I belong to versus the more European-American interpretation of individualistic identity—who I am is defined by myself.

- European Americans tend to seek reassurance in the rules, while Latinos can tend to seek redress in the particulars of each circumstance.

- European Americans tend to be ruled more by the clock, whereas Latinos more by the event—the former making the task at hand the top priority, the latter making the *gestalt* of the whole group most important, making them more likely to stay in the moment rather than cutting it short artificially due a scheduled clock time.

- Latino culture tends to value showing the emotion, while European-American culture can be more about restraining the display of emotion.

- Some of the very things Latinos are criticized for are the very things that are valued and nurtured in Latino culture. Unconsciously, the corporate values that are exalted and held as universal standards for what a great leader and executive looks like are those from the European-American context.

- Corporations need to stop saying they want to hire Latinos for their differences and then coach them into assimilation by asking them to set aside those differences.

Reflection Questions

- Do you see evidence of these culture clashes within your organization?

- If so, specifically how do these culture clashes show up in terms of group dynamics or one-on-one interactions with leaders, managers, and peers?

- Along a spectrum between the two opposites of the seven cultural dimensions shared in the chapter, where would you place yourself?

- Where would you place the cultural norms of that part of the organization that you interact with the most? How much of a gap is there between you and the organization?

- What can you do to help those whose beliefs are different from the Latino cultural norms better connect with the many Latinos who are culturally different from them?

- Where can Latinos demonstrate some cultural adaption to the majority culture without losing their own sense of uniqueness and identity?

Developmental Activities

❏ Read *Riding the Waves of Culture: Understanding Diversity in Global Business* by Fons Trompenaars and Charles Hampden-Turner and *Cultures and Organizations: Software of the Mind* by Geert Hofstede, Gert Jan Hofstede and Michael Minkov. Learn about how the full spectrum of cultural dimensions show up in work environments.

❏ Take the Intercultural Development Inventory (IDI) and have it professionally debriefed to find out your disposition toward differences. Extra credit: Also have your manager take the IDI and share with each other what you learned in the process.

❏ Enroll in one of external Latino leadership programs outlined in the appendix of this book including the course on Latino Efficacy offered by Korn Ferry or the two-day Latino Leadership Intensive program offered by Dr. Robert Rodriguez and Angel Gómez.

❏ Sponsor or fund a younger Latino professional's enrollment in a Latino leadership development program.

❏ Offer to be a resource to your company's recruiting and talent acquisition group on how to best recruit/source top Latino talent.

❏ Meet with someone in marketing at your company and gain insights on how they are reaching out to the Latino consumers and then determine what insights you can offer.

❏ Volunteer for a new assignment or committee at work. Do not wait to be asked.

❏ Define your own personal brand. Establish your own strategy for articulating your own capabilities and contributions without coming across as arrogant.

PART 2
INNER FORCES:
SECRETS TO RISE AS A TRANSFORMATIVE LEADER

"Al Mal Viento, Buena Cara" ("In Bad Winds, a Strong Face")

Chapter 5
Reaching Outward: Education at All Costs

Chapter Summary Points

- Just 15 percent of Hispanics have a bachelor's degree or higher compared to 41 percent for Whites, 22 percent for Blacks, and 63 percent for Asians.

- Pew Research Center's Hispanic Trends reveals that the importance that Latino families place on a college education has markedly increased over the past few years with 88 percent agreeing that a college degree is necessary to get ahead today versus the opinions about college by only 74 percent of Whites. This shift in attitude is a driving factor in the growing numbers of Latinos enrolled in college.

- The expanded horizons produced by a college education create a ripple effect that goes beyond the individual students, spreading through their immediate and extended families and into the Latino community at large.

- As demographic trends continue to prove, the workforce of the future will have an increasingly Latino identity. Latino student success is not only an issue for Latinos, but also for the entire U.S. As Latino education attainment rises, so does economic opportunity for the whole country.

Reflection Questions

- What were the messages you heard from your family regarding education?

- What impact did these messages have on your motivation and the choices you made about your future?

- What were some of the biggest obstacles you had to overcome in the educational system? How did you overcome them?

- What messages are you sharing with your family and community about education?

- What actions are you taking about higher education for Latinos?
- What role could your organization play in helping increase the number of Latinos who go to college?

Developmental Activities

❑ Contribute to the Hispanic Scholarship Fund or any other nonprofit organization that raises money to give scholarships to young Latino students.

❑ Enroll in a degree program to enhance your level of educational attainment.

❑ Consider teaching at a local community college or university to serve as a role model for young Hispanic students and to give back to the community.

❑ Volunteer to be a guest speaker to a Latino student organization.

❑ Advocate for your company to consider recruiting at Hispanic Serving Institutions and to support the Hispanic Association of Colleges and Universities (HACU).

❑ Volunteer to participate in recruiting events attended by your corporation to visibly support such efforts and to advocate for the hiring of Latino graduates.

❑ Offer to serve as a mentor or coach in one of the Latino leadership programs offered by academia, Hispanic nonprofits or internal corporate programs.

❑ Partner with the Latino ERG (employee resource group) at your company to raise awareness of tuition reimbursement benefits offered by your company. This could encourage more Latino professionals to seek additional education.

❑ Serve on your local Parent Teacher Association (PTA) to raise awareness of education issues faced by Hispanic students.

❑ Take your children or Hispanic students to visit college campuses and universities before they reach their sophomore year in high school.

❑ Watch the movie *Stand and Deliver* about Jaime Escalante and his work with Hispanic high school students. Identity key themes that you can help spread across the Latino community.

Chapter 6
How to Be: Three Key Traits of Transformational Leaders

Chapter Summary Points

- The Latino executives tend to have talent and ability, but most importantly, they also have *ganas*, that hard-to-translate Latino term that conveys pursuing any endeavor with total heart, body, mind, and soul. Ambition drives them to dedicate their lives to hard work, the perfection of a craft, long hours, and a willingness to sacrifice for the sake of having the life they wished to attain.

- In the quest to fill the pipeline of future leaders, Latinos must acknowledge that ambition is a good thing and should be encouraged.

- Latino professionals need to give themselves permission to be pioneers and to explore career opportunities that may not have guarantees. They must be open to following a path without a clear roadmap. To be a transformative leader, Latinos must be comfortable taking risks.

- Transformational Latino leaders must also know how to cultivate relationships, both inside their organization and externally.

- While connecting with other Latinos has proven to be a successful way to leverage relationships, Latinos often make the mistake—particularly early in their careers—of cultivating relationships only with people who are similar to them or who are part of their peer group.

- Transformational leaders look outside their immediate circle and develop relationships with people who are not like them.

- The benefits of being able to manage relationships effectively are many and varied. The key distinction for transformational Latino leaders is that for them relationship building was not considered additional work—it *was* the work.

- Apply for promotions and career opportunities for which you may not feel qualified. If not selected, use the feedback to gain insights on areas to better prepare for future opportunities.

- Accept career opportunities when offered that stretch your capabilities and extend you beyond your comfort zone.

Reflection Questions

- Do you struggle with having ambition and taking risks? If so, why?
- What steps can you take to get more comfortable with having more explicit ambition?
- What steps can you take to get more comfortable with taking more risks in your work and career?
- In what ways can you be a mentor and a role model for other Latinos so they will show more ambition and take more risks?
- How strong is your network within the organization (at every level— C-suite, senior leadership, management, peers)?
- How strong is your networking outside the organization (Latino and non-Latino people and organizations)?

Developmental Activities

- ❏ Create a long-term career plan that outlines a path to obtain a position you highly desire.
- ❏ Take the Developmental Network Questionnaire offered by *Harvard Business Review* to analyze your professional network and to identify any gaps.
- ❏ Review your current professional network and reach out to those you have not recently connected with to re-establish and strengthen the relationship.
- ❏ Discuss the issue of relocation with your family and revisit any reservations that may have been preventing you from considering a broader array of career opportunities.
- ❏ If you belong to a professional association or employee resource group, pursue a leadership role within the group.
- ❏ Learn how your company supports the Latino community via their community affairs and foundation efforts. Advocate for more support of the Latino community if current funding is minimal or nonexistent.
- ❏ Volunteer to serve on the board of a nonprofit organization supporting Latinos.

Chapter 7
What to Do: Three Key Competencies of Transformational Leaders

Chapter Summary Points

- Latinos must learn to master the politics that determine how things get done within the corporate culture. A person cannot survive very long when breaking into the leadership ranks without this knowledge. Yet there is a delicate balance here; authentic leaders will recognize the warning signs of nearing the danger zone of compromising their own uniqueness and of losing themselves by hewing too closely to corporate norms.

- When credibility, working within the system, and relationships have been established, transformative leaders don't just stay with the pack—they find ways to differentiate. By doing so, they begin to formulate and shape their unique leadership style. In other words, having mastered the cultural rules, they know when and where to break them. The Latino executives who have done the foundational work of being authentically grounded in their cultural identity can now find outlets through which their diverse views and behaviors can flow outward, and in that, differentiate their leadership.

- Giving back to the community requires the trait of a generous spirit combined with the competence to do it well. The arc of transformative Latino executives is not complete until their accomplishments have elevated them and have spilled over into bettering the lives and prospects of individuals and groups outside the leaders' corporate world.

- Transformational Latino leaders realize that if they don't get involved in the process of making a difference and clearing the way for more Latinos to advance in the corporate world, they cannot complain about the lack of a Latino pipeline.

Reflection Questions

- Where can you demonstrate the three competencies we discuss in this chapter? (understanding corporate culture, establishing and shaping a leadership style, and giving back)?

- When you demonstrate the three competencies, how and where can you contribute even more?

- Where are your shortcomings?
- Where you don't implement the competencies, what are the reasons for your shortcomings, and what can you do to enhance that competency?

Developmental Activities

❏ Read about corporate culture, including Edgar Schein's books, *Corporate Culture and Leadership*, and *The Corporate Culture Survival Guide* and assess your company's culture to gain understanding.

❏ Meet with your mentor or mentee and discuss your organization's corporate culture and its implications.

❏ Use a behavioral assessment tool such as Myers-Briggs, HBDI (Hermann Brain Dominance Instrument) or DiSC to gain insights on your behavioral tendencies and how they impact your leadership style.

❏ Set a goal to visibly and significantly contribute to the broader community within the next six months and hold yourself accountable.

❏ Have an honest conversation with another Latino professional who may not be giving back to the Latino community and see if you can help them get started.

❏ Serve on a nonprofit board to gain governance experience.

Chapter 8
Power Ambivalence: The Achilles Heel

Chapter Summary Points

- In a world with massive forces holding back broader Latino achievement, there is a deeper reservoir of power that Latino leaders could be tapping into to exponentially amplify the positive impact they already have.

- African-Americans in the U.S. have a different relationship to power than Latinos. This is because Latinos and African-Americans have different philosophies about interacting with power, different leadership role models, and different institutional responses—all of which have led to different outcomes.

- Latinos must engage in the dual process of being less ambivalent about power while at the same time differentiating their approach to power in a way that is grounded in, and not in conflict with, Latino sensitivities and ethos.

- When Latinos fail to fully live out our values of *comunidad* (community), we are not only contributing to exclusion in a world that is rife with leaving people out because of their differences, but we are also hurting our collective ability to advance—and that of individual Latinos to rise to the fullness of their potential.

- The Power of Biography—Latinos need to see their biographies as an asset with value that leads to powerful insights and ideas. To gain this perspective, Latinos must engage in cultural reflection and soul searching on a consistent basis as it relates to Latino biography, thus allowing Latino leaders to be guardians of their Hispanic heritage.

- Power of a Global Perspective—Because ours is a history shaped by 27 different nations, Latinos epitomize what it means to be global. We can provide an ideal archetype to corporate America of what a global leader could be. Ours is a community with a rich history of bringing diverse groups together to construct a collective identity. In today's global economy, this essential facility is a unique gift offered by Latinos.

- The Power of Sacrifice—Latino power dictates that supporting the greater Latino community is not an option, but rather an obligation.

- Power will come when forged through collaboration because it leverages our strength in building relationships. Yet let's accept that we won't always maintain *simpatía* (likeability, friendliness, and solidarity) with others while advocating for the advancement of the Latino talent agenda. We have to learn to address uncomfortable power dynamics instead of perpetuating our acquiescence.

- Let's acknowledge that no one will give us power so we must always be in the pursuit of it. Furthermore, let's recognize that when we withdraw from the power game, it is not absolution but rather abdication.

- We must speak truth to power: to the majority culture about both the corporate 4 Percent Shame, and about their need to put action behind their words of valuing diversity. Their words are meaningless, and we would all be better off without them if they are not willing to lead the change. We also need to speak truth to power to those leaders within our Latino community who aren't doing enough to promote Latino advancement and celebrate those who do.

- Our concern for the collective good of the Latino community obligates us to challenge injustices imposed on Latinos. Whenever we feel personal unease in advocating for Latino issues, we can gain strength, courage, and resolve by leveraging our existing mindset where the needs of Latino community supersede any one of our individual needs.

Reflection Questions

- What is your own relationship with power? Beliefs, feelings, and actions around it?
- How are you attempting to gain more power within the position you are currently in?
- What can you do to gain more power and yet do so in a way that remains true to your cultural identify?

Developmental Activities

- ❏ Read *The Power of Latino Leadership* by Juana Bordas. Apply some of the key concepts outlined.
- ❏ Revisit your family's history and assess if you are doing all you can to repay them for all the hard work and sacrifices they made to provide you with a better standard of living and new opportunities.
- ❏ Take a professional development course on conflict management and dealing with conflict. Remember that just because someone may not agree with your point of view does not mean they do not like you.
- ❏ Read about or attend a professional development workshop focused on power and politics in organizations.
- ❏ Take a personal assessment of the power that you possess and identify ways to leverage it for the benefit of the broader Latino community.
- ❏ If you participate in talent review or high-level discussions of potential advancements within your organization, advocate for deserving Latino professionals who are being overlooked.

❑ Actively serve as an executive sponsor for Latino professionals who are performing at a high level and have potential within your organization.

❑ Consider establishing an internal Latino officer caucus consisting of the most senior Hispanics within your company to advocate for Latino talent initiatives.

❑ Take an assessment aimed at determining your emotional intelligence (EQ).

❑ Visibly and actively advocate for Latino causes and issues within your company.

❑ Advocate for the creation of an internal Latino talent summit to bring together the top Latino professionals within your company. Identity ways Latinos can support business initiatives.

❑ Become more knowledgeable of current Latino authors and thought leaders who are advocating for the advancement of Latino professionals. Sponsor these authors and leaders as speakers for organizational meetings.

❑ Review Latino representation in internal management, leadership, and executive development programs and advocate for a higher percentage of Latino participation.

❑ Encourage your company's supply department to diversify and identity Latino vendors and Hispanic-owned businesses who qualify. Connect them with the U.S. Hispanic Chamber of Commerce.

❑ Get involved in initiatives designed to raise Latino voter registration and voter turnout.

❑ Read the book *Cracking the Corporate Code* by Price Cobbs. Conduct your own comparison on how African-American executives deal with the issue of power with the approach taken mostly by Latinos.

❑ Take a professional development course on influencing skills.

❑ Develop a plan of action for gaining more power and influence within your organization.

❑ Support Hispanic-owned business. Watch and attend plays that have a Latino theme. Purchase books by Latino authors. Seek out the services of physicians, attorneys, accountants and financial advisors who are Latino.

Chapter 9
The Next Generation of Latino Leaders: Latinx Learns, Challenges, and Rises

Chapter Summary Points

- Young Latinos are choosing to fight to maintain their Hispanic identity and consider it a worthwhile struggle. In essence, they see their Latino-ness as an asset and as a differentiator, adopting a bicultural identity in which they still embrace their American-ness. They celebrate and accept their Latino identity as another dimension of who they are.

- This is not to say that Latino identity is not a complex issue for young Latinos, it is just that Latinx Millennials are more willing to lean into their identity.

- Young Latinos see their biculturalism as a competitive advantage in the workplace. Unlike some of the Latino executives interviewed who entered organizations when their Hispanic heritage was seen as a disadvantage, today's young Latinos are manifesting their biculturalism as part of their career strategy, viewing it as something that will serve them well in business.

- Young, upwardly mobile Latinos, have a clearer outlook, greater maturity, and a much more sophisticated approach to their careers. They convey a heightened sense of organizational savvy and a more refined career mindfulness.

- While young Latinx professionals embrace the benefits that come with being bilingual and bicultural, they are especially sensitive about programs and initiatives that aim to give them preferential treatment based on their Hispanic heritage. They want to be given opportunities because of the skills and perspectives they bring to the workplace, not because of their ethnic background.

- Latinx professionals collectively felt that older, more successful Latinos are not providing as much help or mentoring as they could. Without role models, Latinos may struggle to find their way and can have difficulty navigating corporate America.

Reflection Questions

- If you are Latinx, what are your career aspirations?
- What steps are you taking now to achieve your aspirations?
- If you are a Boomer Latino, what was the biggest ah-ha for you from this chapter?
- How can Latinos of all generations collaborate with one another to leverage intergenerational diversity?

Developmental Activities

- ❑ Determine ways to leverage your Hispanic ethnicity as an asset in the workplace.
- ❑ Pledge to mentor at least one other Latino professional or student regardless of your age or level of experience.
- ❑ Revisit any hesitation or uncertainty you may have for not manifesting your Hispanic heritage in the workplace.
- ❑ Immerse yourself in at least two deep Hispanic cultural experiences per year.
- ❑ Commit to connect intensely with Latino professionals who have significantly different experiences than yours.
- ❑ Inquire if your company will pay for you to obtain an executive coach to accelerate your advancement.
- ❑ Commit to not falling into a victim's mentality. If someone else believes you were hired or promoted because you are Latino, demonstrate through your performance that you earned the job based on your capabilities.
- ❑ Take a course on personal branding and executive presence to boost your ability to toot your own horn and raise your visibility within the company while simultaneously remaining true to your Hispanic heritage.
- ❑ Learn to master written and verbal communications. Arguably this is one of the most potent ways you can exponentially amplify the other skills and experiences you already have.
- ❑ Network like there is no tomorrow. Meet all kinds of people at all kinds of levels through all kinds of professional and social activities.

❑ Take care of your body, soul, and heart. Exercise, eat nutritiously, hydrate, and get enough sleep. While exerting all the hard work of becoming a leader, keep life in perspective and spend plenty of quality time with your family and friends. Take time away to contemplate, pray, or meditate. Remember, *despacio se va lejos* (Slow and steady you go far).

❑ Take a nap. Have some wine. Go dancing. *Pura vida!* (Full life!)

BIBLIOGRAPHY

Alvarez, Julia. *How the Garcia Girls Lost Their Accents*. Algonquin Books of Chapel Hill, 2010.

Benitez, Cristina, and González, Marlene. *Latinization and the Latino Leader*. Ithaca, NY. Paramount Publishing. 2011.

Bordas, Juana. *Salsa, Soul and Spirit: Leadership for a Multicultural Age*. San Francisco, CA. Berret-Koehler. 2012.

Bordas, Juana. *The Power of Latino Leadership: 10 Principles of Inclusion, Community, and Contribution*. San Francisco, CA: Berrett-Koehler, 2013.

Carbajal, Frank, and Medina, Humberto. *Building the Latino Future: Success Stories for the Next Generation*. Hoboken, NJ. John Wiley & Sons. 2008.

Carr-Ruffino, Norma. *Managing Diversity. People Skills for a Multicultural Workplace (6th ed)*. Boston, MA: Pearson Publishing. 2003.

Cashman, Kevin. *Leadership from the inside Out: Becoming a Leader for Life*. San Francisco, CA: Berrett-Koehler Publishers, 2008.

Chong, Nilda, and Baez, Francia. *Latino Culture: A Dynamic Force in the Changing American Workplace*. Yarmouth, ME. Intercultural Press. 2005.

Cobbs, Price M., and Turnock, Judith L. *Cracking the Corporate Code: The Revealing Success Stories of 32 African-American Executives*. New York: AMACOM, 2003.

Dabbah, Mariela, and Poire, Arturo. *The Latino Advantage in the Workplace: Use Who You Are to Get to Where You Want to Be*. Sphinx Publishing. 2006.

Davidds, Yasmin. *Take Back Your Power: How to Reclaim It, Keep It and Use It to Get What You Deserve*. Los Angeles. Atria Books. 2006.

Diaz, Junot. *The Brief Wondrous Life of Oscar Wao*. New York: Riverhead, 2008.

Gladwell, Malcolm. *Blink: The Power of Thinking without Thinking.* New York: Back Bay Books, 2013.

Gladwell, Malcolm. *The Tipping Point: How Little Things Can Make a Big Difference.* London: Abacus, 2000.

Hyter, Michael, and Turnock, Judith L. *The Power of Inclusion: Unlock the Potential and Productivity of Your Workforce.* Toronto. Wiley, 2006.

Fraser, George C. *Click: Ten Truths for Building Extraordinary Relationships.* New York: McGraw-Hill, 2009.

Marín, Gerardo, and Vanoss Marín, Barbara. *Research with Hispanic Populations.* Applied Social Research Methods Series. 23. Thousand Oaks, CA. Sage Publications, 1991.

Márquez, Gabriel Garcia. *One Hundred Years of Solitude.* New York, NY. Alfred A. Knopf, 1995.

Rodriguez, Richard. *Days of Obligation: An Argument with My Mexican Father.* New York: Penguin, 1995.

Rodriguez, Robert. *Latino Talent: Effective Strategies to Recruit, Retain and Develop Hispanic Professionals.* Hoboken, NJ. John Wiley & Sons. 2008.

Stavans, Ilan. *The Hispanic Condition: The Power of a People.* New York: Rayo, 2001

Tapia, Andrés T. *The Inclusion Paradox: The Obama Era and the Transformation of Global Diversity (3rd ed).* Korn Ferry Institute, 2016.

Trompenaars, Fons, and Charles Hampden-Turner. *Riding the Waves of Culture: Understanding Diversity in Global Business.* McGraw-Hill Companies, The, 2012.

Wyche, Keith R., and Sonia Alleyne. *Good Is Not Enough: And Other Unwritten Rules for Minority Professionals.* New York. Portfolio, 2009.

ACKNOWLEDGMENTS

¡Muchas Gracias!

The two authors are in deep appreciation of:

Networker extraordinaire, **Melissa Wilson Giovagnoli**— book publishing and social media marketing muse who has a long track record of amplifying the messages of those with something to say. You always believed, you always were generous with your time and ideas, and you were the one who introduced us to Michael Nolan, our editor, and Kathy Meis, founder of Bublish, our distributor, who are mentioned below.

Michael Nolan, wow, you were an editorial treasure. Not only as the editor who reviewed every word we wrote, but as someone who actively participated in ensuring we were bringing our best thinking to the surface through your provocative questions and incisive insights. You also played many other editorial roles, including managing the excellent team including **Joy Dean Lee**, the copy editor and indexer, **Rafael Olivas**, the cover concept designer, and **Gretchen Dykstra**, the proofreader. We are grateful to each of you for the professionalism and high caliber of your work.

And thanks to you, Michael, for managing the entire project from start to finish seamlessly, with great dedication, compassion, firmness, and grace. As we traveled all over to meet our client obligations, you kept the project on schedule and moving forward with a very efficient process. Saturday mornings are going to feel a bit empty for some time now that we won't be having our weekly editorial calls. We can't think of a better editorial coxswain to have been able to partner with. (And, yes, since this is the one paragraph you don't get to edit, we are ending that last sentence with a preposition.)

Renee Jackson, Andrés's executive assistant, you chased down multiple individuals to schedule the many phone calls, meetings, and focus groups. You never missed a beat. Always on top of all the details, moving at the speed of light, with bull's-eye accuracy on all the details. Without this energy and effort, we wouldn't have developed the momentum and velocity that we ended up with in this project.

Sofia Suarez, thank you for helping us source so many of just the right literary and historical quotes that now open the book and each chapter. This was work that required someone as erudite, well read, and insightful as you. And, of course, we were always grateful for the cocktails and appetizers that greeted us at the end of various working sessions.

Kathy Meis, our journey with you begins now that the book is complete. We have already learned much from you about the world of distribution and we are ready to follow your lead as we partner to let online and brick-and-mortar bookstores, universities, libraries, and associations know of the book and its messages.

Price Cobbs, we have followed in your footsteps by doing what we can to accelerate the advancement of the many who have been marginalized. We continue to be impressed by the eloquence of your writing and are honored by your foreword, which is a powerful reminder of your tremendous body of work we have enjoyed reading through the years. A toast, *salud!*, for helping to build more bridges between the African-American and Latino communities.

Jorge Ferraez and **Pedro Guerrero**—we thank you both for being publishers of two of the most influential publications related to top Latino talent—*Latino Leaders* magazine and *Hispanic Executive* magazine. We are grateful for your insights on our book project, for helping with the focus groups, and for your friendship. We look forward to partnering with you both for years to come as we build the pipeline of future Latino executives.

Jaclyn Tumberger, Pedro's executive assistant at *Hispanic Executive* magazine, you helped us so much with all you did: directions, signage, parking, water, pens, and your overall gracious, helpful, and pleasant self.

Kate Newbold, thank you for assisting Melissa in the book's marketing campaign in all its multiple channels and myriad details.

A big thank you to the **Consortium of Latino Employee Organizations** (CLEO) in Chicago. Your active involvement in the Chicago focus groups was extremely valuable. Plus, your participation in our professional survey provided tremendous insights. Keep advocating for Latino professional advancement.

Andrés wants to also give gracias *to:*

My friend, collaborator, co-author, and fellow Latino **Robert**. Partnering on this project with you has been a total joy. Our easy and mutually respectful personal and professional relationship made this an enriching and fun project. Your depth of knowledge, experiences, research rigor, and passion for our subject were assets in themselves. But then came the magic of the synergistic thinking whenever we put our two heads and hearts together. It has been an intellectual- and mission-driven high.

My colleagues at **Korn Ferry**: your smarts, insights, professionalism, collegiality—as well as your passion for better leaders, managers, employees, and corporate cultures—have all made me a better consultant and person.

The **Class of '79** of the American High School of Lima, FDR. Our fusion of Latino, American, Asian, and European vibes taking us through smooth salsa and disco dancing nights after sun-baked beach days of surfing and *ceviche* in our *Lima Querida*, all in the midst of *la dictatura*, the military totalitarianism, were so deeply formative to how I view, understand, and experience the world and my Latino identity. *¡Amigos y amigas de toda la vida!*

And, to my lifelong partner, **Lori**, who, as always, supported yet another project. Hey, *amor, tengo una nueva idea…*

Robert has his own gracias *to give to:*

Mi amigo **Andrés**—I've learned so much from you during this collaboration. I'm in awe of your writing style and I wish to thank you for helping to refine my creative voice. I believe that life is about moments and I will always treasure our moment of partnership on this endeavor. You and I are proof that friends can work, create, and thrive together. At times, it felt like we traveling on the same passport. *Un abrazo!*

Our final gracias:

To our interviewees and focus group participants, who gave of their time and energy to share their stories, thoughts, dreams, and aspirations:

Los Angeles Focus Group

Bonizu Ramirez
Erika Maldonado
Ingrid Mendez
Janet Perez
Lorena Martínez
Marlene Luna
Natalie Sanchez
Sandra Calles, PhD
Sandra Williams

Dallas Focus Group

Flor Gonzalez
Gabriel Leal
Isaac Padilla
Lisa Rodriguez
Ramir Camu

Chicago Focus Group

Dario Bolanos
Enrique Juarez
Hector Diaz
Isabel Villegas

Marcus Rodriguez
Sofia Curiel
Xiema Duque
Yoly Valencia

New York City Focus Group

Amanda Garcia
Geraldine Cols Azocar
Leonor Ayala
Robert Rivas
Rosemary Martinez
Salvador Mendoza

Mujeres de HACE Focus Group

Barbara Resendiz
Delia McLaughlin
Edith Pacheco
Edna Castro
Faye Aguilar
Karen Saa
Laurin Bello
Marisol Martinez

INDEX

About the Authors

Dr. Robert Rodriguez

Robert is the founder and president of DRR Advisors LLC, a diversity consulting firm that specializes in Latino talent initiatives, employee resource group optimization, and diversity strategy.

A leading expert on corporate Latino talent programs, he has worked with over seventy-five corporations including Intel, NBCUniversal, PepsiCo, Verizon, Cisco, Facebook, Mass-Mutual, Progressive Insurance, JetBlue, and State Street Corporation. He previously held leadership roles with the Association of Latino Professionals for America (ALPFA), Target, 3M, RR Donnelley, and the *Washington Post*.

He holds a doctorate in organization development and has taught graduate courses at DePaul University in Chicago and in Latino leadership programs at the University of Southern California (USC) in Los Angeles. He has also taught in executive education programs offered as part of the Latino Leadership Initiative in the Cox School of Business at Southern Methodist University (SMU) in Dallas. He is the author of *Latino Talent: Effective Strategies to Recruit, Retain and Develop Hispanic Professionals* (Wiley, 2008).

He was named by *Hispanic Business* magazine as one of the top 100 most influential Hispanics in corporate America. He serves on the advisory council for the Hispanic Scholarship Fund and has collaborated with Latino nonprofits including HACR, NHCC, HACE, HITEC and CHLI.

He was born in Lubbock, Texas, the son of Mexican immigrant parents. He has two teenage sons, Bailey and Benjamin, and resides in Chicago.

Andrés Tomás Tapia

Andrés is senior client partner and the global diversity and inclusion solutions leader at Korn Ferry, a leadership and talent consultancy. He has over twenty-five years of experience as a C-suite management consultant, diversity executive, organizational development and training professional, and journalist.

Prior to Korn Ferry, he was the president of Diversity Best Practices, a diversity and inclusion think-tank and consultancy, and the chief diversity officer and emerging workforce solutions leader for Hewitt Associates. He has worked with dozens of Global 500 organizations such as John Deere, Marriott, United, MassMutual, Allstate, Target, Cigna, HPE, Capital Group, Apple, LinkedIn, and Novartis, as well as non-U.S. multinationals in Brazil, South Korea, and India.

Andrés is the author of *The Inclusion Paradox: The Post-Obama Era and the Transformation of Global Diversity* (Korn Ferry Institute, 2016). He specializes in working with executive teams on developing global enterprise-wide diversity and inclusion strategies while also providing one-on-one executive coaching, He is also a sought-after speaker, the recipient of numerous leadership awards, a trustee with Ravinia Festival, and a board member of the Hispanic Alliance for Career Enhancement (HACE).

Andrés received a bachelor's degree in modern history from Northwestern University with an emphasis in journalism and political science.

He grew up in a bilingual/bicultural home in Lima, Perú. He is married to Lori, a musician. They have one grown daughter, Marisela, who is a professional flamenco dancer.

The Latinx Institute

The Latinx Institute is a collaboration between Andrés Tomás Tapia and Dr. Robert Rodriguez that seeks to capture, understand, and synthesize the realities of Latino professionals and leaders in the workplace. Their collaborations include joint public speaking, research, and writing.

Auténtico: The Definitive Guide to Latino Career Success is the first book published by The Latinx Institute.

To contact the authors:

Andrés: *www.inclusionparadox.com*

Robert: *www.drradvisors.com*